THE
HIDDEN AGENDA
OF THE
POLITICAL MIND

THE
HIDDEN AGENDA
OF THE
POLITICAL MIND

HOW SELF-INTEREST SHAPES OUR OPINIONS
AND WHY WE WON'T ADMIT IT

JASON WEEDEN AND
ROBERT KURZBAN

PRINCETON UNIVERSITY PRESS

PRINCETON AND OXFORD

Published by Princeton University Press, 41 William Street, Princeton, New Jersey 08540

In the United Kingdom: Princeton University Press, 6 Oxford Street, Woodstock, Oxfordshire OX20 1TW

press.princeton.edu

Jacket images © escova/Shutterstock. Jacket design by Lorraine Doneker.

ISBN 978-0-691-16111-2

British Library Cataloging-in-Publication Data is available

This book has been composed in Minion Pro

Printed on acid-free paper. ∞

Printed in the United States of America

1 3 5 7 9 10 8 6 4 2

Contents

Part I

Political Minds

CHAPTER 1

Agendas in Action

MITT ROMNEY WAS DEFEATED BY SELF-INTEREST. Not his own, but the self-interested voting of poor minorities and those meddling kids.

At least that's how he saw things in the week after his 2012 election loss to the incumbent, President Barack Obama. On a conference call with disappointed fund-raisers and donors, Romney offered his post-game analysis: "What the president's campaign did was focus on certain members of his base coalition, give them extraordinary financial gifts from the government, and then work very aggressively to turn them out to vote, and that strategy worked."

Romney and his strategists listed the policy gifts and the beneficiaries. Obama bestowed "amnesty" on certain young immigrants by executive order, a move that "was obviously very, very popular with Hispanic voters." The president passed Obamacare, "which basically is ten thousand dollars a family," a good price for the votes of poorer Americans. As for those meddling kids, they got to stay on their parents' health insurance plans, received cuts in student-loan interest rates, and got "free contraceptives," something that was "very big with young, college-aged women." Romney's summary: "It's a proven political strategy, which is give a bunch of money to a group and, guess what, they'll vote for you."

Romney surely could have added other "gifts" to his list. In the spring of 2012, not long before Obama issued his new directive for young immigrants, he announced his support for same-sex marriage, something that, along with his administration's earlier repeal of the military's "don't ask, don't tell" policy, pleased another solid Democratic group, gays and lesbians. The Obama administration's support for General Motors and Chrysler probably improved his standing with union workers and

Michiganders. His support of payroll tax cuts and extended unemployment benefits particularly helped poorer people struggling through the Great Recession. His appointment of a Jewish woman and also of a "wise Latina" to the Supreme Court showed his support for abortion-rights and civil-rights policies so popular with feminists and lefty Ivy Leaguers.

Liberal columnist Clarence Page, among others, responded to Romney's "gifts" analysis with the inevitable charge of hypocrisy: "That President Obama sure is a clever fellow, giving so many Americans what they want. I wonder why that notion apparently didn't appeal to Romney? Oh, right. It did. He promised seniors, for example, that he'd restore President Obama's $716 billion in Medicare cuts. . . . Romney looked like Santa Claus to upper-income earners with his promises to protect them from Obama's proposed income tax hikes. He also promised Wall Street that he would roll back the Dodd-Frank financial regulations that were legislated to rein in the abuses that led to the 2008 financial crash."[1]

From the right, in a piece for the libertarian website reason.com, Ira Stoll condemned such hypocrisy charges as further hypocrisy: "[T]here's a double standard at work. When reporters suggest that donors to *Republican* causes are motivated by self-interested desire to keep their taxes low and their businesses unhampered by environmental or labor regulations, *that's* groundbreaking investigative journalism. . . . Yet when Romney suggests that *Democratic* voters might have been motivated by self-interest, his comments are condemned."[2]

Perhaps more peculiarly, even some of Romney's supposed Republican allies were as critical as his political opponents. Louisiana governor Bobby Jindal said: "If we want people to like us, we have to like them first. And you don't start to like people by insulting them and saying their votes were bought." Even Newt Gingrich called Romney's comments "nuts."

In certain respects, these strong reactions from both left and right might seem surprising. Elected officials' job, after all, is to advocate policies, and different policies usually work in favor of some people's interests and against others'. The major supporters and opponents of different policies frequently include those most helped or most hurt by the policies. Immigrants tend to prefer immigrant-friendly policies. Lesbians and gays tend to prefer LGBT-friendly policies. Poorer people tend to prefer robust government assistance with health care. Students tend to prefer lower college costs. Those on birth control tend to prefer cheaper birth control. Rich people tend to prefer lower taxes on rich people. Wall Street executives tend to prefer relaxed financial regulation. *Of course* the respective campaigns emphasized how their favored policies would help people. *Of course* different policies appeal to some but not to others. That's sort of the point of elections.

Indeed, as Stoll noted, the hubbub over Romney's comments calls to mind journalist Michael Kinsley's fitting observation: "A gaffe is when a politician tells the truth—some obvious truth he isn't supposed to say."[3] Romney's "gifts" phrasing may have betrayed an unseemly bitterness over his recent loss, but his comments were largely on target: Campaigns try to turn out different groups of voters based on the particular policies those voters favor, and, often, the policies voters favor have a lot to do with their interests. Why is it such a big deal to say this out loud?

In this book, our goal is to explain why people hold the political positions that they do—why, that is, different people hold different views on areas like immigration, government spending on health care and the poor, same-sex marriage, abortion, and so on. A large part of the answer will be found in the kind of (unpopular) explanation Romney offered: it's about people's interests. Identifying where people's interests lie is, in some cases, pretty easy. Sure, as Romney pointed out, people who have less money have an interest in the state moving money from the richer to the poorer.

However, in other cases, while the key issue is still interests, identifying how particular policies advance people's interests can be trickier. Are some people really better (or worse) off under different policy regimes about "cultural" issues surrounding sex and religion? As we'll see, the answer is "yes," and once we figure out who is better off under which regime, we'll have gone a long way to figuring out who favors, and who opposes, different policies.

Looking for where people's interests lie will lead us to many of the familiar demographic features political analysts and pollsters have been looking at for decades. It will lead us to some lesser-known features as well.

By the time we're done, we hope to have provided an explanation—or, at least, a big part of the explanation—for people's political issue positions across the American spectrum. Along the way we'll also explore some key features of the modern coalitional alignments of the parties, and the perplexing reality that it's taboo to talk truthfully about the fact that politicians try to appeal to voters' interests.

To do all that, however, we have to take a careful look at data.

A lot of data.

Slicing and Dicing

As election night unfolded, NBC's Chuck Todd, analyzing incoming returns and exit polls, expressed the emerging conventional wisdom on Obama's impending victory: "The story of this election is demographics. The Republican party has not kept up with the changing face of America. . . . It's the growth of the Hispanic communities in various places. . . . [T]hey look like core Democratic voters tonight. Again, the story of this election is going to be demographics when all is said and done. The Obama campaign was right. . . . They built a campaign for the twenty-first century America. The Republican party has some serious soul-searching to do when you look at these numbers."[4]

Looking at the numbers isn't just for the pros anymore. On election night, the public has access to huge amounts of information from exit polls. Anyone with an Internet connection and a hint of interest in politics can get online and follow along as the commentators slice and dice a deluge of demographic data.

Overall, Obama won 51% of the popular vote to Romney's 47% (with the other 2% going to third-party candidates)—a 4-point win for Obama. But this 4-point margin masks wildly lopsided demographic splits revealed by the exit polls.

By far the biggest deal in American party politics these days is the difference in voting patterns by race and ethnicity.[5] Obama won African Americans by 87 points. Obama won Latinos and Asians by around 45 points. Romney won whites by 20 points.

Another fundamental set of differences involves religion. Romney may have won whites overall by 20 points, but Obama won Jews by 39 points and whites with no religious affiliation by 32 points. Romney cleaned up with his fellow Mormons, winning them by 57 points. Romney also won white Protestants by 39 points and white Catholics by 19 points. Across racial groups, Romney won those who go to church more than once a week by 27 points and weekly churchgoers by 17 points; Obama won people who never go to church by 28 points.

Lesbians, gays, and bisexuals were also huge Obama supporters, favoring the president by 54 points. In fact, according to the exit polls, had the election only included heterosexual voters, the popular vote would have been pretty close to a tie.

Obama took big cities by 40 points (these populations, after all, contain lots of minorities, lots of less religious whites, and relatively more lesbians, gays, and bisexuals). Romney won rural areas by 24 points (these populations, after all, contain lots of white, heterosexual Christians).

Poorer people tended to support Obama and richer people tended to support Romney. For example, Obama won those with incomes under $30,000 by 28 points while Romney won those with incomes above $100,000 by 10 points. These income results obviously relate in part to racial differences, with minorities typically being poorer than whites.

On education, the story starts off in a way that looks consistent with the income differences we just saw: Obama won among those without high school diplomas by 29 points. Those in the middle were pretty evenly distributed, with Obama barely eking out people with high school diplomas but not bachelor's degrees and Romney winning those with bachelor's degrees but not graduate degrees. But then there's a noticeable outlier: Obama, not Romney, won among the most educated group (those with graduate degrees) by 13 points. By the end of the book, we'll see why—why, that is, high income tends to lead to Republican support while high education tends to lead to Democratic support—but it'll take a while to put the pieces together.

The marriage gap shows up: Obama won unmarried people by 27 points; Romney won married people by 14 points. The age gap shows up, too: Obama won young adults (ages eighteen to twenty-nine) by

23 points; Romney won seniors (ages sixty-five and higher) by 12 points. And, of course, the gender gap: Obama won women by 11 points; Romney won men by 7 points.

These last differences, though, aren't in the same ballpark as those we started with for race, religion, and sexual orientation.[6] In fact, despite persistent media talk of the liberalness of young people, note this nugget from the 2012 exit polls: *If the election had only involved white voters between ages eighteen and twenty-nine, Romney would have won by 7 points.*

Political professionals think of voters in terms of coalitions, the key point being that members of various demographic groups tend to respond in different ways to different issues.[7] Groups such as whites with no religious affiliation and African Americans may vote mostly for Democrats, but this doesn't mean they share the same policy views or have the same issue priorities. For example, 70% of whites with no religious affiliation support the Supreme Court's ban on school prayer; only 26% of African Americans agree.[8] When it comes to government spending on African Americans, in contrast, while 73% of African Americans think there should be higher spending, only 30% of whites with no religious affiliation agree. These two groups have different reasons for voting for Democrats.

With ever increasing, data-driven sophistication, political professionals analyze not "the public," generally, but (increasingly smaller) *segments* of the public. Sasha Issenberg's book, *The Victory Lab*, provides a fascinating glimpse into the modern development of "micro-targeting," and other efforts to group the voting population into coherent clusters with shared policy concerns. In his 2004 book, *The Two Americas*, veteran Democratic pollster Stan Greenberg described in detail more than twenty overlapping demographic categories, some solidly in the Republican coalition, some solidly in the Democratic coalition, and some up for grabs. The book was a detailed example of demographic political analysis, flowing from various demographic features, to groups' different policy priorities and positions, to party allegiances and voting patterns that ultimately reflect demographic-driven coalitions of diverse policy preferences.

In discussing Latino Americans, for instance, Greenberg stated that they have tended to be attracted to Democrats because of shared support for civil rights for immigrants and policies providing greater economic security for people with lower incomes. In other words, the Democratic pollster in 2004 gave practically the same analysis as the Republican candidate in 2012, who described on his postelection conference call how Latinos had been wooed by Democrats primarily through Obama's "amnesty" efforts and the economic subsidies in Obamacare. Romney wasn't, then, out on a political limb; he was expressing a widely held view of pollsters and strategists in both parties.

Sometimes the demographic labels of pollsters make their way into the public's political conversation. Often the focus is on various groups of swing voters—soccer moms, office-park dads, Walmart moms, NASCAR dads, and a host of others. Our own approach will be to look closely at how and why different demographic features relate to different kinds of political issues. Someone who goes to church regularly, for example, is likely to be more conservative on abortion and related lifestyle issues, but how much people go to church doesn't have much at all to do with being conservative on immigration or affirmative action or Social Security. Once we've seen how and why different demographic features relate to different issue opinions, we'll get into the real slicing and dicing, breaking up the public into lots of different groups with various collections of views. This will lead to an expanded perspective on the variety of modern political positions.

The Bichromatic Rainbow

Sometimes it can seem that there's little need for the demographic obsessions of political professionals who target specific "messages" to narrow groups. Aren't there really just two big groups—liberals/Democrats on one side and conservatives/Republicans on the other—and, thus, really just two big "messages"? Comedian Jon Stewart and the team behind *The Daily Show* put it this way in *America (The Book)*: "Each party has a platform, a *prix fixe* menu of beliefs making up its worldview. The candidate can choose one of the two platforms, but remember—no substitutions. For example, do you support universal healthcare? Then you must also want a ban on assault weapons. Pro–limited government?

Congratulations, you are also anti-abortion. Luckily, all human opinion falls neatly into one of the two clearly defined camps. Thus, the two-party system elegantly reflects the bichromatic rainbow that is American political thought."[9]

These remarks were made with tongue firmly placed in cheek, of course. But a number of other very smart people have made essentially the same point without any hint of humor. Economist Bryan Caplan in his book, *The Myth of the Rational Voter*, asserted (with his tongue in its usual non-cheeky place): "There are countless issues that people care about, from gun control and abortion to government spending and the environment. . . . If you know a person's position on one, you can predict his views on the rest to a surprising degree. In formal statistical terms, political opinions look one-dimensional. They boil down roughly to one big opinion, plus random noise."[10] In a *New York Times* online opinion piece, psychologist and linguist Steven Pinker made similar claims: "Why, if you know a person's position on gay marriage, can you predict that he or she will want to increase the military budget and decrease the tax rate . . . ? [There may] be coherent mindsets beneath the diverse opinions that hang together in right-wing and left-wing belief systems. Political philosophers have long known that the ideologies are rooted in different conceptions of human nature—a conflict of visions so fundamental as to align opinions on dozens of issues that would seem to have nothing in common."[11] Caplan and Pinker didn't just make this stuff up; plenty of political scientists have stated that people typically show a general left-right coherence in their policy views.[12]

In the course of the 2012 campaign, in response to complaints about a misleading ad attacking Obama over welfare, Romney's chief pollster, Neil Newhouse, said: "We're not going to let our campaign be dictated by fact-checkers." But for social scientists like us, fact-checking is what it's all about. So, when it comes to liberal-conservative coherence among the general public, what are the facts? Do Americans really take their political positions from a prix fixe menu, or is it more like a buffet?

Let's consider two items from the U.S. General Social Survey (GSS), a large database on Americans' lives and politics that we will rely on heavily throughout the book. One item asks whether the person agrees that homosexual couples should have the right to marry; potential answers range from strongly agree to strongly disagree, and the respondent can also indicate that they don't have an opinion one way or another. Answers to this question correlate strongly with answers to the question of whether people view themselves as "liberal" or "conservative" overall. (Throughout the book, we're using the terms "liberal" and "conservative" in the way that politically aware contemporary Americans typically use them.)[13] The other item asks whether the person thinks that government should do something to reduce income differences between rich and poor, or whether the person thinks that government should not concern itself with income differences; here, the respondent can give a response leaning heavily one way or the other and can also land in the middle, indicating weak or mixed opinions. Answers to this question have a big correlation with answers to the question of whether people generally prefer Republicans or Democrats.

If we take the assertions from Caplan and Pinker (not to mention Stewart) seriously, we should be able to take people's views on one of these issues and know their views on the other issue. People who favor same-sex marriage should generally favor government reduction of income differences. People who are opposed to government reduction of income differences should generally be opposed to same-sex marriage.

The data are decidedly less tidy. In the GSS sample over the past ten years, 21% of people were liberal on both same-sex marriage and government reduction of income differences, 19% were conservative on both, 18% were conservative on marriage but liberal on income, 12% were liberal on marriage but conservative on income, and the other 30% had in-the-middle responses on one or both items. In other words, around 40% of the public were either consistently liberal or consistently conservative on these two items, around 30% had mismatched views (liberal on one and conservative on the other), and around 30% expressed no opinion one way or the other on at least one of these issues.

Pinker asserted that if you know a person's views on same-sex marriage you will also know their views on redistributive issues. In fact, though, most people aren't so accommodating. In the GSS data, people who support same-sex marriage have a 50% chance of wanting government to reduce income differences, a 20% chance of being in the middle, and a 30% chance of opposing income redistribution. On the other side, people who oppose same-sex marriage have a 42% chance of opposing income redistribution, a 17% chance of being in the middle, and a 41% chance of supporting it.

One possible reason that Pinker and Caplan overstate the liberal-conservative coherence of public opinion is that it fits their own experience (and, in fact, ours as well). That is, liberal-conservative coherence is more common among some groups than others, and the group where it is most common is that of people like us—white voters with bachelor's degrees.[14] Even among this group, however, only around 50% land either consistently liberal or consistently conservative on same-sex marriage and income redistribution (as opposed to a mere 40% of the general public, as we noted above). White voters with bachelor's degrees, while probably a tremendously high percentage of the people Pinker, Caplan, and we hang out with, constitute only around 20% of American adults. The other 80% are not of European ancestry, or don't have bachelor's degrees, or don't vote.

Roughly 40% of American adults have two but not three of these features—white voters without bachelor's degrees, African American voters with bachelor's degrees, and so on. The other 40% have one or none of these features, and among them, *liberal-conservative coherence is fundamentally absent*—about a third land either consistently liberal or consistently conservative on same-sex marriage and income redistribution, about a third have mismatched views, and the other third hold neutral opinions on one or both issues. Among these individuals, that is, one learns *exactly nothing* about a person's view on one issue by learning their view on the other. Caplan and Pinker may have phrased their conclusions in terms of *people*, but these conclusions hold primarily for *people like them (and us)*.

Crucially, we've been talking about only two issues here—same-sex marriage and government income redistribution. If we add others—affirmative action, immigration, abortion, health care, Social Security, and so on—simple views of liberal-conservative coherence fall apart even further. Now, it is true that certain subsets of these issues do hang together pretty tightly. If you know someone's view on same-sex marriage, for example, you've got a good shot at guessing their view on abortion. If you know someone's view on government income redistribution, you've got a good shot at guessing their view on government support for health care (which typically involves, after all, some kind of economic redistribution). But things break down when one strays too far in issue domains. Occasionally, indeed, the safest bets involve ideological mismatch. Americans who want to reduce immigration levels (a "conservative" position) are actually more rather than less likely to want to increase funding for Social Security (a "liberal" position). Americans who support affirmative action for women (a "liberal" position) are more rather than less likely to think that the Supreme Court should allow school prayer (a "conservative" position).

There may be only two significant political *parties* in the United States (Democratic and Republican) and two or three frequently discussed ideological *labels* (liberal, conservative, and perhaps libertarian), but people defy simple categories, holding every possible combination of views on various issues.

Even for people with high levels of liberal-conservative coherence, the kinds of demographic properties we described earlier when looking at exit polls often drive the overall skew to the left or to the right. We'll take a close look later at Ivy League graduates, for example, and see that their overall liberalism or conservatism relates strongly to things like race, sexual orientation, gender, religion, and income.

The demographics are especially interesting because they often provide better insight into what causes what. No one would believe, for instance, that being a liberal or a Democrat can cause whites to become African Americans, or heterosexuals to become homosexuals, or men to become women. It also seems a stretch to say that a liberal ideology frequently causes people to abandon Christianity in favor of Judaism or agnosticism, or causes people to be poorer rather than richer. There may be some connections like these—people committed to income equality choosing nonprofit jobs over Wall Street positions, for example—but it would be nuts (as Gingrich might say) to suppose that the connections between demographics and politics are *mostly* or even largely a matter of people adjusting demographics to political ideologies. When one sees political patterns relating to demographics, then, one can rule out at least some of the possible causal pathways. The arrow doesn't lead from ideology to demographics, at least most of the time.

In this book, our main questions are the *why* questions. We are psychologists, not political professionals. When analyzing political opinions, our job differs from those seeking to maximize vote-getting. Political professionals are usually satisfied when they identify *that* connections exist between demographics and policy preferences, using this information to help candidates and marketers craft specific messages to woo specific voters and get them to the polls. Our job is to go a step deeper.

Our conclusion will sound familiar to political professionals and commentators who are used to thinking in terms of complex issue combinations that are driven by different demographic features, but we'll provide a fresh focus on the interests driving these connections. We'll look at how people tend to support policies that are in the interests of themselves, their families, their friends, and their social networks. We'll look at how people tend to support coalitions that work to advance their own policy preferences. And, yes, we'll look at how the demographic features typical of political targeting (race, religion, gender, sexual orientation, income, education, etc.) are often key signs of diverse underlying interests that drive different issue positions.

We'll take it step by step, looking at a few different areas of political conflict, tracing people's competing interests, identifying demographic features that relate to those interests. These efforts will produce a small number of essential insights that highlight the major connections. Then, using these lessons, we'll see how to combine them to produce more complex pictures of different groups.

We'll supply some of the tools needed to keep up with modern politics. We'll provide some insights to make pretty good guesses about why, in a given campaign, a politician might run different ads in different markets and highlight different themes in speeches to different interest groups. On election night, when commentators pore over exit polls and talk about Latinos, white churchgoers, college-educated women, or a host of other groups, our discussions will illuminate what's really driving the differences. As the parties consider how to alter their positions to attract new voters—something that Republicans wrestled with on the subject of immigration after the 2012 election—the lessons of later chapters will show many ways in which these changes would help with some specific groups of voters while inevitably hurting the party's chances with other specific groups of voters.

Ignoring Some Usual Suspects

Our approach resonates well with that of some political scientists, particularly those with closer ties to the concrete world of political professionals. In contrast, our approach runs counter to that of others, especially those that take a more abstract approach.

For many political scientists, interests aren't very interesting and demographics are mere "controls" in statistical models, items to be brushed over as the more central determinants of political views are revealed. Often these central factors include ideologies, values, political personality items, and other "symbolic" foundations of the political mind. Our perspective, however, includes some very deep worries about these analyses.

To see one of our key worries, consider parties—not political parties, but party parties, where lots of people get together, mix, mingle, listen to music, nibble on snacks, have a few drinks, and so forth. Some people really like parties while other people don't. Why is that? Ask an undergraduate who has recently taken an intro psychology course, and they might give an answer that sounds pretty smart: It's because some people are extraverts and others are introverts.

But consider a follow-up question: How does one know that some people are extraverts and others are introverts? The answer, it turns out, is that people are asked a series of questions that often includes questions about . . . whether they like parties. Here are a few questions measuring extraversion and introversion from one of the most popular scales used by psychologists:

- Do you enjoy meeting new people?
- Can you usually let yourself go and enjoy yourself at a lively party?
- Can you easily get some life into a rather dull party?
- Do you like mixing with people?
- Can you get a party going?

Psychologists call people who answer "yes" to these kinds of questions "extraverts" and call people who answer "no" to these questions "introverts."

So what does it mean, then, to say that someone enjoys parties *because* they're an extravert? Personality psychologists often think of extraversion/introversion as an underlying trait that is doing the causing. But one has to be careful when it comes to actually studying these things. It's easy to slip into empirical results that boil down to simple circularity. Some people enjoy parties because they are extraverts, which we know they are because they enjoy parties. If we label people who answer "yes" to those questions above "party-likers," then the circularity becomes even more transparent: Why do some people like parties? Well, it's because they're party-likers.

The pattern is common in social science: Think of something one wants to explain (e.g., why some people are more outgoing than others); give people a set of survey questions that measures the very thing one wants to explain (e.g., a set of items about whether they're outgoing); give survey-takers' answers to those questions a name (e.g., extraversion); and then claim to have solved the puzzle (e.g., some people are outgoing because they're extraverts). It's such a common pattern, surely it deserves a name of its own. We'll call it: Direct Explanation Renaming Psychology Syndrome, or *DERP Syndrome* for short.

Examples abound across the social sciences, and are often particularly transparent when it comes to politics. In a 2002 article in the journal *Political Psychology*, for example, the authors wanted to explain why some people oppose government spending to assist African Americans, why some people think it's not the government's job to guarantee equal opportunity for different racial groups, why some people think minority groups should help themselves rather than having the government help them, and why some people oppose race-based affirmative action.[15] It's an interesting set of issues. So what's the answer?

The answer, according to the authors, is that the main explanation for conservative racial policy attitudes is found in *symbolic racism*. But now ask the follow-up question: How does one know whether someone suffers from symbolic racism? The answer here is classic DERP Syndrome. One knows that someone suffers from symbolic racism because the person answered survey questions generally indicating that they oppose efforts and rationales underlying minority advancing policies. Specifically, to measure "symbolic racism," the study had people answer the following questions, some of which were simple statements with which survey-takers could agree or disagree:

- Some say that black leaders have been trying to push too fast. Others feel that they haven't pushed fast enough. What do you think?
- How much of the racial tension that exists in the United States today do you think blacks are responsible for creating?
- How much discrimination against blacks do you feel there is in the United States today, limiting their chances to get ahead?
- It's really a matter of some people not trying hard enough; if blacks would only try harder they could be just as well off as whites.
- Irish, Italian, Jewish, and many other minorities overcame prejudice and worked their way up. Blacks should do the same.
- Generations of slavery and discrimination have created conditions that make it difficult for blacks to work their way out of the lower class.
- Over the past few years, blacks have gotten less than they deserve.
- Over the past few years, blacks have gotten more economically than they deserve.

Is it any wonder that "symbolic racism" is such a strong "explanation" of "racial policy preferences"? Literally translated, the claim is: The reason many people oppose efforts to advance racial equality is that they think, for example, that minorities should work their way up, that black leaders have been trying to push too fast, and that blacks have gotten more economically than they deserve. In short, people oppose these efforts because they oppose these efforts.

There are lots of other examples. A popular explanation for why people tend to oppose equality for women, gays and lesbians, and religious minorities is *right-wing authoritarianism*.[16] How does one know if someone has a bad case of right-wing authoritarianism? One asks them whether they agree or disagree with items like:

- Women should have to promise to obey their husbands when they get married.
- Gays and lesbians are just as healthy and moral as anybody else.
- Atheists and others who have rebelled against the established religions are no doubt every bit as good and virtuous as those who attend church regularly.
- Everyone should have their own lifestyle, religious beliefs, and sexual preferences, even if it makes them different from everyone else.
- A "woman's place" should be wherever she wants to be. The days when women are submissive to their husbands and social conventions belong strictly in the past.
- Homosexuals and feminists should be praised for being brave enough to defy "traditional family values."

Here's the Twitter version of explaining discriminatory views by citing right-wing authoritarianism: Some people oppose equality for women, gays, and religious minorities because they oppose equality for women, gays, and religious minorities. #DERPSyndrome.

When political scientists point to political "personality" features or "symbolic" predispositions or "values" as explanations for policy preferences, there's often an underlying DERPishness that leads back to the starting point. One asks questions about why people favor different policies. The answers are that it's because they favor those policies, or because they think it would be better if those policies prevailed, or because they approve of the people who advocate those policies. And it's back to square one.

We should note that we of course don't object to all uses of symbolic racism or right-wing authoritarianism (or egalitarianism, or social dominance orientation, or moral traditionalism, or countless other similar political measures). Such measures reflect people's differing policy views in important areas and could be used to investigate the ways in which such policy views influence, for example, voters' choices among candidates. Our objections involving DERP Syndrome arise when these measures are used to predict policy views that are basically the same as those in the measures themselves. Our main goal in this book is to better understand the sources of competing views in widely contested policy areas, and it doesn't advance the ball to learn, for example, that people who oppose income redistribution oppose income redistribution, or that people who support meritocracy support meritocracy, or that people who favor the moral condemnation of promiscuity favor the moral condemnation of promiscuity. We hope to provide more informative accounts of these kinds of political positions.

Other items that are often used to explain particular issue opinions are political party preferences and ideological labels. One asks questions about why people favor different policies. One is told that whether people favor Democrats or Republicans correlates with their policy views. One is told that whether people say they're liberal or conservative correlates with their policy views. And one is told, in the end, that a big *cause* of having a left-leaning policy view in a given area is being a Democrat and being liberal.[17]

Party preferences, liberal/conservative labels, and DERPish variables are often cast as causes of particular policy views because of an important assumption: When it comes to political views, people go from general to specific, from broad "ideological commitments" and "party identifications" and slightly more generally worded DERPish measures to the particulars of individual policies.[18] Yet the opposite could well be true. It could be the case, for example, that many people choose to call themselves "liberal" or "conservative" (or "libertarian" or something else or none of the above) based on a kind of summation of their particular policy views.[19] It could be that many people prefer either Democrats or Republicans *because* they favor the policies of one or the other party.[20] It could be that many people endorse general kinds of "value" items (e.g., "it would be better if people were more equal") in large part *because* they have in mind some specific areas (race, sexual orientation, income, etc.) that make the general language appealing.[21]

Nonetheless, it's clear that, having picked a political party, people use that partisan preference to interpret all kinds of information. People favoring a party tend to view the economy as doing better when their party is in power, tend to worry less about foreign military action when their party calls the shots, and so on.[22] Further, when presented with policies that are vague or complex or unfamiliar, knowing that one's favored party is behind the policy goes a long way in helping people to make quick judgments about whether they think the policy is a good idea.[23]

In these ways, we don't doubt that preferring a party and giving one-self an ideological label exert some causal influence on political opinions. A key question, though, is what causes the party preferences and ideological labels in the first place. On this question, our view is that it probably has a lot to do with people's preexisting positions on many of the central policy fights that we examine in this book.

For example, someone might be drawn to the Republican party primarily because of its stances on tax-and-spend policies, and then, once there, might be more likely to support fellow coalition members by providing answers to questions about other issues the person doesn't care or know as much about in ways that lean more to the right than the answers might otherwise. But, in this example, the party affiliation itself was an effect (rather than a cause) of the person's views on another set of issues (i.e., tax-and-spend policies).

All this causal presumption and DERPish question begging might be intellectually harmless if researchers simply pointed to these kinds of correlations and said, You know, these sure are big correlations. Fine. But they go further, frequently, and say, And other things that are not so big (like demographic features) are basically irrelevant. This is like noting a really big correlation between the height of identical twins and then saying: Taller twins are taller *because* they have taller twins, and, now that we know that, we can ignore the less interesting fact that taller twins *also have taller parents*.

Our preference is to largely ignore DERPish and other causally presumptuous "higher-level" variables, even though they are among the usual suspects political researchers turn to in accounting for policy opinion differences. Given that we're trying to understand the sources of diverse opinions on various well-known policy fights, we don't want to rely on items that often have big *correlations* with policy views, but are arguably not big *causes* of the kinds of commonly discussed policy views we examine in this book.[24]

Instead, we favor collections of demographic variables that offer a more secure basis on which to propose (in a noncircular way) *why* things turn out the way they do. Again, it's typically the case with demographic features (such as race, gender, education, sexual orientation, income, etc.) that one can make pretty plausible guesses that correlations with political opinions really do involve causation flowing (through various direct and indirect routes) from demographics to politics. To echo our earlier comments, no one would entertain the notion that being opposed to income redistribution could turn racial minorities with lower incomes into rich, white men; when we find that rich, white men are especially likely to have conservative views on income redistribution, then, it's pretty unproblematic to conclude that there's something about the rich, white maleness that's somehow doing the causing (again, through various direct and indirect routes).

Further, there's no real DERP Syndrome problem when it comes to demographic correlates of political issue opinions. For example, when we find atheists strongly opposing discrimination against atheists, it might be *obvious* why they would do that—it's out of self-defense—but it's not DERPish. We're not asking people whether they favor policies reducing discrimination against atheists and using that to "explain" why they favor policies reducing discrimination against atheists. We're looking at whether their real-life interests are advanced by reducing such discrimination (whether they would admit this or not), and pointing out something that, weirdly, many political discussions simply ignore: It turns out that lots of people who oppose discrimination against atheists are the kinds of people whose lives would be worse off if other people discriminated against atheists.

We're looking for where the rubber of policy opinions meets the road of everyday life. We don't view people as fundamentally philosophical but as social animals driven by practical concerns. When we clear away the questionable variables and just look for connections between lives and policy views—a project that dominates most of the later chapters in this book—we will find them.

Where We're Headed

Our main goals in the pages that follow are to understand how everyday interests drive public opinion when it comes to some widely debated issues, how members of different demographic groups pick and choose mixtures of liberal and conservative views across these different issues, and how members of these different groups with their idiosyncratic positions end up favoring one political party or the other. By the end we'll be engaged in a pretty sophisticated political exercise, dividing a quirky public into a number of coherent groups with complex contrasts in their political opinions. But the core themes in this cacophony are really rather simple. When we take it one note at a time, the melodies won't be hard to spot.

We've divided the book into four parts, covering political minds, political issues, political coalitions, and political challenges. In the remainder of this first part, on political minds, we look at some key ways in which psychological research sheds light on how people arrive at and defend their political positions. Chapter 2 addresses the question of what it means for something to advance a person's interests. The big lesson here is that the academic view of "self-interest" often sees things through a too narrow economic lens, as though most of what people care about comes down to immediate monetary payoffs. We widen this view by using the latest theory and research to consider other fundamental social goals (including those involving social status and sex lives) and stress how people's everyday goals involve family members, friends, and wider social networks.

Chapter 3 uses psychological research to explain the surprising ways in which human minds divide up their many jobs. A key conclusion of this research is that, while people often pursue their interests, part of this pursuit occurs through self-deceptive efforts to portray one's own preferences and actions as not so much about one's interests, but about one's competent and generous character. Human minds engage in ongoing spin control, with consciousness being generally clueless about the nature of the game. This division of labor helps explain, for example, why people in political disagreements tend to see themselves and their allies as reasonable and kind while seeing their opponents as stupid, greedy, and mean. One result, as with the reactions to Romney's postelection conference call, is that it becomes *insulting* to say accurate but not-nice-sounding things about other people's motives, the sorts of things people tend only to point out about their opponents rather than themselves. Our discussion here relies on a broad range of psychological material, including a book by one of your authors, Kurzban, *Why Everyone (Else)*

Is a Hypocrite (a book that, without a hint of self-interest, of course, we recommend highly).

In part II, we move to political issues. Chapter 4 focuses on issues relating to premarital sex, pornography, abortion, birth control, and marijuana legalization. This chapter draws heavily from some of the major threads in our own research efforts over the last decade or so, which have focused on people's sexual and reproductive lives, the competing interests that arise from different lifestyles, the competitive nature of moral conflict, and how these themes explain people's positions on issues like abortion and marijuana legalization. Our studies focus on the underlying strategic interests at work in moral conflict over lifestyles. What look to others like "cultural" or "religious" issues look to us like the manifestation of interests, albeit cleverly disguised.

In chapter 5, we move to a different set of issues, those involving group-based policies (relating to same-sex marriage, school prayer, immigration, affirmative action, and others). We examine the ways in which these kinds of fights don't just pit a minority group against a majority group, but involve wider issues over "meritocracy" and over what kinds of factors should matter in determining social advantages.

In chapter 6, we turn to our third and final set of issues, those relating to income redistribution and spending on entitlements and social safety nets. Here, most people have a pretty good sense that poorer people tend to be more liberal on these issues and wealthier people more conservative. We expand on this theme, looking at other ways in which demographic features relate to differing interests.

In short, part II of the book provides the demographic building blocks and the interest-based rationales behind them. We'll rely mostly on American data, but we'll see in broad strokes that the basic connections between demographic features and specific policy areas hold up worldwide.

With the building blocks in place, in part III, on political coalitions, we'll see how complex amalgams of interests produce varieties of people with shades of political color well beyond Jon Stewart's bichromatic rainbow. We'll find distinct clusters of demographics and see how they tend to favor the Republican or Democratic coalitions. These demographic groups, while distinct, will not be arbitrary, but rather they will follow a logic grounded in everyday interests across the different sets of issues we will have explored in earlier chapters. In this way, part II will provide the building blocks for the analysis we construct in part III.

In part IV, we'll wrap up, exploring how far an interest-based perspective can take us while acknowledging that it can't take us the entire way. To be clear, we don't want to oversell our perspective. We think we can shed substantial new light on diverse political positions, but any such explanation of politics is limited because people are incredibly complex. For every two or three people who look typical in some facet of their issues opinions, there's probably one who doesn't. We are engaged in social science, not biography. We deal in generalities, typicalities, and averages, and there are always exceptions. Further, while we cover many important areas of modern political disagreement, there are some we've left out, and we'll discuss those.

This is a book on politics but it is not a political book. We're not trying to figure out how candidates can win elections. We're not trying to argue that people who share our own policy objectives are good and right while our opponents are bad and wrong. In this we depart from a well-worn path. Most writing on politics carries a clear underlying message about the righteousness of some set of policy positions that just happen to be strongly favored by the authors and the audience. Compared with such pleasing endeavors, our premise—that interests are key in understanding different positions on different issues—will probably feel like a kind of political attack to partisans on all sides. The best we can say is that we've worked hard to give a perspective that stands up to the facts.

In the end, the hardest part of understanding people's political opinions isn't the complexity of the material—this stuff is hard, but, taking it one step at a time, it's not *that* hard. Instead, the hardest part of understanding these opinions is *quieting one's own noisy biases long enough to hear the real themes being played*. We're going to make the case that minds are built for results, to advance their own everyday interests. But part of people's results-oriented agenda involves making themselves and others on their side look good and making their opponents look bad. We argue that all sides are in an important sense doing the same thing— advancing competing interests—in a way that doesn't naturally lead to one side looking better than the other. But minds are built to resist such accounts, to latch on to more satisfying alternatives that rescue the moral privilege of one's own positions.

Still, we're not saying that people shouldn't favor their own side in political competitions. It's what democracy is about, for better or for worse. Speaking for ourselves, for example, there's nothing about our analyses in this book that has changed who we, your authors, vote for—we have policy preferences typical of our demographic group and will continue to support candidates who represent our views.

In this book, we're scratching a different itch. Our intention is not to advocate, but to understand and explain political positions. Along the way, we'll needle our own policy friends as much as our own policy opponents. As a reader, one has to make choices—is it worth it to try to put aside one's own comforting stories (for a moment, anyway) and simply try to figure out what's going on, even if the resulting portrait isn't particularly flattering to anyone?

CHAPTER 2

Investigating Interests

MITT ROMNEY BLAMED HIS 2012 ELECTION LOSS on self-interested voting. Many leading figures in the academy, however, are, to say the least, skeptical of this kind of explanation:

> [S]elf-interest ordinarily does not have much effect on the mass public's political attitudes.   *—David Sears and Carolyn Funk, professors (1990)*[1]

> Unless the material outcomes from a public policy or issue are very clear, very large, and very imminent, self-interest does not determine opinion or action.   *—Charles Taber, professor (2003)*[2]

> The current scholarly consensus holds that self-interest is not a major determinant of issue attitudes or voting choices.
> *—Michael Lewis-Beck, William Jacoby, Helmut Norpoth,*
> *and Herbert Weisberg, professors (2008)*[3]

> Self-interest has no more than sporadic marginal effects on political views.
> *—Bryan Caplan, professor (2012)*[4]

> [S]elf-interest is a weak predictor of policy preferences.
> *—Jonathan Haidt, professor (2012)*[5]

These folks are very well-respected researchers at top universities who have written numerous influential articles and books on political opinions. They understand that they're saying something that would surprise most people, but it's their sincere view—Romney's analysis must be wrong because people don't typically prefer policies or candidates based on self-interest.

The self-interest-denying message hasn't generally impressed the chattering class. Commentators regularly claim that self-interest is kind of a big deal in politics:

[A]s is so often the case with people who spend heavily on elections, [their] worldview does happen to coincide pretty neatly with the economic interests of the people who hold it.   —*Ross Douthat, political pundit (2013)*[6]

The sense of fairness is so often a moralised stalking horse for personal interest.   —*Will Wilkinson, political pundit (2013)*[7]

The traditional conservative anti-government economic agenda is getting less and less popular in large part because it appeals to the economic interests of a small minority of capital owners and high-income earners.
                        —*Jonathan Chait, political pundit (2013)*[8]

[H]uman beings are very good at convincing themselves of whatever their self-interest would have them believe.
                        —*Ezra Klein, political pundit (2012)*[9]

So which is it? On the one hand, many influential columnists think that self-interest matters. A lot. On the other hand, a number of respected researchers confidently assert that self-interest isn't all that important, often without bothering to hedge their declaratives with the usual academic "mights," "coulds," and "suggests."

These views are so diametrically opposite that someone—really, many someones—must be wrong. We think we know who.

Self-Interest Is Dead, Long Live Self-Interest!

Consider an influential set of claims from the 1998 edition of *The Handbook of Social Psychology* from a chapter by political scientist Donald Kinder (another deservedly well-respected figure) reviewing findings on political opinions:

> For the self-interested citizen, then, the question is always and relentlessly, What's in it for me and my family—what's in it for me and mine now? Defined in this way, self-interest is surprisingly unimportant when it comes to predicting American public opinion. . . . Consider these examples. When faced with affirmative action, white and black Americans come to their views without calculating personal harms or benefits. The unemployed do not line up behind policies designed to alleviate economic distress. The medically indigent are no more likely to favor government health insurance

than are the fully insured. Parents of children enrolled in public schools are generally no more supportive of government aid to education than are other citizens. . . . Women employed outside the home do not differ from home-makers in their support for policies intended to benefit women at work. On such diverse matters as racial busing for the purpose of school desegrega-tion, antidrinking ordinances, mandatory college examinations, housing policy, bilingual education, compliance with laws, satisfaction with the reso-lution of legal disputes, gun control, and more, self-interest turns out to be quite unimportant. . . . American society is marked by huge differences in income, education, and wealth, but such differences generally do not give rise to corresponding differences in opinion.[10]

This take on the state of the art in political science has been highly influential in academic circles. The quote from Charles Taber above is from a discussion quoting Kinder at length. In his recent book, *The Righteous Mind*, Jonathan Haidt cites the Kinder article in summarizing the role of self-interest in political opinions. We quoted a bit of it earlier, but here's more context from Haidt: "Many political scientists used to assume that people vote selfishly, choosing the candidate or policy that will benefit them the most. But decades of research on public opinion have led to the conclusion that self-interest is a weak predictor of policy preferences."[11]

Five of Kinder's claims can be evaluated reasonably straightforwardly with the main source of data used in this book, the U.S. General Social Survey, which has measured public opinion on a wide range of topics going back to the early 1970s.

Affirmative Action. In 1994 the GSS asked whites whether they thought it was likely that they or anyone in their families would not get a job or promotion while an equally or less qualified African American received one instead. African Americans were asked the inverse ques-tion, whether they thought it was likely that they or anyone in their fam-ilies would not get a job or promotion while an equally or less qualified white received one instead. The survey asked these respondents about their support for or opposition to preferences in hiring and promotion for African Americans.

Recall that Kinder's claim was that people take positions on affirmative action "without calculating personal harms or benefits." If that claim is right—if people's views don't track their perceptions of their interests—then whether one stands to gain or lose under affirmative action should have no effect on whether one is for it or against it.

However, in sharp contrast (we present fuller analyses of this issue and the others that follow in the Data Appendix for Chapter 2), we find that the biggest supporters of race-based affirmative action were African Americans who indicated that it is likely that they or a family member would lose a job or promotion to a white—62% supported it and only 22% strongly opposed it. The biggest opponents of race-based affirmative action were whites who indicated that it is likely that they or a family member would lose a job or promotion to an African American— only 8% supported it and 77% strongly opposed it.

Crucially, there were significant differences among African Americans and among whites based on whether they said that they or a family member was at risk. Among African Americans who did not perceive a risk of losing jobs to whites, support for race-based affirmative action dropped to 47% (compared to 62% of African Americans who did perceive the risk). Among whites who did not perceive a risk of losing jobs to African Americans, strong opposition to race-based affirmative action dropped to 65% (compared to 77% of whites who did perceive the risk).

Self-interest deniers might point to the fact that African Americans at lower risk are more likely to favor affirmative action than whites at lower risk as some kind of confirmation that there's *more* than self-interest at work in these opinions. We agree with this, in a way, as we'll describe as we get deeper into this chapter. But the claim at issue here is simply whether self-interest enters the picture at all.

One could quibble at the margins. Is it really "self"-interest to ask about risk to one's "family members" in addition to one's self, for example? (Still, Kinder started it; his formulation explicitly included "me and my family.") Also, it's true that these percentages don't allow us to infer without question that people are "calculating personal harms or benefits." But to the extent these numbers tell us anything, it's that people's own interests are, on average, clearly related to their stated positions.

Unemployment. The claim: "The unemployed do not line up behind policies designed to alleviate economic distress." On a GSS survey item asking whether it should be the government's responsibility to provide a decent standard of living for the unemployed, 74% of the unemployed think it should be, but only 46% of those working full-time agree. On a GSS survey item asking whether government spending on unemployment benefits should be increased, left the same, or decreased, 57% of the unemployed think it should be increased, but only 27% of those working full-time agree. The unemployed actually *do* "line up behind policies" that help the unemployed.

Government Health Insurance. The claim: "The medically indigent are no more likely to favor government health insurance than are the fully insured." A closely related GSS survey item asks whether the government should have a responsibility to help pay for doctors and hospital bills or whether people should take care of themselves. Among individuals in the bottom half of the income distribution who lack health insurance coverage, 65% lean to the government-responsibility side and 13% lean to the take-care-of-yourself side. Among individuals in the top half of the income distribution who have health insurance, 46% lean to the government-responsibility side and 19% lean to the take-care-of-yourself side. One might be surprised that the differences aren't greater than they are, but it's not the case that the uninsured poor are "no more likely" than others to favor a government role in health insurance.

School Funding. The claim: "Parents of children enrolled in public schools are generally no more supportive of government aid to education than are other citizens." The GSS doesn't ask questions that address precisely this claim, but we can come reasonably close. We can look at people whose children do or did attend public schools, on the one hand, and the childless and those with children who do or did attend private school, on the other hand, splitting both groups into younger and older adults, approximating those with children still in school versus those with grown children. Among these groups, the highest level of support for increased school spending comes from adults under fifty whose children exclusively attend/attended public schools—to the tune of about eight in ten supporting higher spending on public education. The lowest levels of support for increased school funding come from older individuals, whether or not their (by now probably grown) children attended public school. Among these older folks, two-thirds support higher spending on education. Unlike the three cases above, these differences, while statistically significant, are not very big in practical terms, and especially unimpressive when we add the fact that almost three-quarters of younger people without children in public schools also support higher spending. These results, then, don't really provide an unequivocal answer one way or the other on the claim, especially given the use of the term "generally." Score this one as unclear.

Working Women. The claim: "Women employed outside the home do not differ from homemakers in their support for policies intended to benefit women at work." For this topic, we compared, on the one hand, women working full-time (whether married or not) with, on the other hand, women who report they are "keeping house" (to use the GSS's term) and are also married to full-time workers. For these two groups of women, we looked at two items: (1) views regarding employers hiring and promoting women, and (2) whether women should receive paid maternity leave when they have a baby. There were no significant differences between these groups on these items. Thus, we think the claim with respect to working women is supported by these data.

So, in the five cases in which we can relatively cleanly assess the claims with the GSS, only one—the one regarding working women—is true. The statement about education was unclear, but leaned toward being untrue. In the other three cases—affirmative action, unemployment, and health insurance—self-interest relates to people's positions in exactly the way Kinder's statements denied.

Bilingual Education and Gun Control. In additional areas—including bilingual education and gun control—Kinder suggested that self-interest is "quite unimportant," a suggestion whose accuracy depends on one's view of how big an effect would have to be before it graduated to being important.

On bilingual education, in fact, in the GSS data, the strongest support for eliminating the programs is among those who speak only English (24% want to eliminate; 24% are strongly opposed to eliminating), while the strongest opposition to eliminating bilingual education is among those who speak Spanish and English but no other language (13% want to eliminate; 45% are strongly opposed to eliminating). We think these differences are large enough to be important, and certainly not small enough to be "quite unimportant."

On gun control, the GSS has included gun ownership and a range of gun-related policy views over the years. Typically, on policy items involving permits, background checks, and limiting semiautomatic or high-powered weapons to police or military, restrictions are supported by around 85% to 90% of people who do not own guns, but support for restrictions drops to the 50% to 70% range for gun owners. That is, there is typically around a 25-point gap between gun owners and non-owners, a gap that strikes us as plainly important.

Socioeconomic Status. Finally, Kinder made the following broad claim about political views: "American society is marked by huge differences in income, education, and wealth, but such differences generally do not give rise to corresponding differences in opinion." We'll investigate the relationships among education, income, and political opinions at length in the pages to come, but for now let's take a look at two examples of issues that are central matters of difference between Democrats and Republicans on which one might expect people with different income levels to have different opinions. We'll compare those in the bottom 20% of family income, the middle 20%, and the top 10% (as with all these issues, we present the full data in the appendixes).

On the question of whether the government should be taking steps to reduce income disparities, 57% of the poorest group lean left of center in their responses, dropping to 49% of those in the middle, and dropping substantially to only 30% of the wealthiest group. A recent study looking at this GSS item went further, using data from the same individuals over time. The finding was that when people experience unemployment or a loss in income, their views on reducing income disparities become significantly more liberal than they were before the unemployment or income loss, providing powerful evidence that there really is a causal connection leading from one's economic circumstances to one's political views on redistribution.[12]

On the related question of whether the government should be taking action to help the poor or whether the poor should help themselves, lots of people (reasonably, we think, given how the question is worded) land in the middle, agreeing with both positions. But, still, more than twice as many of the richest Americans (39%) than the poorest Americans (17%) head to the right on this question; and more than twice as many of the poorest Americans (40%) than the richest Americans (17%) head to the left on this question. Americans in the middle of the income distribution are practically evenly split on this item.

So, for questions like these—questions that relate directly to income redistribution—does income "give rise to corresponding differences in opinion"? It sure looks that way to us.

The evidence that people's policy views really do track their interests raises the question of how the self-interest-denying meme got started in the first place. Kinder's summary, after all, isn't based on nothing, but in fact relies on a large number of studies by several researchers over many years. Nonetheless, we have major concerns about these studies. We've provided what we believe to be a key piece of the puzzle at the end of the Data Appendix for Chapter 2, but our argument is rather technical and, to many, we predict, not particularly interesting (it's a thrilling tale of how the use of DERPish and other noncausal variables as predictors in multiple regressions leads to plainly misleading coefficients for both noncausal and causal variables). For those uninterested in such academic Urkel-jerking, our summary is this: The self-interest-denying claims from academics are based on complex effects from complex studies with questionable assumptions, but the summaries of these studies make it sound like these are simple conclusions from simple studies. When one strips out the complexity and just looks at the simple statements, as we did above, the simple statements are often untrue.

In sum, our fact-checking indicates that self-interest often plays an important and substantial role in key areas of policy opinions, and yet strongly worded self-interest denials regularly pop up. One example is the well-known book, *What's the Matter with Kansas?*, by journalist Thomas Frank. The central claim in Frank's book is that whites with lower incomes in red states are ignoring their economic interests by voting Republican. Several political scientists have since debunked Frank's claim,[13] including a thorough treatment in *Red State, Blue State, Rich State, Poor State*, by Andrew Gelman and colleagues. Gelman finds that while wealthier states often have more Democratic voters, richer people *within* any given state are more likely to vote Republican. It's simply not the case that people (even Kansans) generally ignore income in choosing political parties, though income is not the only thing that matters. Frank's is a comforting tale for big-city liberals who want to think that middle-American conservatives are suckers; but, sadly perhaps, it just ain't so (or, at least, it ain't so in the way that Frank claims it is).

Reports of the death of self-interest have been greatly exaggerated. We don't want to replace one extreme with another by saying that some narrowly defined version of self-interest is all that matters—to be clear, we're not saying that. Indeed, the rest of this chapter examines some of the complexities and widens the typical view.

The Nature of Interests

What do people mean when they say that something is in a person's interests? Mainly, it's that something advances a person toward getting what they want. It's more complex than this, of course, in no small part because people want many things, some of which are mutually exclusive. A heroin addict might want to get more heroin, and people wouldn't normally say that doing so would be in their interests. Why not? Because people think that getting more heroin will interfere with the person achieving their (presumed) long-term goals—looking after their own health and safety, success at a job, developing and maintaining relationships with friends and partners, taking care of their children, and so on. People can have goals, after all, that conflict.

In a related way, one often hears that something would be in someone's interests even though they might not know it themselves—it's in people's interests to eat less trans fats, it's in teenagers' interests to wait to have children, and so on. People are comfortable saying what's in someone else's best interests because they assume that people share some very basic goals. People should eat less trans fats because most people want to be healthier. Teenagers should wait to have children because having children too early often leads to being poorer over one's lifetime, something few people presumably want.

What people usually mean by something being in a person's interests, then, is that it advances them toward getting what they want overall, but such claims always rest on a set of background assumptions regarding what people usually want and how to prioritize those various goals when they conflict. It's not an airtight way to think about it, but for many purposes it's close enough.

So what, then, do people want? To figure this out, we start with our friend and colleague Doug Kenrick. Kenrick has been an influential researcher for decades, and in recent years he has been usefully integrating social psychology, evolutionary psychology, cognitive science, dynamical systems theory, and behavioral economics. These days he's been combining his academic efforts with popular books bringing social science to the masses, including *Sex, Murder, and the Meaning of Life* and *The Rational Animal* (coauthored with Vlad Griskevicius).

Kenrick and his colleagues maintain that people are trying to put together lives that advance fundamental, everyday motives, including satisfying immediate physiological needs (breathing, eating, drinking, finding shelter, etc.), defending themselves and those they value, establishing social ties, gaining and maintaining social status and esteem, attracting and retaining mates, and parenting. People are not abstract beings, after all, but social animals.

Economic goals don't appear explicitly on Kenrick's list, but are interwoven in various ways. Money isn't viewed as a fundamental motive in itself, but as something useful to satisfying various fundamental motives—securing food, shelter, health care, and protection; gaining and maintaining social status, alliances, and mating relationships; providing advantages for one's children and other family members. Economists are sometimes accused of believing that humans mostly care about economic outcomes, but most modern economists don't believe this. The standard views in economics see people as maximizing their *preferences*, whatever these happen to be. These preferences can include having more money, but can also include gaining prestige, or having sex, or having one's children fulfill their own preferences, or a range of other goals.[14]

There are further goals that derive from the high-level goals. Some key subgoals relate to managing how one is thought of by others. In establishing social ties, for example, people seek to come across as reliable, predictable, competent, consistent, admired, nice, powerful, reasonable, likable, generous souls—just the sort of people, that is, that other people might rationally view as someone who would be a good friend to have.

The list of fundamental motives is relatively straightforward, but matters become more complex because motives and the priorities among them differ across individuals, across sexes, across stages of life, across cultures, and across situations. To take a simple example, young men often do dangerous things (football, skateboarding, motocross, fighting) in substantial part—whether they know it or not—to gain attention from young women. It's not that they stop caring about their safety, but that, for some individuals in some situations, safety motives are trumped by mating motives.[15]

Furthermore, motivation is dynamic, frequently sensitive to context. For instance, Kenrick and his colleagues have run clever experiments regarding the widely discussed tendency toward loss aversion—where people fear losses more than they desire equal-sized gains. The studies show that, in fact, loss aversion depends on what motives are salient at the time. Get people thinking about their safety, and they show typical loss aversion patterns. Get young men thinking about hooking up with young women, however, and their loss aversion disappears as they seek to gain the kinds of things (money, status) that might be attractive to women.[16]

Our view of political interests draws heavily from the work of researchers analyzing how people's lives and minds reflect humans-as-social-creatures kinds of goals. These goals can be complex, contradictory, and overlapping, they can involve short-term or long-term agendas, they can differ between individuals, and they can differ within the same individual over time.

Contrast this somewhat catholic view with typical definitions of "self-interest" from political science, which tend to be very narrow. Self-interest, by the usual standards, is invoked only when a person gets some material gain now or soon. A typical definition involves "relatively short-term tangible benefits."[17] Getting some money today is in a person's self-interest, but—somewhat oddly—entering into an agreement to get some money a few years from now is not. Gaining social status isn't in a person's self-interest—again, on many traditional definitions—because it's not "material" or "tangible," despite the fact that status usually translates in the real world into more control over the levers of power that distribute resources over time.

By the restrictive definitions, getting a college education is not in a person's self-interest because it leads to immediate loss of income (while in college) in exchange for long-term gain. To take another example—again confounding most people's intuitions—by the restrictive definitions, two single adults who want to marry but are legally prevented from doing so (e.g., because of laws against interracial marriage or against same-sex marriage) would not have their self-interests advanced by removing the legal barrier (self-interest is about money, not relationships).

The perversities that the standard definition introduces penetrate into any number of policy domains. On the restrictive definitions, being denied access to birth control is not against the self-interest of someone who wishes to be sexually active while avoiding pregnancy (it's not material in the short term). On the usual definition, wanting publicly funded unemployment insurance to be available is only in the self-interest of people currently unemployed, despite the fact that lots of other people might need it in the future. On the restrictive definitions, it's not against the self-interest of sexually active young women when others engage in moralistic "slut shaming." On the usual definition, it does not advance the self-interest of young minority men to eliminate racial profiling by the police.

We simply reject the restrictive definitions of "self-interest." In real life, people have agendas that involve more than the short term and more than just money. Viewing "self-interest" in such a limited, counterintuitive way strikes us as arbitrary. Instead, generally—and we concede somewhat less cleanly—we view self-interest as advancing any of a range of people's typical goals, whether directly involving material gain or not, whether involving immediate gain or something more subtle that advances someone's progress over the longer term.

Somewhat oddly, typical definitions of self-interest *do* include immediate material benefits to one's family members. (Recall Kinder's formulation, which included "me and my family.") Even by the restrictive definitions, then, "self-interest" isn't really just about one's self. We agree with this expansion, primarily because it captures something fundamental about human life—people typically care deeply about outcomes for close family members, particularly their children. Indeed, evolutionary biology, on Richard Dawkins's famous "selfish gene" frame, views an organism as a machine that advances the interests of its own genes, genes that are shared, to one degree or another, by parents and children, siblings, nephews and uncles, grandparents and grandchildren.[18]

For all these reasons, we think it's probably best to jettison the term "self-interest" altogether. To replace it, we'll borrow from evolutionary biologists, who use the term "fitness" to describe reproductive success, which is evolution's bottom line. When evolutionary biologists want to talk about the combined gene-level reproductive success of a person and that person's relatives, they refer to "inclusive fitness." So, we'll refer to "inclusive interests." Something is in a person's "inclusive interests" when it advances their or their family members' everyday, typical goals.

But even this leaves out something important.

Life Is a Team Sport

There is no deeper truism in economics than the idea that people compete over scarce resources. Indeed, this is true not only for people, but for animals generally. Animals are built for competing. In the nonhuman world, they compete with one another for territory, food, and anything else that contributes to survival and reproductive success. Often they have built-in equipment for competition, like the large antlers of bucks used to compete with other bucks for access to does.

Humans don't have much by way of natural armaments, but two human traits stand out: big brains and big social groups. Relative to their relatives, humans have large, dense social networks and huge numbers of both negative and positive social interactions. People spend incredible portions of their time in close proximity—sometimes, these days, virtual proximity—to other people. Indeed, humans cooperate with one another arguably more than almost any other species, except maybe some kinds of insects.[19] People cooperate with one another on many scales across many domains, from division of labor within families to modern large-scale military enterprises.

The fact that people are so social means that they can advance their interests not only by making use of physical tools, but also by making use of social tools (i.e., their relationships with other people). There is one crucial difference. When someone uses a rock to beat on a rival, the rock is no better (or worse) off. Not so with social tools.

The fact that people use one another does not mean that the individuals who are being so used might not also stand to benefit. People use one another to reach goals they couldn't if they acted separately, goals whose benefits are typically shared to one degree or another. They rely on their social networks to help carry them through hard times. And when someone gains, it's often a gain for others in their social network as well.

Indeed, anthropologists have emphasized that a pervasive, even universal, feature of human societies is that people cooperate with one another to produce goods and services that benefit the group, or at least some subsection of it. Such activities range from hunting in small-scale societies—in which meat is frequently shared broadly among members of the larger community—to Wikipedia, a planetary outpouring of cooperative effort to benefit anyone with an Internet connection.

A related, if perhaps less encouraging, point is that psychologists have documented that humans reliably play favorites, disposed—to put it very roughly—toward helping those that are more like them rather than those who are less like them. The data from psychological experiments dating back several decades have suggested to some that nearly any feature, no matter how arbitrary or inconsequential, can motivate in-group favoritism. In classic early studies, subjects estimated the number of dots on a screen and were (randomly) informed that they were "over-estimators" or "under-estimators" of the number of dots. Assigning these (trivial, artificial) labels influenced subjects' subsequent choices of allocating rewards to other subjects, with people favoring those who were "like them" in terms of their style of estimation.[20]

In the real world, cooperative groups are formed and dissolve on an ad hoc basis all the time. People participate in pickup games of soccer or basketball for a short period, dissolving at the end of an afternoon. The film industry illustrates a similar phenomenon, with groups of specialists—actors, directors, technicians—working cooperatively on a particular project, and more or less disbanding when the task is complete.[21] And people are choosy about the groups they join and stay members of. In laboratory experiments in behavioral economics, people often exit groups that are not meeting their standards of being sufficiently cooperative.[22]

The point is that one's interests are often enhanced by advances generally among one's social network. Life is competitive, not just for individuals and families but for various, wider, overlapping social circles as well. Life is a team sport, and we're all on several teams. The benefits spill over; the harms trickle through.

And so our earlier notion of "inclusive interests" needs to be expanded further. People's everyday, real-life endeavors are enhanced by various kinds of material and nonmaterial gains, over shorter-term and longer-term horizons, received by themselves, their family members, and their friends, allies, and social networks.[23]

An Interest by Any Other Name

Self-interest deniers are often quick to point out that while *self*-interest doesn't really matter, *group* interests matter quite a bit when it comes to political issues. Kinder puts it this way: "In matters of public opinion, citizens seem to be asking themselves not 'What's in it for me?' but rather 'What's in it for my group?'"[24]

Our notion of inclusive interests skates over it, but the self/group distinction has always been pretty messy. To begin with, we've noted that typical definitions of self-interest nonetheless explicitly include a group—family members.

But the bigger problem is that group interests, as typically conceived, overlap with the interests of individual members of the group. Groups, after all, are made up of individuals. Take Kinder's discussion of groups, for example. He points to large average differences between whites and African Americans on issues relating to racial discrimination and safety-net programs and in party affiliations. There is no doubt that these differences exist. The issue is what to make of them.

When a particular African American supports policies that attenuate the negative effects of racial discrimination, sure, those policies are good for other African Americans. Should the individual's support for the policies be understood as advancing the interests of the person (and their family), and helping other African Americans as a side effect? Or should support for the policies be understood as advancing the interests of other African Americans, helping the self (and kin) as a side effect? Or some combination of both?

It's certainly not obvious, to us anyway, that supporting policies in this way is properly described as looking out for one's group as opposed to looking out for one's self and one's family. When one widens the circle to social allies, taking account of the common sharing of benefits among them, the problem is compounded. If I'm an African American with a social network consisting mostly of other African Americans, and if having more African Americans hired and promoted within companies would place more people in my social network in positions to control hiring and promoting decisions themselves, and if that might help me and my family members get hired and promoted down the road, then it becomes something of a mess to try to unravel what the "self" and "group" interests are.

Psychologist Jonathan Haidt in his book, *The Righteous Mind*, takes things further than most social scientists and views advancing group interests as a kind of self-sacrifice. When it comes to politics, he views people as choosing a team and transcending their own interests in favor of group interests.[25] We resist this move as applied to most real-world political issues. If most African Americans support policies that attenuate the negative effects of racial discrimination, and most African Americans benefit from these policies, and few African Americans are harmed by these policies, then we don't see why supporting one's group would be self-sacrificial. We view most examples of things that advance "groups" as basically equivalent to things that advance the individual interests of lots of members of those groups.[26]

In some cases self-interest and group interests might genuinely diverge. An obvious example would be wealthy African Americans and income redistribution. African Americans have, on average, lower incomes and lower income social networks and might therefore benefit from more robust income redistribution. But the immediate individual interests of wealthy African Americans pull the other way. What do the data show? As we'll discuss in chapter 6, average views on income redistribution are predicted by a mixture of race, income, and a few other factors. Among those most opposed to government income redistribution are, unsurprisingly, wealthy whites. Among those who most support income redistribution are poorer and middle-income African Americans. Wealthy African Americans are in the middle—neither as routinely opposed as wealthy whites nor as routinely supportive as poorer African Americans.

Such patterns would seem to us to undermine Haidt's view that people typically sacrifice their own interests to those of their salient groups. We hasten to add that such patterns similarly don't support the view that people solely care about immediate individual interests. Instead, these patterns suggest a messier formula, one that combines self-interest and group interests into something more like: What's in it for me, my family, my friends, my allies, and my wider social network? This combination is what we're calling "inclusive interests."

From our perspective, it's not surprising that politicians routinely talk about "you and your family," or that circumstances that threaten people's physical safety (like the attacks of 9/11 or large hurricanes) serve as such potent motivators of political will, or that issues relating to sex and reproduction (like abortion and birth control) can for some people in some circumstances become as or more important than issues relating to income redistribution, or that politics can often appear to be as much about people's own groups as their own selves.

In later chapters, we'll take a close look at how particular demographic features relate to differences in people's inclusive interests with respect to particular policy disputes. First, however, we'll address a lingering and important concern. If people are driven by their interests, why is it that, when asked why they have the policy preferences they have, people hardly ever say that it's because it's in their interests? Instead, people often claim that they, themselves, are largely magnanimous, interest-free creatures, while viewing their opponents as, at best, creatures of self-interest (and, at worst, evil people actively trying to sabotage society). If interests so obviously matter, why won't people just admit it?

CHAPTER 3

Machiavellian Minds

So convenient a thing it is to be a *Reasonable Creature*, since it
enables one to find or make a reason for every thing one has a
mind to do.

—*The Autobiography of Benjamin Franklin*

SUPPOSE A JOURNALIST WANTED TO KNOW WHY Big Regional Bank
(BRB) sponsored the Local International Arts Festival. To find out, the
journalist might ask BRB's corporate office. The reply would probably
come from its public relations department and say something about
BRB's views on the importance of being a good corporate citizen and
the role that the arts play in the quality of life of the region's citizens—
especially the children. *BRB is proud to be a part of this life-affirming
educational and cultural event . . .* and so on.

Suppose a journalist wanted to know why a presidential administration was pushing for increased government support for medical payments for seniors. To find out, the journalist might ask the administration's press office, which would probably say something about the
president's views on the importance of the nation's health and our obli-
gations to seniors. *The president believes it is an important part of who we
are as a nation that we look out for those who worked hard and played by
the rules and now seek to retire with dignity . . .* and so on.

Most observers of business and politics these days are pretty savvy
and cynical, and are unlikely to confuse the spin that banks and presidential administrations put on their actions with the truth of the matter.
Public statements come from the part of the organization that handles
public relations, and such statements often have little or nothing to do

with the real reasons that the bank sponsored the event or the administration is trying to expand payments to seniors. Any journalist who reported these press-office statements as simple facts about the underlying motives would be viewed as hopelessly naïve at best and on the take at worst.

Complex organizations such as large businesses and presidential administrations generally have a set of principal goals. For businesses, it's typically maximizing profits or shareholder value. For presidential administrations, it's typically advancing the ability of the administration and its party to win further elections and filling the policy gift baskets of their donors, activists, and voters.

For both businesses and administrations, the organization's success depends in part on maintaining a particular image. Businesses seek to attract customers with brand images emphasizing things such as reliability, value, and an association with excellent basketball players; many firms also cultivate a reputation for being nice, friendly, a generous supporter of communities and children, a good neighbor, and so on. Administrations seek to advance their policy objectives and attract voters with images of competency, strength, compassion, and love for all things American, from apple pie to Yellowstone.

Businesses and administrations, then, have a set of principal objectives that are about advancing the interests of themselves and their stakeholders. However, *as part of advancing those objectives*, they must engage in public relations that cover up the fact that the bases for their decisions have to do with advancing their principal interests, replacing the real motives with nice-sounding stories. In short, they have to engage in "spin," the polite way of saying they have to lie—a lot.

Firms and administrations organize themselves in ways that enhance their ability to spin. One way they do this is simply to limit who actually knows the truth of the matter: important decisions are generally made behind closed doors—whether in top-floor board rooms or hermetically sealed situation rooms—out of view of the prying press and the public. Such meetings aren't leak-proof—let alone subpoena-proof—but, under the usual circumstances, outsiders can't easily find out the details of the decision-making process that gave rise to a particular choice.

In other walled-off spaces are dedicated public relations staffs. These staffs often don't care *why* the decision-makers come to the decisions they do in their top-floor board rooms or hermetically sealed situation rooms. The jobs of public relations departments are made easier by the fact that the same decision might, plausibly, have been motivated by a number of different reasons.[1] Disconnected from the deliberations of decision-makers, public relations departments are free to pick and choose among a range of motives, selecting or inventing ones that work best for public consumption.

And, so, when Big Regional Bank decided to sponsor the Local International Arts Festival, the decision was probably made by the bank's executives and board of directors, who based their decision on a cost/ benefit analysis, a calculation regarding how much increased business they would get from the exposure the sponsorship provides. And when an administration decided to push for expanded funding for seniors' medical care, the decision was probably made in consultation with pollsters and key industries and donor groups, with a keen eye on the potential effect on future elections and fund-raising.

But then the public relations team does its job. In separate offices, it crafts its messages with a focus on manipulating public perception in favor of the organization. For the bank, the decision is presented not as one driven by profit maximization, but instead by a desire to promote the good of local communities . . . especially the children. For the administration, the decision is presented not as one driven by electoral and fund-raising advantages, but instead by widely shared concern for the well-being of grandparents. The public relations office doesn't get to set policy, but it does come up with ways to defend it. Public statements, in the end, have little to do with accurately describing why organizations do the things they do; in fact, public relations efforts actively seek to throw the public off the real trail.

In some cases, such messages are relayed to the public by spokespersons with minimal knowledge of how the decision was actually made and who perhaps had no direct role even in crafting the public relations story. At the extremes, they are essentially actors on a stage, delivering messages that are made all the more earnest by the spokespersons' own ignorance of the underlying, uglier, strategic facts. The blissful ignorance of the talking head is the icing on the cake of effective spin control. By virtue of their ignorance, spokespersons can tell the *organization's* lies without, themselves, lying. True, they are passing on misleading information; but they themselves remain willfully innocent of the facts.

There is no "I" in "Mind" (Well, there is, but . . .)

Advances in research in psychology over the last half century suggest that the human mind resembles large businesses and administrations: it consists of a large number of specialized systems, each with their own jobs, with information flows being limited among the different departments.[2] Human minds are complex bureaucracies.

Even people unfamiliar with much contemporary psychology probably know a little about some of the specialized systems of the mind. For example, there are systems whose job is narrowly focused on seeing. Starting with the photoreceptors in the retina and leading ultimately to dedicated groups of neurons in the brain, the cells of the visual system carry out the narrow but difficult task of building an image of the world.[3] There are also specialized systems for tasks such as understanding and producing language, moving the body's limbs, storing information about events that have occurred, and so on.[4] These systems are, loosely, analogous to a company's billing and collections department or payroll department or shipping department—departments that help the organization collect the information it needs and execute the decisions it makes.

Our concern here is not with these nuts-and-bolts systems, but rather with another way that the organization of the human mind parallels the organization of large corporations or administrations: the division of labor between decision-making and public relations. Human minds can be thought of as containing Boards of Directors engaged in high-level agenda setting in back rooms, Public Relations Departments that craft effective spin, and Spokespersons that have no real sense that they're telling made-up stories concocted by their Public Relations Departments.

A classic study from the literature in psychology illustrates the basic point. Richard Nisbett and Timothy Wilson conducted an experiment in which they laid out four pairs of panty hose and people had to say which pair they liked best, as one might be asked to do in a traditional marketing survey.[5] In this case, however, there was a twist: all four pairs of panty hose were identical. Because they were all identical, the experimenters could be sure that people weren't basing their decisions on some property of the panty hose, such as their color or their texture.

By and large, people chose the panty hose laid out on their right. That is, the cause of people's decisions was the *position* of the panty hose, not the *properties* of the panty hose. When asked to explain their choice, however, people did not say it was because of where their chosen item was on the display. Rather, they said they chose based on some (imagined) property that differentiated their selected pair from the others.

The claim that Nisbett and Wilson made was emphatically not that the people who participated were lying, intentionally deceiving the experimenters. The claim was that subjects literally did not know—have conscious awareness of—the reason for their choice. The Board of Directors of the mind did its job and picked one of the objects from the display, but didn't pass on the reason for its choice to the Public Relations Department of the mind. The Public Relations Department then did its job and made up a reason for the choice that was consistent with the story it likes to tell: *When I say something is preferable to other things, I don't do so irrationally or at random but, rather, I do so based on the fact that my chosen thing really does have better qualities.* Then the Spokesperson did its job, earnestly believed that the Public Relations Department's story was the actual source of the Board's decision, and made the case publicly, sincerely, and with a straight face.

Research over the last several decades suggests that people's inability to report the actual reasons that guide their decisions is by no means limited to panty hose choices, but is, in fact, pervasive. Several recent books—including *Blink* by Malcolm Gladwell and the somewhat less well-known *Strangers to Ourselves* by Timothy Wilson—document the large number of domains in which people lack conscious awareness of the reasons behind their choices.

Most of people's decisions, of course, are not as trivial as in the panty hose example. Usually, as we discussed in chapter 2, people, like big corporations and presidential administrations, have a set of principal objectives—trying to advance a number of everyday goals. And, like corporations and administrations, people need to maintain positive public images that are typically most effective when stories are spun to disguise these principal objectives.

To craft its public image, the mind combines tactics from Dale Carnegie's *How to Win Friends and Influence People* with Niccolò Machiavelli's *The Prince*. A person needs to appear to be a valuable asset: competent, smart, reasonable, talented, powerful, connected, wise. Such traits imply that a person can be of use to others. But a person also needs to appear *not* to be too self-interested. Others want allies who are altruistic and generous, genuinely invested in the interests of their confederates rather than in their own narrow interests.

In short, in the service of winning friends and influencing people (something that advances a person's own interests), the person encourages others to believe things about the person that are in *others'* own interests—that the person is a useful ally because of the person's competence, and also that the person is a useful ally because the person cares about others and is not really governed by concerns over the person's own interests. Minds pull off these Herculean feats of spin control the same way complex businesses and administrations do it—by sequestering the sources of their preferences and decisions away from their Public Relations Departments and, ultimately, their Spokespersons (i.e., their conscious minds). The Public Relations Department feeds the Spokesperson inaccurate but highly useful stories about how the Board's desires and actions really are simple reflections of competence and generosity.

The beauty of this compartmentalization is that this dynamic plays out unconsciously. Lies, after all, can be detected. But the conscious mind doesn't have to lie to tell the story that the underlying mental bureaucracy wants told. Instead, the conscious mind is simply fed made-up stories, believes them, and makes the case publicly. People's conscious Spokespersons usually literally don't know the true origin of their minds' own positions, and so have no qualms about pressing the only stories they're given, the nice-sounding stories their Public Relations Departments make up.

For instance, suppose we give a set of experimental subjects a test of "social intelligence"—a pleasantly ambiguous term—and tell some of them that their scores were on the high side and others that their scores were on the low side. Further, suppose the scores are actually assigned at random, having nothing to do with their actual test performance. We then ask the subjects why they think they got their impressive or unimpressive score. When researchers conduct these kinds of studies, subjects who are told they got a high score generally say that the result has to do with their inherent competence: their high social intelligence. But those who are told their scores are low generally resist explanations that call their competence into question—they say it has to do with bad luck. This is a very general pattern observed in psychological research: people often take credit for having brought about good outcomes, and blame others, chance, fate, or the gods for bad outcomes.[6]

In one version of this study, researchers went a step further and wired up some subjects to a lie detector that subjects believed accurately measured whether or not they were telling the truth.[7] One might have thought that when so wired up subjects would be slower to take credit for good scores and faster to admit blame for bad ones. Not at all. The results with and without the lie detector showed the same bias toward taking credit for the good score and denying responsibility for the bad one. The point is that there is no lie to detect—the Spokespersons of the mind are quite sincere in their belief in the accuracy of the Public Relations Departments' stories.

Thinking of the mind as a kind of modern organization with a Board of Directors, a Public Relations Department, and a Spokesperson helps explain the discrepancies between what people do and what people say about what they do. Still, there is an important way in which the analogy between corporations and administrations on the one hand, and minds on the other, does not hold up. In particular, corporations have CEOs; administrations have heads of government. There might well be no equivalent in the mind. The part people typically think of as their CEO—the conscious mind—is in fact just a bit player, a Spokesperson eager to stay on script but not actually in charge of much.

Consider the classic work of Benjamin Libet. He would have a subject sit in front of a clock and move their hand at a moment of their choosing. Subjects then reported the exact second they had decided to move their hand. While subjects were doing this, the electrical activity in their brain was being monitored, giving Libet an accurate measurement of when the decision was actually made (by monitoring the activity in the motor systems that execute such decisions). Though moving the hand feels like a "conscious" decision, people reported having made the decision to move their hand *after* the brain activity began, strongly suggesting that the decision was made before the subject was aware of having made it.[8] In other words, the conscious Spokesperson didn't learn of the decision until after it was made by some other part of the mental bureaucracy.

Other particularly striking evidence comes from work with epileptic patients. Epilepsy can act as a kind of uncontrolled electrical storm in the brain, starting off in one area and then quickly spreading across connected areas. In some patients, one procedure used to help control the effects is to sever the bundle of connections between the two halves of the brain; that way, when a storm arises in one half of the brain, it won't spread to the other half. In these split-brain patients, then, there's no direct communication between the two halves of the brain.

Michael Gazzaniga has used the unusual cases of split-brain patients to cast further light on the Public Relations Departments and Spokespersons in human brains (systems he calls the "left-hemisphere interpreter").[9] In one setup, Gazzaniga and colleagues had split-brain patients look at a screen and told them to follow any command presented on the screen. The researchers quickly flashed the word "laugh" on the left-hand side. Because of the way the nervous system is organized, this information gets sent only to the right hemisphere of the brain. The right hemisphere interprets the command and complies—the person chuckles. The left hemisphere, at this point, knows that a chuckle just came from their own mouth, but doesn't know why—the "laugh" command only went to the right hemisphere.

What happens when Gazzaniga asks the patient—really, their language-using left hemisphere—why they just laughed? Does the left-hemisphere Spokesperson say "holy crap, that's weird; I have no idea why I just laughed"? Does it fret? Does it panic? Not at all. It takes things utterly in stride. "Oh," it says, without any hint of distress, "you guys are really something!" In other words, it passes along a more or less reasonable-sounding answer to the question of why the person laughed—because other people in the room were being funny. It was the wrong answer in this case (really it had to do with the "laugh" command sent to the right hemisphere), but it's the kind of answer that in most situations would have been perfectly plausible.

In such cases the Spokesperson doesn't miss a beat because the Public Relations Department is doing what it always does, what it's designed to do—providing reasonable-sounding interpretations of what a person does despite the fact that the Public Relations Department is often ignorant about the underlying causes. It makes stuff up. That's what it's there for.

As with the case of Libet's clock-watchers, the Spokespersons in Gazzaniga's studies are happy to take credit for decisions made elsewhere in the neural bureaucracy. The Spokespersons have a funny feature not found in corporations or administrations—they believe they are the CEO/President, calling the shots. But it's largely an illusion.

Emotional Intelligence

Instead of a single CEO of the mind, there is something more like a Board of Directors, a collection of systems responsible for setting the agenda and determining which outcomes count as good ones that should be pursued and bad ones that should be avoided. These systems are, speaking very roughly, the emotional systems that motivate behavior and produce so-called gut feelings or intuitive reactions.

In the past, emotions were seen as in conflict with reason. Modern psychology takes a very different view. These days, many, perhaps most, psychologists don't view emotions and reason as fundamentally different from each other. Instead, they view minds as engaged in various kinds of information processing, some of which is faster and more automatic and some of which is slower and more deliberative. Behavior comes from a combination of systems using a mix of processing styles. Daniel Kahneman's *Thinking, Fast and Slow* is an extended look at how modern psychologists approach emotion and cognition; Malcolm Gladwell's *Blink* is something of a catalog of some striking cases, such as the opening chapter about experts' ability to intuit that a piece of art is a forgery without being able to articulate how they know.

The large number of systems that together make up an individual mind need coordination and guidance; these systems need to know what's important at any given moment, what sorts of problems they should be focused on, and what sorts of outcomes are desirable. These tasks fall to the mind's motivational systems, what we're referring to as its Board of Directors.

A textbook definition of emotions these days (rephrased in the kind of language we're using in this book) runs something like this: An emotion is a commonly occurring, results-oriented reaction to some external event that serves to coordinate the systems in a person's brain and body (e.g., to focus attention on something important, to get lots of the brain's subsystems processing information about the situation at hand, to get one's muscles ready to act fast if needed), helping the person to interact with the world in ways that advance the person's goals.[10]

Consider an emotion such as anger. Someone does something that harms the interests of a person or the people that person cares about. The person gets angry. Systems in the person's mind that might have previously been focused on, say, getting something to eat, now get new marching orders: Focus on the object of the anger and figure out ways to fight back. Blood starts pumping away from the digestive system and toward the person's muscles, preparing the body for action. The person's face takes on a characteristically angry look, signaling in a quick and effective way to others around the person that there's a storm a-brewing, so they better either back off or get ready for business. The anger can then quickly go away if the person quickly gets what they want. As explained elegantly by Robert Frank in *Passions within Reason*, anger is an effective means of deterrence. If I get (visibly) angry when you have hurt me or are about to do so—if I get prepared and motivated to harm you—then you are less likely to hurt me in the future. Far from being irrational, then, emotions such as anger typically guide people toward useful outcomes.

Emotions often reflect the sorts of social goals we discussed in chapter 2—safety, health, mating, alliances, status, family, and so forth. Anger, for example, is often a response to a threat to some aspect of one's inclusive interests. Someone threatens the safety of one's self, family, or friends. Someone steals one's property. Someone doesn't hold up their end of a bargain intended to be mutually beneficial. Someone is disrespectful, implying that one has low social status. Someone flirts with one's long-term romantic partner (or one's partner flirts back).

Other emotions have similar interpretations. Fear and anxiety focus mental resources to deal with potentially dangerous situations. Disgust keeps people away from pathogens and toxins. Familial love helps guide people in caring for and seeking care from people who have shared interests in one another's well-being. Sexual passion and romantic love get people to put up with outrageous levels of nonsense in the service of their mating goals. Envy focuses a person's attention on ways to even out status competitions that the person appears to be losing. Romantic jealousy reduces the chance of a person's partner cheating on them or abandoning them. Shame and guilt help people in navigating complex social interactions to make amends for the strategic harms they sometimes inflict on others. Emotions, in short, guide the fundamentals of navigating social life and getting what one wants.

When we talk about a mind's Board of Directors, we mean these kinds of motivational systems, designed to identify and advance people's inclusive interests. They are the shadowy emotions, the "gut-level" responses—the things that get people to care about issues in the first place, determine their basic positions, and spur them to action.

People often think of the products of their motivational systems as mysterious, but that's just Spokespersons noticing that they're not privy to the deliberations of the Boards of Directors. People's lack of insight regarding their own motives doesn't mean that what the Boards are doing is unsophisticated or irrational—far from it. As authors such as Gladwell have discussed, it just means that the conscious parts of minds don't receive certain kinds of information about the workings of the unconscious parts of minds. People often know the results of the deliberations, but are not privy to the deliberations themselves. People also often think of the products of their motivational systems as unmoved by rational thought—the heart wants what it wants, after all. But this is just their Spokespersons noticing the limits of their own role in the bureaucracy.

In recent years, some political scientists have integrated lessons from the psychology of emotions, recognizing that emotions are coordinating mechanisms that are goal-directed and that generally work in people's interests,[11] and that emotions give people a kind of sophistication with the politics of everyday life even among those who are mostly ignorant of national politics.[12] These efforts to integrate nuanced work on emotions are a welcome development.

Politicians are similarly getting more sophisticated in speaking to citizens' emotions. People's mental Boards of Directors deal with concrete consequences for themselves, their families, their friends, and their social networks. In political contexts, Boards seem to respond best to examples of real people like themselves who are helped or harmed by particular policies. And so the savvy politician, when advocating some policy or another, places Ordinary Americans nodding appreciatively in the camera's frame standing behind the politician. The politician tells stories about ordinary people being tangibly hurt by the politician's opponents' favored policy but tangibly helped by the politician's own favored policy—*you know, I met a woman, Jane Public, yesterday, and she told me that her child can't afford to go to college or get a life-saving medical procedure, but we're going to make sure no one has to go through what Jane and her family have gone through.* Cue applause from the Ordinary Americans. Persuasion is in no small part a matter of winning over people's (emotional) Boards of Directors.

Eternal Spin of the Political Mind

In summary, the mind has an agenda—advancing inclusive interests in the context of real-life goals. This agenda is set by the Board of Directors, a set of motivational systems whose internal workings are sophisticated, but kept out of one's own consciousness (and thus outside of public view). Other specialized mental systems deal with various kinds of tasks needed to gather information and carry out activities consistent with the Board's agenda. One such set of systems is the Public Relations Department, primarily responsible for developing arguments and narratives that advance the mind's goal of appearing to be competent and generous. The creation of these stories also occurs largely outside of conscious awareness. Down the line is the Spokesperson, who is fed limited information, often including the basic directives of the Board along with the talking points of the Public Relations Department. The Spokesperson takes credit for the entire operation, claiming that the person does the things the person does and advocates the things the person advocates for the reasons listed in the talking points.

The result, when it comes to political opinions, is a messy combination of preferences for policies that advance people's own inclusive interests coupled with a stubborn set of talking points used to insist that, in fact, these policy preferences *really* just come from a well-reasoned concern for the welfare of everyone. I have the positions I have because I am a smart person and my favored policies are smart policies. I have the positions I have because I am a good person and my favored policies are good for society.

On the flip side, when human minds are confronted with people who disagree with their preferred policies, the mental machinery builds competing narratives. *Those people* have the positions they have because they are stupid people with stupid ideas. *Those people* have the positions they have because they are bad people who are at best brazenly selfish and at worst actively seeking to destroy what is good in society.

The Spokespersons are not *lying* when they pass along the stories that paint themselves as clever and noble and paint their opponents as clueless and nefarious. Still, even if they're not lying, that's not to say that they are not, in an important sense, often *wrong*. In fact, the stories typically are systematically and self-servingly mistaken. The mind has an agenda, but it's a hidden agenda, buried beneath self-serving spin, hidden not only from others but from its own conscious Spokesperson.

Evidence for these views has been accumulating for some time. Consider a study by psychologist Geoffrey Cohen, who had subjects evaluate a proposal on welfare reform.[13] Cohen varied the content of the proposal—generous or stringent—and, crucially, also varied the information he provided to subjects about whether the proposal was favored by Democrats or Republicans. What mattered more, the content of the policy or the group that endorsed it? As Cohen put it: "For both liberal and conservative participants, the effect of reference group information overrode that of policy content. If their party endorsed it, liberals supported even a harsh welfare program, and conservatives supported even a lavish one."[14] Subjects were also asked about the extent to which their evaluation of the policy was influenced by the information they received about which party endorsed or opposed the policy. Because Cohen's design was experimental, it's clear that the information about the party that endorsed the proposal was the cause of subjects' views; yet subjects denied that the party positions determined their views.[15]

Subjects in Cohen's studies show the mental bureaucracy at work. The Board announced its position, which was to not bother thinking too hard and just use the Democrat/Republican tag to make a quick judgment in line with its preferred party coalition; the Public Relations Department provided the spin, which was that the person's position had little to do with lazily playing favorites but was instead based on being considerate and reasonable; and the Spokesperson did its job of earnestly claiming to have adopted the Boards' bottom-line position *because of* the well-spun reasons.

Jon Haidt's research illustrating "moral dumbfounding" has produced other examples.[16] In one case, subjects were told a story about a brother and sister who have sex with each other. They use two forms of birth control, they enjoy it, and they never do it again, though they believe the experience improved their relationship. Subjects were asked whether what the pair did was right or wrong, and, if it was wrong, why. Subjects generally believed that what the siblings did was wrong, of course. When subjects provided a reason for their judgment, they frequently offered one that was contradicted by the story, such as the possibility of a deformed child (which was negated in the story by the use of reliable birth control). Haidt found that subjects eventually gave up, and indicated that the act was wrong even though they couldn't provide a reason to justify this judgment.

Moral dumbfounding illustrates the Spokesperson's limited purview. The Spokesperson doesn't determine moral preferences (that's the Board's job), but just passes along stories about those moral preferences.

Challenging those made-up stories doesn't typically cause people to change their moral preferences; the Spokesperson just gives up . . . *Hey, I've got my orders and this stuff is above my pay grade.*

A particularly relevant line of research comes from psychologists Nicholas Epley and David Dunning, who have investigated people's beliefs about their own motives versus others' motives. Subjects in one study had to choose which of two tasks they themselves would do, and which task they would assign to another person. The "self-interest" of the assignment was manipulated—the unpleasant task would last either thirty minutes or only ten minutes. And the "moral sentiments" of the assignment were manipulated as well—the other person they assigned the other task to was either a male college student or a ten-year-old girl (in general people feel worse about assigning unpleasant tasks to little girls). The results? While people predicted that they themselves wouldn't be as strongly influenced by self-interest as other people and would of course be strongly influenced by moral sentiments, in fact self-interest mattered a great deal: four times more people took the unpleasant task when it was only ten minutes long rather than thirty minutes long.[17]

As Epley and Dunning put it, in a remark that closely echoes the thesis we pursue in this chapter: "participants correctly anticipated that others would be strongly influenced by self-interest, but erroneously predicted that they themselves would not. . . . On the other hand, participants inaccurately predicted that moral sentiments would influence both their own and others' behavior. Although participants generally overestimated the impact of moral sentiments, they did so particularly when predicting their own behavior."[18] Summarizing these findings, they wrote: "Participants tended to predict that their own behavior would be influenced only by the level of moral sentiments inherent in the situation and not by the level of self-interest. Actual behavior, in contrast, was influenced only by participants' self-interest."[19]

Similar patterns of results have been found by other researchers. In studies in which people are asked to indicate how important various motives—"extrinsic" incentives, such as pay, compared to "intrinsic" motives, such as "accomplishing something worthwhile"—are for themselves and for others, people tend to think that others are extrinsically motivated while claiming that they themselves are intrinsically motivated. *Other people do it for the money; I do it because it's worthwhile.* For example, in one study, a majority of prospective lawyers indicated that they were pursuing the career path because of its intellectual appeal as opposed to the financial rewards; but they thought that their peers were on average pursuing the field for the money.[20] In another study, college students estimated that *other students* would be nearly twice as likely to donate blood if they were paid fifteen dollars compared to the case in which there was no payment at all. Crucially, however, the students reported that they themselves would be nearly as likely to donate in both cases, suggesting that subjects felt that others respond to financial incentives in a way that they themselves would not.[21]

Once people's Boards of Directors have adopted their favored positions, additional processes help people preserve these views. For instance, in one study looking at gun control, subjects were given the choice of reading arguments from various sources that could reasonably be inferred to be either in line with their own position on the issue or from contrary sources (the NRA, Citizens Against Handguns, etc.). Do people investigate relevant arguments evenhandedly? As the authors of the work put it: "[P]roponents of the issue sought out more supporting than opposing arguments, and this difference was quite substantial for sophisticates. . . . When given the chance, sophisticated respondents selected arguments from like-minded groups 70–75% of the time. For example, on average sophisticated opponents of stricter gun control sought out six arguments of the NRA or the Republican Party and only two arguments from the opposition."[22] Such results imply that instead of dispassionately seeking out information in the services of determining the most sensible, reasonable positions based on the facts of the matter, people try to find arguments that can be used to bolster their Boards' existing views.

A recent study by Yale law professor Dan Kahan and colleagues illustrates a similar point.[23] Kahan measured people's political views and then showed them data from one of two (fake) studies. In one experiment, subjects were shown information about rates of recovering from an illness for medical patients who had received a particular treatment versus those who had not received the treatment. In a second experiment, subjects were shown information presented in exactly the same way, but this time comparing crime rates in cities with gun bans versus cities without such bans. The math was identical in both cases, but the animating idea behind the study was that subjects might be motivated to see the answer they wanted to see in the case of guns as opposed to medical treatment. Indeed they did. Numerically sophisticated Democrats, when seeing data that gun bans reduced crime, correctly identified this pattern. But when numerically sophisticated Democrats were presented with data that indicated that the gun bans were ineffective, their number-interpreting performance was significantly worse. Reciprocal results were found for Republicans. The Public Relations Department sees what it wants to see in data, even if what it wants to see isn't there.

Passions and Reasons in the Abortion Debate

To see, concretely, how these ideas work in the context of an important policy domain, we'll now take a look at the work of Boards of Directors, Public Relations Departments, and Spokespersons in the particularly thorny case of abortion. Putting it a bit roughly—and we'll revisit this idea in more detail in the next chapter—people who support abortion rights are often people who spend big chunks of their early adult lives having sex but not having children. That is, they have an interest in the availability of the tools that aid family planning. Their opponents, in contrast, tend to be people who have an interest in making casual sex socially more costly and difficult; as a result, they seek to limit family planning. These interests, we think, explain why many people have their varying intuitive reactions to abortion—their Boards are mostly thinking about how abortion affects adults' lifestyles.[24]

This lifestyle-driven view helps explain some otherwise puzzling empirical details of people's abortion views (as we'll see shortly) but, like most interest-based sources of issue opinions, makes for terrible public relations. The pro-life side can't say things like: *It would be better for people like us if other people didn't sleep around very much, so we favor things that make casual sex riskier.* The pro-choice side can't say things like: *We want to spend big chunks of our lives sleeping around without having babies, so it's really better for us if we have the tools to make that easier.*

There are, of course, far better stories to be told. Some of the favorite protagonists in the political stories of Public Relations Departments are women and children. For the pro-choice side, their Spokespersons get handed a useful story rallying around women: *We support the right of women to control their own bodies.* And for the pro-life side, their Spokespersons get handed a different useful story rallying around children: *We oppose abortion because it kills babies . . . babies, not fetuses, because, it turns out, we believe that life begins at conception.*

Both stories provide good spin but are bad explanations for the actual sources of people's views. The life-begins-at-conception account sits very uneasily with the reality of pro-life attitudes: While pro-life Americans routinely oppose abortion in cases in which women willingly have sex but don't (currently) want to have (more) children, the majority of pro-life Americans do not oppose abortion in cases of rape, incest, or fetal deformity. To see the point, imagine a survey asking someone whether they support a mother's right to kill her two-year-old. Everyone would answer no to this, of course. Fine, the survey continues, but what if the mother had been raped? Or if the child were developmentally disabled? Now is it OK? Neither situation, we think, would change anyone's answer. People don't take circumstances into account when the issue is killing two-year-olds. But they do when it comes to abortion.

These kinds of exceptions are inconsistent with the life-begins-at-conception account but quite consistent with our lifestyle-driven theory. Rape and fetal deformity are circumstances that don't have much to do with casual sex or family planning—these are cases in which women who engage in no casual sex or family planning at all might nonetheless want abortions. Pro-life Boards of Directors make exceptions because their judgments are based in large part on adults' lifestyles.

On a related note, sometimes the pro-choice side is confused by the fact that the pro-life side often opposes expanding the availability of birth control and comprehensive sex education, both of which could reduce the need for abortions in the first place. Surely, choicers think, if the goal is to reduce the number of abortions, then an obvious step in the right direction would be anything that reduces the number of unplanned pregnancies. If one views pro-life opinions as primarily aimed at casual sex and family planning, however, there's no confusion. Readily available birth control makes casual sex less risky, explaining lifers' enhanced opposition.

The pro-life side, of course, is seeking to interfere in other adults' lives, for which it's helpful to have some higher authority. Their Public Relations Departments distance themselves from responsibility for undermining anyone's lifestyle: *Blame God, not me*. One often sees talk that abortion opponents are "biblical literalists" who simply get their views from the Bible.[25] This proposed basis for the sources of pro-life views is implausible. First, while the Bible covers a lot of topics (including adultery, divorce, and homosexuality), it contains nothing—really, nothing—that directly speaks to when life begins or whether abortion is wrong. (It's hard to prove a negative, but we'll just point out that one of your authors once offered a hundred dollars to the first person in a large undergraduate course who could provide a clear biblical source for pro-life views. He left the offer open for several weeks and never had to pay.) Second, there are a ton of things that the Bible literally says that are literally ignored by biblical literalists. The book of Leviticus, for example, contains wide-ranging directives that are really quite specific. To take just a few examples: Don't wear clothing woven of two kinds of material; don't plant your field with two kinds of seed; don't cut your hair at the sides of your head; don't get tattoos; treat foreign visitors the same as native-born people. So, the biblical-literalism account of abortion is a double failure—abortion isn't in the Bible, and people quite often ignore things that actually are in the Bible, even when they claim to take it literally.

The Public Relations Departments of choicers don't do much better with their favored stories. These stories tend to be about how pro-choice people believe that women have a fundamental right to control their own bodies and view attempts to force women to carry a pregnancy to term as a kind of reactionary misogyny, even part of a "war on women."

First, however, the "war on women" story leads to the expectation that men are more likely to oppose abortion rights than women, yet the differences between women's and men's views on abortion are in fact trivial. If anything, women are a bit more likely than men to be consistently pro-life. Abortion might be an issue that relates particularly to women, but pro-choice views are not more common among women.

From our lifestyle-driven point of view, this is not surprising—we don't view abortion restrictions as aimed at women generally, but at casual sex and family planning, which involve (some) women (but not other women) and (some) men (but not other men). As we discuss in more detail in chapter 4, opposition to abortion tends to come from both men and women with more traditional sexual and reproductive lifestyles, while support for abortion rights tends to come from both men and women who are less traditional.

In a related point, as Kristen Luker examined in *Abortion and the Politics of Motherhood*, the activists on both sides of the abortion debate are typically women. This is inconsistent with a simple "war on women" framework. But it's highly consistent with our lifestyle-driven viewpoint given Luker's emphasis on the different features of pro-choice and pro-life women activists—the pro-choice side tends to attract unmarried professional women while the pro-life side attracts more stay-at-home wives with lots of kids. It's not tough to spot the group with a bigger interest in family planning versus the group that might be really nervous by the notion of a society with lots of casual sex.

Another weakness in the women-controlling-their-bodies explanation is that there are plenty of ways in which most pro-choice people otherwise agree that women (and men) should be restricted in what they do with their bodies: seat belt laws, prostitution laws, restrictions on trans fats and giant sodas, mandatory health insurance, and so forth. Hardly anyone holds views actually consistent with the idea that people should be able to do whatever they want with their bodies.

The pro-choice side engages in its own interpretative contortions when it comes to sacred documents, viewing the U.S. Constitution as guaranteeing a "right to privacy" that prohibits laws that outlaw abortion prior to fetal viability. This interpretation is, to put it mildly, on thin ice when it comes to the actual text. People favoring a right to privacy don't claim to be "strict constructionists" but rather view the Constitution as a "living" document that changes with the times. However, these sorts of principles don't drive judicial outcomes so much as they are themselves driven by one's favored outcomes. It's a classic case of what psychologists call "motivated reasoning." In short, practically no one who wasn't already in favor of abortion rights would read the U.S.

Constitution and infer that it prevents states from limiting abortion, just as practically no one who wasn't already opposed to abortion would read the Bible and decide that it takes the position that abortion is a serious moral issue.

A common portrait of abortion opinions presents a nation polarized into warring tribes by deeply held, plainly incompatible principles.[26] But these stories don't really explain what's going on. Instead, the minds-as-bureaucracies account, though more complicated, pays off in doing a good job of explaining the whole package. We can understand the positions taken by people's Boards (the positions are mostly driven by considerations of adults' promiscuity and family planning); we can understand why people's Public Relations Departments would want to hide these real sources behind made-up, noble-sounding stories about how it all comes down to protecting women or children; and we can understand why people's Spokespersons defend the stories so adamantly, despite the fact that the stories fail both empirically and logically.

From Minds to Issues

In part I of this book we've sketched the psychological foundations that will help in figuring out why people have the political views they have. In chapter 1 we saw that it's just not the case that people typically fall consistently either to the left or to the right in their political opinions. In chapter 1 we also argued that many of the typical policy-laden "value" or "personality" variables used to account for political opinions end up creating plainly circular explanations that provide lots of renaming but few actual answers. In chapter 2 we saw that self-interest often matters in political opinions, despite claims to the contrary. In chapter 2 we also argued that typical notions of "self-interest" are too limited to be of much use; instead, we argued for an expanded notion of "inclusive interests" to better connect to the kinds of concerns that drive real people in everyday life.

In chapter 3 we made our case that minds are Machiavellian bureaucracies, driven by the agenda-setting commands of a back-room Board of Directors, filtered through a speech-writing Public Relations

Department that seeks to give the Board's commands a public-friendly veneer, and presented to the public by the earnest Spokesperson more widely known as the conscious self. The agenda of the secretive Board—advancing the person's everyday, real-life, competitive interests—typically goes unrecognized by the happy-talking Spokesperson, who cheerfully adopts whatever story will make its wider bureaucratic home seem most principled, altruistic, responsible, consistent, considerate, and reasonable. A key implication is that *people can't just introspect their way into figuring out why they have the political preferences they have* but, instead, have to piece together the puzzle in other ways.

Together, these considerations lead us to a view of the political animal as ultimately driven not by ideologies or philosophies or values, but by the desires of individuals to advance their inclusive interests, to support societal rules that aid themselves and their families and their allies in achieving the kinds of fundamental goals that drive everyday life.

Sometimes advancing a person's own inclusive interests advances most other people's interests as well, and so there's little conflict. Residents of a given city, for example, all want a safe and reliable water system, and one doesn't see a lot of political conflict with a given side favoring safe and reliable water and the other side opposing it. But sometimes there are real conflicts in which some people benefit from one regime and others from another. Income redistribution is one example, generally benefiting the poor at the expense of the wealthy. Some of these conflicts in a given time and place become so widespread, recurring, and unresolved that they appear as standard themes in political and moral conversations.

We now shift from the generalities of political minds to the specifics of political issues. The next set of chapters will explore why different people take different positions on widely contested issues. Why do some people oppose legalizing marijuana and others support it? Why do some people oppose same-sex marriage and others support it? Why do some people oppose expanded immigration and others support it? Why do some people oppose race-based affirmative action and others support it? Why do some people oppose expanding government safety nets and others support it?

Our view of minds leads us to ignore some of the usual suspects scholars identify when addressing these questions: ideologies, values, political personality variables, biblical literalism, constitutional principles, and so on. We're less interested in the press releases penned by Public Relations Departments. Instead, we're trying to gather clues about the closed-door meetings of people's Boards of Directors. We're looking for the ways in which the policies people support affect their everyday lives and how different features of different people give rise to competing interests and competing political positions.

In the next few chapters, our tools will largely consist of demographic information that figures heavily in the work of political professionals— race, gender, religion, income, education, and so on. Our goal is to explain not just *how* different demographic features connect with different policy disputes, but *why*.

A key insight from political targeting has been that different demographic features relate to different kinds of issues. People's religious lives might relate to their views on abortion, for example, but that doesn't mean they have much to do with their views on immigration. People's income might relate to their views on taxes, but that doesn't mean that income has much to do with their views on legalizing marijuana. As we've argued, thinking about people as being generally "liberal" or generally "conservative" can advance the ball only so far. The connections between people's lives and politics occur in the details. And so, in the next few chapters, we won't be talking about how being a racial minority makes a person generally "liberal," for example. (On some issues, in fact, we'll see that racial minorities tend to be more "conservative.") The key is to focus issue by issue. What are the competing interests at stake for a particular issue? What are the demographic features that relate to different individuals' interests for a particular issue?

Moving now to part II of the book, we'll split up the sets of policies we examine into three chapters covering issues relating to sex and reproduction (e.g., abortion and pornography), group-based issues (e.g., same-sex marriage and affirmative action), and economic issues (e.g., government spending on health care). For each of these three sets of issues, different aspects of people's lives and interests are implicated, and, as a result, different sets of demographic features come into play.

PART II

Political Issues

CHAPTER 4

Fighting over Sex: Lifestyle Issues and Religion

WHEN IT COMES TO SEX AND FERTILITY, the United States and other developed countries are incredibly diverse. It's easy to look at the sexual revolution, for example, and think that the road from the 1950s to the present in the United States led from *Father Knows Best* to *Sex and the City*. A closer look shows that the country moved from one in which most people had lasting marriages and lots of kids to one in which there is tremendous variety. The old patterns didn't die out; they just shrank.

The generation born in the 1930s that came of age around the 1950s by and large had a typical pattern when it came to marriage. By the time they were in their fifties, around 95% of them had married and only about a third had divorced; that is, there was a roughly two-thirds majority of people who married and never divorced.[1] Among the baby boomers, born between 1946 and 1964, marriage rates were also very high but the rate of divorce climbed from a third to a half. Generations subsequent to the baby boomers have married less, with a related rise in nonmarital cohabitation. Still, plenty of people these days get married once and never divorce, but nothing like two-thirds of the country. The nation went from—statistically speaking—typicality to variety.

Related shifts occurred in Americans' sexual activity and fertility. Among women born in the 1930s, only 10% of those in their fifties reported having had more than five sex partners in their adult lives. Among baby-boom women in their fifties this figure rose to 25%. For birth rates, close to 60% of the 1930s generation had three or more children, while baby boomers were equally spread among having three or more children, having exactly two children, and having either one or none. Having few sex partners and lots of kids was once highly typical of American women, but now it's just one pattern among others.

In recent years, television shows such as *Sex and the City* and *Girls* have portrayed the lives of young women in big cities as being filled with a series of sexual affairs. The media often write about "hook-up culture" in a way that implies that everybody's doing it.[2] From popular accounts, one might be forgiven for having the impression that modern young women are as homogenous as their midcentury counterparts, but at the opposite extreme.

In fact, despite the fictional escapades of Carrie, Charlotte, Miranda, and Samantha on *Sex and the City*, almost one in ten women in their twenties these days are virgins; almost another three in ten report having had sex with only one person since age eighteen. Fewer than two in ten report having had sex with seven or more people. True, about a third of women in their twenties have no children and go to bars about once a month or more—something resembling *Sex and the City*—but then just as many have children and don't go to bars as often as once a month. Roughly a quarter have no children and still don't go to bars as often as once a month.

College students show similar patterns. We've given anonymous surveys on these topics to a couple thousand undergraduates at a half-dozen American universities. Contradicting the media portrayal of students as sexually voracious, a fifth in our samples have never had intercourse or hooked up and almost another fifth have had intercourse or hooked up with only one or two partners. On the other end of the spectrum, about a quarter have had ten or more intercourse or hook-up partners. About a third report rarely if ever drinking, another third drink a couple of times a month, and the other third drink more than that. Around three-quarters rarely if ever use recreational drugs.

The wilder groups of college students make for juicier gossip, better TV, and more interesting press coverage—few people would be interested in reading an article headlined "Arizona State Undergraduate Stays in Dorm Room, Studies on Friday Night"—so the wilder kids are more visible. This asymmetry in media coverage makes it easy to overestimate their prevalence. But for every college kid who goes wild, there's another who is abstinent.

College itself represents another way that America has become increasingly diverse. Relatively few people, especially women, got college degrees prior to the baby-boom generation. But, again, the pattern goes from typicality to variety. Most people reading a book like this are college educated and tend to overestimate how many other Americans these days are as well. The reality is that, even among Americans in their thirties, only 35% have a bachelor's degree or more, 28% have some college or an associate's degree but no bachelor's degree, and the other 37% never completed even a year of college.[3]

Marriage, sex, fertility, and education interact in complex ways. For instance, most highly educated people delay starting families compared with those with less education.[4] Women who don't go to college typically have their first child in their late teens or early twenties; women with bachelor's degrees generally wait until their mid-twenties to early thirties. Women with less education are more likely to have children outside of marriage; at higher education levels, few do.

Also, marriages are less stable among those who marry young. First marriages for people their late teens have about a 50% chance of ending within ten years, but people first marrying in their late twenties have only around a 25% to 30% chance of splitting up within ten years.[5] Divorce rates also relate to sex and nonmarital cohabitation. Putting it somewhat bluntly, people who have sex with many people are less likely to stay married to one person. Overall, people first marrying at around age twenty-four have a little over a 30% chance of splitting up within ten years. But for those who had prior sex partners and who lived together before getting engaged, the ten-year divorce rate is over 40%; among those who were virgins until around the time they married, the ten-year divorce rate is tiny, less than 15%.

In sum, there's a lot of diversity. Many people have lots of kids; others don't. Lots of people wait until getting married before having kids; lots of people don't. Lots of young people are hooking up and drinking and using drugs; lots of young people are not. Lots of people have several sex partners and cohabit before getting married, if they marry at all; lots of people don't. Lots of young adults are highly educated and delay having kids; lots of young adults are not and do not.

Freewheelers and Ring-Bearers

To make things easier to follow, we'll use the terms "Freewheelers" and "Ring-Bearers" to describe different broad categories of sexual and reproductive lifestyles. Freewheelers include people who sleep with more people, are sexually active outside of committed relationships, have more same-sex partners, party, drink, go to bars, and use recreational drugs more, live together outside of marriage, are less likely to marry at all, get divorced more when they do marry, and have fewer kids. Ring-Bearers include people who wait longer to have sex, tend to have sex only in committed relationships (often waiting until getting engaged or married), go to bars and party less, don't cohabit outside of marriage, have long-lasting marriages, and have more kids.

People don't, of course, all fit tidily into the Freewheeler and Ring-Bearer categories, and many exist in the places in between. Further, lots of people have predominantly Freewheeler patterns at some points in their lives and predominantly Ring-Bearer patterns at others. Still, by and large, the categories tend to hang together. People who sleep with more people are more likely to drink more, use recreational drugs, and cohabit outside of marriage, all of which relate to lower marriage rates and less stable marriages over the long term, which in turn are associated with having fewer children. Freewheelers, by our terms, are people who lean in that direction on the whole, while Ring-Bearers are people who lean in the opposite direction.

While we can distinguish broadly between people who lean in either the Freewheeler or Ring-Bearer direction, the details of their sexual and reproductive patterns have complex intersections with race and education. African Americans have lower marriage rates than whites (a Freewheeler trend), but they also drink less on average (a Ring-Bearer trend). People with more education tend to delay having children and end up with fewer of them (Freewheeler trends), but they also tend to delay having sex and end up with lower divorce rates (Ring-Bearer trends). Among Ring-Bearers, the less educated are more likely to marry early and have higher divorce rates down the line. Among Freewheelers, while those with less education are more likely to have kids conceived in the context of their younger partying, those with more education tend to put off having kids until much later in life and often end up having none at all—an arc all too familiar to the characters in *Sex and the City*.

The Interests of Freewheelers and Ring-Bearers

In sorting out how these lifestyle differences translate into different interests and, consequently, different political views, let's start with an easy case, one that we suspect will sound very familiar to many readers. Consider a person who gets lots of education and goes into a high earning career path. The person also enjoys a Freewheeler lifestyle, involving late teens and early twenties with plenty of partying and a certain number of low-commitment sexual experiences. Later, there might be a nonmarital cohabitation (or two, or three), leading ultimately to one or more marriages and a small number of children later in life. As familiar as this sounds, people who get college degrees, delay having children, and pursue Freewheeler lifestyles constitute maybe a fifth or a quarter of modern Americans.

From the point of view of someone with such a lifestyle pattern, does it help or hurt their interests when *other people* morally condemn low-commitment sexual activity? Moral condemnation from other people isn't something abstract; there are negative consequences for the condemned person's social goals of winning friends and influencing people. Obviously, the people who suffer from moral attacks on adventurous sexuality are more adventurous people, and they should be expected to defend themselves by recruiting others to the position that moral attacks on low-commitment sex are not OK. They might even lead their own moral counterattacks against anti-promiscuity moralization, bringing collective pressures to bear in opposition to those who engage in "slut shaming" and related kinds of lifestyle intolerance.

What about their interests in having alcohol and recreational drug use be legal and not viewed as serious moral issues? Members of this group are especially likely to have active party phases in the service of their hooking-up agenda, and they benefit when these activities don't have high legal or social costs.

Is it in their interests for birth control and abortion to be widely available? Certainly. These are people who engage in sexual activity for long periods of time outside of committed relationships while they're climbing educational and professional ladders; for such people, it's *really important* not to be forced to have children at inconvenient times. They want to wait until their ducks are in a row before having children, who will then themselves reap the rewards of their parents' high education and income. These are people who, more than most, have stakes in "family planning."

These highly educated Freewheelers are relatively easy to understand. People who party and sleep around have an interest in other people not bringing legal or moral costs to bear on them for doing so. People who want to delay having children while partying and sleeping around have an interest in the availability of family planning, including the backstop of legal abortion. Their mental Boards of Directors will prefer moral and political policies that help them live the lives they want to live.

Less straightforward is figuring out why anyone would want to stop them. Aren't these the classically "victimless" misdemeanors? If I want to go all hippie or high roller, have some hooch, inhale a hookah, hook up with a hottie, hole up with a honey—ain't nobody's business if I do, right? And so what if I want to do all this without having children? Seriously, wouldn't everyone *prefer* that, if I do these things, I do them without having children? Why would anyone's Board of Directors object to any of this?

Consider a very different, but equally common, lifestyle pattern. Consider people who get moderate amounts of education, marry in their early or mid-twenties, and have relatively higher numbers of children. A key, recurring problem with this pattern is that, if the marriages don't last, the women and children are often faced with potentially crippling economic hardship.[6] (In fact, these days, in large part because of Social Security and Medicare, the elderly are rarely impoverished compared with earlier eras, and the typical demographic profile of American poverty has shifted away from the elderly poor to unmarried women with less education and higher numbers of young children.)[7]

Plenty of such couples do, of course, have marriages that last. What predicts a lasting marriage? Waiting; getting married later in life without already having had children.[8] But for people who get married earlier (in no small part, often, *because they want to end up with more children*), sexual commitment is important. The marriages most likely to last for those marrying younger are those in which the members of the couple don't have sex at all before marriage (even among teens, only about one in five of these marriages split up within ten years). Short of waiting until marriage, the marriages that last are between people who have premarital sex but only with their eventual marriage partner and don't live together before marriage. Next down the list, they are people who have sex with only their eventual marriage partner and live together only once they are engaged to be married. If, in contrast, a couple comes to the marriage with a more storied sexual history, among people who marry younger and have had other premarital sex partners, the divorce risk is really high, with well over half splitting up within ten years, when there are typically young children to be cared for.

Highly educated Freewheelers seem to want to tell less educated Ring-Bearers that they should not want to prioritize family stability over sexual experimentation. Related messages from Freewheelers to Ring-Bearers are that they should not want to have lots of kids, or that they should only have kids the way highly educated Freewheelers sometimes do it, by waiting until they are substantially older, and then relying on some combination of luck and expensive reproductive technology. Ring-Bearers, however, have their own plans and make their own lifestyle choices, preferring to work things the old-fashioned way.

The problems faced by people who choose Ring-Bearer lifestyles explain why they might find it in their interests to discourage other people from engaging in lots of low-commitment sexual activity. For young Ring-Bearers, a big problem is finding suitable partners to share Ring-Bearer lives with. Young women asking their boyfriends to wait for sex have to compete with young women offering more immediate rewards.

For both sexes, the fewer people fooling around, the more suitable candidates there are for long-term Ring-Bearer relationships.

For married Ring-Bearers, infidelity can have an especially serious impact. Ring-Bearer women often rely on the continued support of their husbands to improve the odds that having lots of kids won't lead to poverty. These women often curtail their own educations and careers, a sacrifice that is increasingly risky to the extent that their husbands are more likely to leave. As for the men, they're offering to spend most of their time and resources over the whole of their lives supporting their wives and children. While one might argue over whether it *ought* to matter to such men whether those children are his rather than the offspring of sexual infidelity, it's clear that for most men it *does* (as Maury Povich and his daytime talk-show emulators can attest).

For both Ring-Bearer men and women, the chances of maintaining a faithful marriage depend in part on what people around them are doing when it comes to low-commitment sex. Ring-Bearers have an increased interest in minimizing the temptations faced by their mates, and the fewer people fooling around, the less likely it is that one's mate will succumb.

An obvious way to make Freewheeling less common is to make it more costly. Moral condemnation of low-commitment sex imposes social costs. Outlawing recreational drugs imposes legal costs on hard partyers. Outlawing abortion and limiting the availability of birth control makes it harder to engage in casual sex without jeopardizing plans to delay having children, which would surely be a powerful deterrent to promiscuity, especially among the highly educated crowd.

Another way to reduce levels of (local) Freewheeling is to surround oneself with other Ring-Bearers who similarly support placing high costs on Freewheeler lifestyles. The Amish, for example, isolate themselves in rural communities centered on strict family morals and high levels of neighborly support, something especially important for large families with modest incomes. While the Amish example is extreme, there is more than a passing resemblance between it and couples moving to smaller communities and becoming heavily involved in Ring-Bearer churches when it comes time to have and raise children.

There's also an element of strategy that's a bit more subtle. Ring-Bearer women want their men to believe that the women are faithful and that the children are the husband's own (so that the men will have more incentive to stick around and support the family). Ring-Bearer men want their women to believe that the men are faithful and reliable (so that the women will feel more comfortable having additional children without worrying as much about future poverty). One way to convince someone of one's seriousness in these areas is to make it more costly to break one's promises.

So, think of two people, both of them currently in committed relationships (not with each other, but with different people). One of them often goes on about how terribly wrong it is for people to fool around; the other takes a more tolerant position, saying that, you know, sometimes fooling around is understandable. Now imagine that both get caught cheating on their significant other. Both will be seen as having done something wrong, but the pious moralist will bear the enhanced moral costs of being judged a deeply hypocritical blowhard. It matters in these cases whether a person ups the ante by announcing publicly that they think a given set of behaviors is especially worthy of moral punishment. The ante is upped even further for people (like active members of Ring-Bearer churches) whose social allies similarly condemn promiscuity.

In sum, the interests of Ring-Bearers are advanced both when they actually reduce levels of Freewheeling around them and when they are seen to be the kinds of people who want to reduce levels of Freewheeling. Either way it comes to the same thing—supporting policies that make Freewheeling more costly.

The Politics of Ring-Bearers and Freewheelers

Lifestyle information is crucial in making sense of why some people support and others oppose various policies relating to sex and reproduction. In fact, one of the reasons we're relying heavily on data from the U.S. General Social Survey (as opposed to something like the American

National Election Studies) is that the GSS is one of the very few large studies that not only asks about politics, but also collects information about sexual history, how often respondents go to bars, education, marital history, cohabitation, and children.

We'll explore five moral and political areas: (1) views on whether premarital sex is morally wrong or not, (2) views on whether pornography ought to be legally available to adults, (3) views on whether abortion should be legally available across a range of circumstances (when motivated by rape, by fetal deformity, by not wanting more children, by being poor, and by being single), (4) views on whether teens should have access to birth control without parental consent, and (5) views on whether marijuana should be legal. This last one—marijuana legalization—might seem off topic, but our own studies have shown that it belongs on the list. In the United States, Europe, and Japan, views on marijuana legalization share a uniquely powerful relationship with views on casual sex.[9] People's Public Relations Departments might come up with press releases couching views about recreational drugs in terms of public safety, health care, and children (always the children!), but their Boards of Directors are thinking mostly about how pot helps people to hook up.

As a simple exercise, think of someone, and make the following calculations. Add 1 point for each of the following: The person has had five or more sex partners since age eighteen; the person goes to bars or taverns about once a month or more; the person is lesbian, gay, or bisexual; the person is living in a nonmarital cohabitation. And subtract 1 point for these features: The person has had none or only one sex partner since age eighteen; the person pretty much never goes to bars or taverns. If the result is a positive number, then the person you have in mind is a Freewheeler; if the result is a negative number, he or she is a Ring-Bearer. If the number is 0, then think of the person as somewhere in between the other two groups. On these very rough categories, 39% of American adults are Freewheelers, 34% are Ring-Bearers, and 27% are in the middle.

Even using this very coarse metric, the GSS data show strong connections between sexual and reproductive lifestyles on the one hand and lifestyle politics and morals on the other. Among Freewheelers, two-thirds report that they think premarital sex is "not at all wrong";

only one-third of Ring-Bearers agree. More than three-quarters of Free-wheelers believe pornography should be legal for adults; only half of Ring-Bearers agree. Two-thirds of Freewheelers think that teens should have access to birth control without parental consent; less than half of Ring-Bearers agree. Most Freewheelers think marijuana should be legal; only a quarter of Ring-Bearers agree. (Additional details on these and other data-related points in this chapter are presented in the Data Appendix for Chapter 4.)

Education doesn't play a big role in the issues we just reviewed, but it does when it comes to abortion. Among Freewheelers who have bachelor's degrees, over two-thirds think abortion should be legally available in practically any circumstance the GSS asks about. In contrast, among Ring-Bearers without bachelor's degrees, while almost two-thirds think abortion should be legally available in cases of rape or fetal deformity, almost three-quarters think abortion should be illegal when motivated by not wanting more children, by being poor, or by being single. Freewheelers without bachelor's degrees are split basically 50/50 on these latter kinds of abortion circumstances. Ring-Bearers with bachelor's degrees land somewhere in between less educated Freewheelers and less educated Ring-Bearers.

Across all these sexual and reproductive lifestyle issues, those with liberal views are more likely to have features such as higher numbers of sex partners, nonmarital cohabitation or sexually active singledom, more frequent bar visits, and fewer children. The conservatives on these issues are more likely to be married or widowed with few past sex partners or not currently sexually active at all, to avoid bars, and to have had more children.

In our analyses using a range of demographic information (holding religion aside, which we'll get to shortly), we find other variables that matter, but no variables are more important than people's sexual and reproductive lifestyles. Summarizing some of these smaller effects: Older people are more likely than younger people to disapprove of pornography, teens having access to birth control without parental consent, and marijuana legalization; women are more likely than men to disapprove of pornography but to approve of teenage birth control; and Southerners are particularly likely to disapprove of premarital sex and abortion.

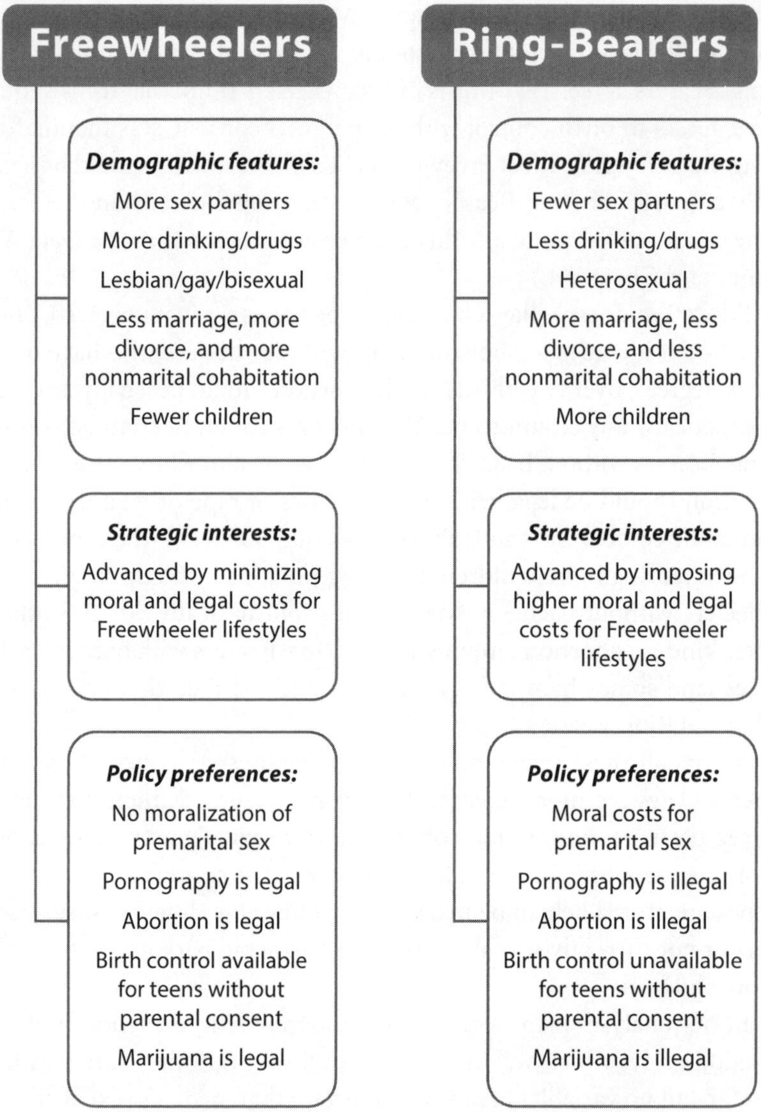

Freewheelers	Ring-Bearers
Demographic features: More sex partners More drinking/drugs Lesbian/gay/bisexual Less marriage, more divorce, and more nonmarital cohabitation Fewer children	**Demographic features:** Fewer sex partners Less drinking/drugs Heterosexual More marriage, less divorce, and less nonmarital cohabitation More children
Strategic interests: Advanced by minimizing moral and legal costs for Freewheeler lifestyles	**Strategic interests:** Advanced by imposing higher moral and legal costs for Freewheeler lifestyles
Policy preferences: No moralization of premarital sex Pornography is legal Abortion is legal Birth control available for teens without parental consent Marijuana is legal	**Policy preferences:** Moral costs for premarital sex Pornography is illegal Abortion is illegal Birth control unavailable for teens without parental consent Marijuana is illegal

Figure 4.1 Freewheelers vs. Ring-Bearers

Viewing issues such as abortion as purely "symbolic" or based on abstract values or religious motives, as they are in some political science circles, misses the important point that people's lives mesh coherently with their lifestyle politics.[10] When it comes to sexual and reproductive policies, the real-life effects of having restrictive or unrestrictive regimes differ based on how people live. These competing interests translate into competing positions. Freewheelers prefer policies that benefit Freewheelers. Ring-Bearers prefer policies that benefit Ring-Bearers. Not always, of course, but usually. In short, demographic features often reflect diverse interests, and diverse interests often lead to competing policy positions. The key is in matching the relevant demographics to the relevant interests to the relevant policies. Figure 4.1 summarizes things to this point.

Churches: Ring-Bearer Support Groups

So far we've largely skirted the issue of religion. It's time to stop beating around the burning bush.

There are lots of ideas about religion floating around. A somewhat quirky psychological perspective known as Terror Management Theory proposes that perhaps religion serves to provide comfort in the face of the horrors of mortality. Well-known biologist Richard Dawkins and philosopher Daniel Dennett suggest that religious ideas may be like viruses that infest human minds, ultimately serving their own interests rather than the interests of their human hosts.[11] People who favor the idea that between-group competition is especially important propose that ideas about invisible, rule-enforcing gods evolved to help humans cooperate in large-scale groups, providing extra incentives for members of groups not to lie to and steal from one another (because they're always being watched by the invisible, rule-enforcing gods).[12] Or maybe the notions of gods and souls are just by-products of human tendencies to interpret all kinds of mindless phenomena as though they are caused by intentional beings.[13]

But perhaps the most common view in social science is the simple socialization account: People are raised one way or the other when it comes to religion, soaking it up like sponges from friends and family. Here's an example from a recent political science book discussing Republican/Democratic identification: "The classical view of party identification argues for the similarity of party identification with religious attachments precisely on the grounds that both are acquired early in life, and more or less reflexively in response to parents and peers."[14]

It is certainly true that there are correlations between the religious patterns of parents and children, particularly when it comes to religious identities (i.e., calling oneself Catholic versus Jewish versus something else). But the general claim about parent-child resemblance doesn't extend as easily from religious *identities* to religious *participation*. Close to 40% of young adults these days were raised in households in which one or both parents attended church about every week; but by their mid-twenties, fewer than 20% are attending that frequently.[15] These results illustrate a continuation of prior trends. Over half of baby boomers' parents attended services about weekly or more when the boomers were growing up. However, in their late teens to mid-twenties, less than a quarter of baby boomers were themselves attending about weekly or more. By their late thirties, this fraction had risen to about a third and has stayed there since. In short, people attend church a lot less as they make the transition from childhood to early adulthood.

Changes in religious participation are even more complicated than these patterns might seem to imply. Of the fewer than 20% of young adults frequently attending church, only a bit over half came from the 40% with high-attendance parents. Looked at another way, among the 40% raised in high-attendance families, *by the time the kids are in their mid-twenties, fully three out of four of these raised-religious kids are no longer attending services all that frequently.*

Now, it's true that kids from low-attendance upbringings are even less likely to become big churchgoers themselves by their mid-twenties. While one in four from high-attendance families are weekly churchgoers by their mid-twenties, only one in nine are weekly churchgoers when they come from families where neither parent attended services weekly. This results in a real correlation—sure enough, kids from high-attendance families are more likely to end up as high-attendance adults themselves. But that doesn't mean that most young adults from high-attendance families end up "more or less reflexively" looking like their parents. Instead, three out of four have joined the ranks of those with low-attendance young-adult patterns.

Because we don't think people absorb their parents' religious practices by osmosis, we have instead tried to understand religious participation as something that is useful in some people's everyday lives but not in others.[16] So here's a simple observation and a simple question. First the observation: When it comes to church attendance, developed countries are incredibly diverse. In the United States these days, for example, roughly 40% of adults never or hardly ever attend religious services while about 30% attend about once a week or more (and the other 30% attend at levels in between). And the simple question: What distinguishes those who go to church a lot from those who don't?

The big, distinguishing features, it turns out, involve sexual and reproductive lifestyles. People tend to go to church more when they are virgins or are married to the only person they've had sex with in their adult lives, when they rarely go to bars, and when they have more children. In short, people go to church more often when they have Ring-Bearer lifestyles. People tend to avoid church when they're in nonmarital cohabitation, when they're sexually active but never married, when they've had higher numbers of sex partners over time, when they go to bars pretty regularly, and when they have children out of wedlock. People, that is, more often eschew organized religion when they lead Freewheeler lifestyles.

Race, it turns out, also matters—African Americans go to church more than other Americans. But if you can ask someone just one question about their lives in order to guess how often the person attends religious services, you should simply ask (politeness permitting) how many people the person has slept with. In the GSS, the typical person who has had sex with five or more people in their adult life goes to church once a year; the typical person who has slept with none or only one person goes to church two or three times a month.

The roles of race and lifestyle in religious-service attendance are summarized in figure 4.2. These graphs show, for each group, the percentage attending religious services about once a year or less (the left-side bars), about once a week or more (the right-side bars), and somewhere

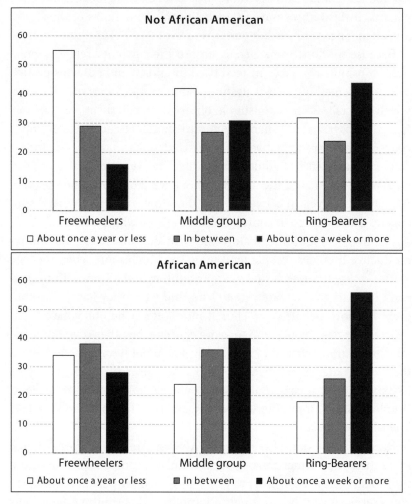

Figure 4.2 Religious service attendance by race and lifestyle category

in between (the middle bars). For non–African Americans who are Freewheelers, people are almost 3.5 times more likely to hardly ever attend services than to attend about weekly (55% versus 16%). For non–African Americans who are Ring-Bearers, in sharp contrast, people are more likely to be weekly attenders (44%) than very infrequent attenders

(32%). For African Americans, overall attendance rates are higher, but there are still big differences that depend on lifestyle. African Americans who are Freewheelers are a bit more likely to go very infrequently (34%) than about weekly (28%). But, African Americans who are Ring-Bearers are about three times more likely to be weekly attenders than very infrequent attenders (56% versus 18%).

In short, there are close relationships between people's sexual lifestyles and their religious participation. Most people, though, when they see these relationships, assume that the causal arrow points from religion to sex. Isn't the right explanation that people end up with Ring-Bearer lifestyles *because* they're religious?

Actually, no. Or, at a minimum, it's not that simple. Recall our discussion of young-adult attendance patterns. Roughly 40% of contemporary young adults were raised in high-attendance households. Three out of four in this group stopped attending this frequently by their mid-twenties. This leaves about 10% of people in their mid-twenties who were raised in high-attendance families and who are themselves attending services regularly. But then there's another group, almost as big, who are attending services regularly in their mid-twenties with parents who didn't attend religious services frequently when these children were in their teen years.

Why do so many individuals' level of religious worship change so much? We turned to the National Longitudinal Surveys of Youth 1997 (NLSY) to find out.[17] This is a great study that has followed a group of young people born in the early 1980s with yearly surveys starting in 1997, when the people in the sample were teenagers. Crucially, the survey asks respondents about sex, alcohol, drugs, cohabitation, marriage, and children, in addition to questions about church attendance. With the NLSY sample, then, we have a nice window onto how the big decline in young-adult church attendance happens.

The change is fairly straightforward. Around 40% of the people in the sample were raised in high-attendance households, but lots of these kids ended up partying, becoming sexually active before marriage, living in nonmarital cohabitation, and/or having kids outside of marriage. In such cases—that is, when, despite their high-attendance upbringings, they adopted Freewheeler lifestyles—they generally stopped going to church. Most of the kids from high-attendance upbringings who retained the pattern chose strongly Ring-Bearer lifestyles—they mostly abstained from hard partying and premarital sex.

On the flip side, many kids from low-attendance households also pursued Freewheeler lifestyles. These kids were spectacularly unlikely to start attending services as young adults. But there were also plenty of kids from low-attendance upbringings who adopted Ring-Bearer lifestyles, and some (not most, but some) became far more religious than their parents. In fact, and we can't emphasize this enough, even with italics, *people raised in low-attendance households who spent their teens and early twenties with Ring-Bearer lifestyles were more likely to be attending services in their mid-twenties than people raised in high-attendance households who spent their teens and early twenties with Freewheeler lifestyles.* Still, it's true that those with Ring-Bearer lifestyles and low-attendance upbringings are much less likely to be frequent churchgoers than those with Ring-Bearer lifestyles and high-attendance upbringings.

In short, *as young people start making their own decisions about their lives, they tend to match their religious participation to their lifestyles.* Parental attendance does have an effect on whether their kids become Freewheelers or Ring-Bearers, but the effect becomes pretty small by the time people are in their mid-twenties.

The net result is that, yes, being raised one way or the other matters to some extent when it comes to religious attendance. Upbringing does have a small effect on the lifestyles people choose and, more importantly, Ring-Bearers are much more likely to *maintain* a high-attendance pattern from childhood than they are to develop such a pattern from scratch. But that's far and away not the whole story. Find the Freewheeler young adults, and you'll also find that, regardless of how they were raised, very few are attending church regularly. As Doug Kenrick put it when discussing his own transition from high-attendance upbringing to Freewheeler lifestyle in *Sex, Murder, and the Meaning of Life*: "If there was anything the nuns had really drummed into our heads, it was that sex was sinful. . . . I no longer wanted to feel guilty about sex, so I decided it was time to choose another set of beliefs."[18]

Religious groups in developed countries tend to serve the interests of high-commitment/high-fertility Ring-Bearers but not the interests of low-commitment/low-fertility Freewheelers. In particular, first, religious groups often provide social insurance benefits and other club goods for attendees, including day care and schools for kids, and collections for hardships such as illness or loss of job. Second, religious groups often provide communities within communities, frequently united around anti-promiscuity morals. Modern religious groups are a pretty good deal for heterosexual, married, less promiscuous folks with more children, as well as for older people who are well past indulging in wilder lives. For others . . . not so much. As a result, we see that lots of parents go to church with their kids; later, if those kids become adults who themselves are Ring-Bearer types, the kids tend to stick with church (because it's a good deal for them); but if the kids set off in a Freewheeler direction, they drop church like a bad habit.

Attending church, then, can be thought of as a tool that helps some lifestyles but interferes with others. When people know how to use the tool (because they were raised religious) and have a use for the tool (because they are pursuing a Ring-Bearer lifestyle), then they use it. Others know how to use it (they were raised religious) but have no use for it (because they are pursuing Freewheeler lifestyles)—so they don't use it. Still others would perhaps find it useful, but didn't have the sort of childhood to know how useful it would be; such people don't often use it either. It isn't hard for Freewheeler types to figure out that they're going to get more hassles than benefits from most religious groups—even teenagers are able to work it out (including a young Doug Kenrick)—and that's basically all it takes to explain most of the connections we find between religiosity and lifestyles.

It's well known that church attendance strongly relates to the kinds of lifestyle policies we're discussing in this chapter—relative to people who don't go to church much, regular churchgoers are especially conservative on issues like premarital sex, pornography, abortion, birth control, and marijuana legalization. The usual explanation for this relationship is that those with conservative lifestyle views get them from religious upbringings and those with liberal lifestyle views get them from secular upbringings. But our read of the data is that the story is more complex. In particular, *much of the correspondence between these moral and political topics and religiosity results from young adults adjusting their religious patterns to their lifestyles.* Many kids are raised religious, but when they adopt Freewheeler lifestyles that create incentives to adopt liberal life-style politics, *they stop being so religious.* A big part of the correlation between religiosity and politics derives not from people soaking up religious views like sponges, but from people rejecting religion when it interferes with their lifestyle.

So is church attendance a cause or an effect of anti-promiscuity opinions? Our view is that it's both. People with Ring-Bearer lifestyles, who have an interest in morally condemning promiscuity, are frequently drawn to organized religion. They embed their high-commitment/high-fertility families within supportive communities of like-minded, promiscuity-discouraging, materially supportive fellows. Church attendance is, then, an *effect* rather than a cause of conservative political views on lifestyle issues. But then attending church doubtless reinforces and creates additional coalitional interests in lifestyle conservatism, amplifying those views further in the direction they already leaned—to this extent, it's also a *cause.*

Divorce American Style

New Atheists commonly charge that religious people don't live up to their conservative norms. Here's Daniel Dennett in *Breaking the Spell:* "[W]hen it comes to 'family values,' the available evidence to date supports the hypothesis that brights [i.e., nonbelievers] have the lowest divorce rate in the United States, and born-again Christians the highest."[19]

One way to evaluate this claim is to ask what percentage of adults have divorced compared with the adult population as a whole, which includes people who have never been married in the first place. Data from the U.S. General Social Survey come close to supporting Dennett's claim: 34% of Christians who report a born-again experience have been divorced, compared with 28% of Christians without a born-again experience, 26% of the nonreligious, and only 20% of those in non-Christian religions.[20]

However, because these percentages are of divorced people relative to the entire adult population—including people who have never married—it seems perverse to calculate things this way. The interest, after all, is in the extent to which people keep their commitments. This is closer to what typical readers have in mind when one uses the phrase "divorce rate": the chance that a given person will divorce *assuming the person gets married in the first place*. So a better question is to ask what percentage of ever-married people have ever divorced, putting aside people never married. This question gives a different answer: 44% of ever-married people with no religious affiliation have divorced, compared with 42% of ever-married born-again Christians, 37% of ever-married non-born-again Christians, and 29% of ever-married people who identify with a non-Christian religion.

Looked at in this more intuitive way, the "divorce rate" is actually *highest* among nonbelievers, though still pretty high among born-again Christians. The difference is driven by the fact that nonreligious people are more likely to never have been married in the first place—41% of adults with no religious affiliation have never been married, compared with only 20% of born-again Christians.

From just these figures, our sense is that claims like Dennett's are at best misleading, even if there are ways to make the claims technically kinda true. These claims are driven, we think, by a desire to engage in emotionally satisfying eye-poking.

A better look at religion in relation to divorce rates requires bearing a couple of additional points in mind. First, the connections between religiosity and lifestyles are more a matter of religious *involvement* (e.g., service attendance) than religious *labels* (e.g., calling oneself "Christian" or "born-again"). One's denomination matters less than one's level of participation. Second, education plays a key role. Christians are far more likely to identify as "born-again" (or "fundamentalist" or "evangelical") at lower education levels, and, importantly, people at lower education levels are more likely to get divorced (in large part because they tend to marry younger and are more likely to have children before marriage). In a related point, highly educated folks who don't attend religious services are more likely to say they have no religious affiliation than are less educated folks who don't attend religious services—people with less education are strongly likely to keep calling themselves "Christians" (including lots of "born-again" Christians) despite the fact that their everyday lives have very little religious about them. Thus, comparisons singling out the "born-again" versus those with "no religion" (as Dennett's did) stack the deck with folks with less education versus folks with more education.

So, looking only at those who have ever married, and breaking it out by education, what's the likelihood that someone has been divorced?

- People with bachelor's degrees:
  - o 24% of those who attend services weekly.
  - o 33% of those who identify with a religion but do not attend services weekly.
  - o 39% of those who do not identify with a religion.
- People who do not have bachelor's degrees:
  - o 33% of those who attend services weekly.
  - o 47% of those who identify with a religion but do not attend services weekly.
  - o 50% of those who do not identify with a religion.

Put this way, it becomes clear that there's a nice relationship between religious participation and staying together, with education giving an added bump across the board. Not only are religious people more likely to have married in the first place, but those who have married are also less likely to have divorced. As we've been saying, religious worshipers are more likely to have Ring-Bearer lifestyles.

The more interesting question, to us, is whether these connections indicate that religious involvement is truly a *cause* of increased marital stability. Maybe. Another possibility, which we have raised, is self-selection: Ring-Bearers seek out religious groups while Freewheelers avoid them. The right answer probably involves both ideas—Ring-Bearers seek out churches (so going to church is in part an *effect* of being less likely to divorce), but then churches provide social environments that help stabilize marriages.

The Politics of Sex and Reproduction

We're now ready to take a broader look at the demographic predictors of views on premarital sex, pornography, abortion, teen birth control, and marijuana legalization (more details can be found in the Data Appendix for Chapter 4). The most important predictors include both religious variables and lifestyle variables, but the single dominant factor is frequency of church attendance. Of the roughly 7% of American adults who regularly attend services more than once a week, fully 83% believe that premarital sex is always or almost always wrong. About seven in ten of these super-attenders think pornography should be illegal. Fewer than 15% approve of abortion in cases motivated by not wanting more children, by being poor, or by being single, and only about four in ten approve of legal abortion for rape or fetal deformity. About seven in ten think birth control should be unavailable to teenagers without parental consent. Fewer than one in five would legalize marijuana.

By far the most liberal profile comes from people who are not Christian (mostly including people with no religious affiliation, but also including Jews, Buddhists, etc.), attend services less than about once a week, have at least a high school education, and have had at least five sex partners in their adult lifetimes—in other words, people who are less religious, have Freewheeler lifestyles, and have at least a modest amount of education. For this group, eight in ten say premarital sex is not wrong at all; nine in ten think pornography should be legally available to adults; around three-quarters support legal abortion in every circumstance; almost eight in ten think teens should have access to birth control even when their parents disagree; and at least three-quarters support marijuana legalization. We admit that this category includes us and most of our friends and, yeah, these numbers sound about right.

Most groups are, of course, between the extremes of super-attenders and Freewheeling non-Christians. Among the less extreme conservatives when it comes to lifestyle issues are people who usually go to church "only" about once a week, who have more lifestyle diversity than the super-attenders. Weekly churchgoers who have married and have had few sex partners (i.e., who lean toward being Ring-Bearers) are more conservative on lifestyle issues than those who are either never married or have had five or more sex partners since age eighteen (i.e., who lean toward being Freewheelers). Weekly attending Freewheelers hold views that are pretty conservative overall but less consistent: About four in ten think premarital sex is always or almost always wrong; about four in ten think pornography should be illegal; only about three in ten support legal abortion for those not wanting more children, who are poor, or who are single; roughly half disapprove of birth control for teens without parental consent; only around a third would legalize marijuana. Weekly attending Ring-Bearers hold views that are somewhere in between these Freewheeling weekly attenders and the super-conservative super-attenders.

Among the less extreme liberals on these issues are people who are not Christian, have less than weekly attendance, and have high school diplomas—but who have fewer than five adult lifetime sex partners. For these less Freewheeling non-Christians, positions on lifestyle issues are pretty liberal overall, but in each case somewhere in the neighborhood of 10 points less liberal than their more Freewheeling analogues (so, e.g., instead of nine in ten supporting legal pornography, only eight in ten do). Among Christians who don't go to church weekly and have high school diplomas (or more education), the results depend a bit on age—the seniors in this group are almost as conservative as the weekly attending Freewheelers we looked at earlier, while the younger folks (especially those with more education) are almost as liberal as less Freewheeling non-Christians. People who both don't go to church weekly and don't have high school diplomas are on average in the middle in their views on all these lifestyle issues, except abortion, about which they have generally conservative views.

International Comparisons

We close out our empirical work in this and the next two chapters by briefly comparing the United States with the rest of the world. Here, we use the World Values Survey (WVS)—an international database with around three hundred thousand individuals from over ninety countries—which has put similar questions to people around the world over the past few decades, though with fewer consistently repeated demographic details than the GSS.

In one of our studies, using this source of data, we looked at how religiosity relates to sexual and reproductive morals in comparison with cooperative morals (such as injunctions against lying and stealing).[21]

Overall, we found that the worldwide connection between religiosity and sexual and reproductive morals (relating to casual sex, abortion, divorce, recreational drugs, etc.) is really strong, and that, once we take this connection into account, cooperative morals don't indicate anything further about who is more or less religious. The least religious people worldwide, really, are those who think there's nothing wrong with Freewheeler lifestyles but who still disapprove of lying and stealing—they're Freewheelers, but not anarchists or sociopaths.

Drilling down in more detail, we found that less developed countries tend to have lots of religious people (except in places like China, where there has been recent state suppression of religions) and lots of lifestyle conservatives, but the individual-level relationship between religiosity and lifestyle conservatism isn't that strong. In modern developed countries around the world, in contrast, there's a lot of diversity in both religiosity and in sexual and reproductive views, and the individual-level relationship is very strong. That is, people in developed countries aren't routinely religious, but when they are, they tend to have conservative views on sexual and reproductive lifestyle issues in particular.

The WVS, happily, has frequently measured views on abortion. Overall, people in the Western world outside of the United States hold the most liberal views on abortion on average, those in the non-Western world hold the most conservative views on abortion on average, and those in the United States tend to be in the middle on average. Of course, all these regions contain people all over the map on abortion, but the averages differ significantly.

As in our earlier look at American views on abortion, across the world, people who are less religious and more educated tend to be substantially more liberal on abortion than people who are more religious and less educated. Among the most religious and least educated, in particular, there's not much difference between Western and non-Western countries on abortion attitudes—such folks tend to be against abortion in the United States, in other Western countries, and in the rest of the world. (We present more details in the Data Appendix for Chapter 4.)

The biggest differences are among those who are less religious and more educated. In Western countries, such individuals tend strongly to be pro-choice. Outside of Western countries, such individuals are scattered around the center on abortion. Overall, then, there's more variation in views in the Western than the non-Western world as a function of religiosity and education, but the directions of this variation are similar worldwide.

One Step at a Time

We have tried to convey a set of simple ideas in this chapter: There are strong connections among sexual and reproductive lifestyles, sexual and reproductive interests, and sexual and reproductive politics. These connections have been widely overlooked primarily because of how strongly each of these also connects with religion. The common assumption has been that religion is the Great Initiator of the Causal Chain. This assumption looms so large that people rarely ask *why* religion has the connections it has.

As we have tried to show, debates that can seem to involve the least rational aspect of politics—issues about when life begins, or what God thinks about sex, or whether "victimless" misdemeanors like promiscuous sex or pornography or marijuana should be morally condemned or criminalized—are comprehensible once the old assumptions are abandoned and attention is paid to the right kinds of lifestyle factors. People with Freewheeler lifestyles often have interests advanced by avoiding churches and minimizing the moral and legal costs of their Freewheeler lifestyles. People with Ring-Bearer lifestyles often have interests advanced by affiliating with churches and supporting moral and legal restrictions that make Freewheeling more costly or difficult.

It does little good to try to explain how the kinds of stories people themselves use to advance their own policy positions lead them to the positions they have—those stories are press releases, issued by the Public Relations Departments of their minds. Believing that those stories are true glimpses into the back offices of their minds is tantamount to a political reporter passing along the canned statements of a press secretary as true glimpses into an administration's internal meetings.

As we mentioned earlier in the book, people often talk about "liberals" and "conservatives" as though there are basically two kinds of people, even though, in reality, people regularly hold idiosyncratic mixtures of liberal and conservative views. Based on what we've covered in this chapter, the conclusion isn't that people who go to church a lot and have Ring-Bearer lifestyles are usually conservative, for example, but that *they're usually conservative specifically on sexual and reproductive lifestyle issues.* For other issues, the underlying strategic interests will differ, as will the demographic features that matter. How much people go to church, how many people they sleep with, how often they go to bars—these features may indicate a great deal about people's views on sexual and reproductive items, but they're not going to indicate very much about, for example, who supports liberal immigration policies or race-based affirmative action. Instead, the demographic stars of this chapter will become bit players in the productions that follow, as some bit players from this chapter take their star turns.

CHAPTER 5

Rules of the Game:
Group Identities and Human Capital

THE NEW YORK YANKEES HAVE MADE THE PLAYOFFS in sixteen out of the last eighteen seasons. (The exceptions were 2008 and 2013.) Given that there are thirty Major League Baseball teams, only a quarter of which reach the playoffs, this is an astounding record.

They have also consistently spent more on player salaries than every other team. In 2012, for instance, they spent just shy of $200 million, nearly four times as much as the San Diego Padres, who spent $55 million. The Yankees spent $20 million more than the next most spendy team, the Philadelphia Phillies.

This circumstance could not occur in the professional football or hockey leagues, both of which have rules that specify how much can be spent in total on player salaries, with both caps and minimums. Professional baseball does have one leveling mechanism, a "luxury tax," a fine that teams pay when they go above a specified maximum figure. This value was $178 million in 2012. The Yankees chose to exceed the threshold, as they had every year since 2003, and simply paid the tax, roughly $19 million.

The Yankees are able to pay their players so much for the obvious reason that they play in New York City, a large, wealthy market. With twenty million potential fans in the New York metropolitan area, the Yankees enjoy in excess of an order of magnitude more population nearby than the Brewers of Milwaukee, with a metro population of about a million and a half.

While many (including the owner of the Brewers) complain that the luxury tax is insufficient and that a salary cap is required to impose some equity and fairness in baseball, there are forces lined up against it. In particular, the people who own the Yankees oppose such a cap for the obvious reason that they would be most adversely affected. It would prevent them from using their financial advantages on the field. Another group that opposes such a cap is only slightly less obvious: the baseball players' union. Caps limit the size of the pie that the unions' players can be paid, making them as a group—and some players individually— worse off. We presume, but do not know, that fans in larger markets tend to oppose caps, while fans in smaller markets tend to favor them.

We would venture to guess that the owners of the Yankees don't care much one way or the other about salary caps in other sports. This isn't as trivial an observation as it might at first appear. It could be that because of their self-interest in caps in one domain, people "internalize" an overarching moral principle along the lines that salary caps are bad— "players should be paid what they're worth, and caps force underpayment of players, which isn't fair!"—and generalize this principle broadly to other sports. While this might be the case, it probably isn't.

The key (if slightly obvious) point: A good way to predict who will support/oppose a particular rule regime is to ask cui bono, who benefits, under the regime.

Consider the racial segregation of American baseball leagues that ended when Jackie Robinson played for the Dodgers in 1947. Before Robinson, all the players' jobs in Major League Baseball were guaranteed to go to white players. This policy gave white players an advantage over African American players. But this puts the notion of advantage too coarsely. There are important differences in who, precisely, is better off and who is worse off under the two possible regimes, whites-only versus integrated.

Clearly, the best African American players are better off under the integrated regime. Because slots on the roster are allocated based on how well one plays baseball as opposed to the color of one's skin, excellent African American players will get higher paying jobs they otherwise would not get.

However, because our present interest is very narrowly on the issue of jobs as opposed to the symbolic elements of an integrated league— which we admit is a tremendously important element to hold aside—

the issue is less clear for African American players who aren't as tal-ented. Some weekend baseball players, for example, wouldn't be talented enough for a professional league, whether integrated or not. These play-ers have no job-related issue at stake. Other African Americans might be good enough for a smaller, less competitive league, but wouldn't be good enough for a highly competitive integrated league. For them, whether they are better off or worse off from integration might depend on how integrating the Major League affects the availability or desirability of jobs in less competitive leagues. Overall, from the (again, admittedly narrow) perspective of job prospects, the most talented African Ameri-can players stand to gain the most from integration, the least talented are unaffected, and for those in the middle, it's complicated.

Applying similar logic, the people who lose the most from the inte-grated regime are white baseball players who are just talented enough to make it into a segregated league, but not talented enough to make it into an integrated league, given that such a league draws on a wider pool of talent. In other words, white players who would have a job in the seg-regated regime (because they are among the best white players) but not in the integrated regime (because there are African American players better than them, pushing them below the hiring threshold) are worse off under the integrated regime.

For the very best white players, however, the calculation is more complex. Opening up the league to additional very talented hopefuls wouldn't directly harm the very talented white players' job prospects; they're good enough to survive the new cutoff. Integration might in-troduce increased competition for media coverage and prizes, such as Most Valuable Player, but at the same time an integrated league would increase the sport's fan base and revenues, potentially making top player positions more valuable.

If one were to imagine that support for integration among players came only from players who stand to gain (materially) from it and re-sistance to integration came only from players who stand to lose from it, one would predict the best African American athletes to favor inte-gration and the second-tier white athletes to oppose it. The very best white athletes and less talented African American athletes should fall somewhere in the middle.

In sports, the rules matter. And, crucially, different rules help some people and hurt others. Salary caps might help teams in smaller markets and hurt teams in larger markets. Race-based limitations might help second-tier whites and hurt top-tier African Americans. And there are countless other examples, of course. Raising the pitcher's mound helps pitchers and hurts hitters. Requiring both feet in bounds for a catch in football hurts wide receivers but helps defensive backs. The foul-out rule in basketball hurts high-impact players but helps bench players get more minutes. Time limits in golf help speedier players and hurt slower players.

Unsurprisingly, athletes know where their interests lie and tend to support the rules that help themselves.

Back to Reality

In life as in sports, people fight over rules that help some and hurt others. Over the past decades, as with integrating baseball, many political fights have been over the role of group identities in determining a range of social advantages. In the United States in the early and middle twentieth century, some of the most important fights were about whether to eliminate overt barriers to full participation in society for racial and ethnic minorities, women, and religious minorities. In the years since, the fights over race and gender have evolved to become more nuanced and less overt: school funding regimes and voter registration rules that might disproportionately harm racial minorities, for example, or continuing bias that might create a "glass ceiling" preventing women from competing for top positions in big business and government, to say nothing of affirmative action programs at universities and businesses for racial minorities and women.

In recent years, a rise in immigration to the United States as well as U.S. involvement in Middle Eastern conflicts have brought new dimensions to old fights involving national origin and religion. A hundred years ago, battles were fought over attempts by native-born Protestants to hold back immigrant groups such as Irish Catholics or Eastern European Jews. Catholics and Jews have since thoroughly integrated into

American life, but new conflicts have taken their place, now involving primarily Muslim immigrants and immigrants from Latin America. While overt barriers to full participation have largely been eliminated for most groups we're discussing here, immigrants still face obvious obstacles. The most apparent include legislative and administrative rules governing who can legally enter the United States. Other barriers to full participation exclude documented and/or undocumented immigrants from government benefits of varying kinds, from poverty and health care programs to university admissions and scholarships.

While old immigration-based fights between Catholics and Protestants have waned, fights between Christians and non-Christians remain, including between Christians and the nonreligious. Superficially, it might appear that some of these are purely symbolic conflicts. There doesn't seem to be much materially at stake in the context of placing the Ten Commandments in courthouses, having crosses or nativity scenes displayed in public parks, or allowing school prayer. Still, the results of these battles have real-life implications. Commandments, crosses, and prayers connote a general endorsement of Christianity and thus of Christians, potentially sending a message that people in other religions or with no religion are outsiders and appropriate targets of disapproval. It is not hard to imagine that these signals affect decisions regarding hiring, promotion, and other important real-world outcomes.

Another recent change is that battles over sexual orientation have heated up considerably. The contemporary conflicts echo two key fights from the middle of the twentieth century over racial integration, first over eliminating barriers to full participation in the armed forces (a process that unfolded in the 1940s and 1950s for African Americans, and in the 1990s and 2000s for homosexuals, in both cases primarily through executive orders) and subsequently over eliminating barriers to marriage equality (a process that unfolded through a combination of state-level initiatives and federal court rulings in the 1950s and 1960s for interracial couples and is still unfolding though similar avenues for same-sex couples).

Today, federal laws generally prohibit explicitly imposing barriers based on race, gender, national origin, and religion in areas such as voting, contract rights, education, and employment. Some barriers remain for homosexuals, but current trends suggest that these are eroding. Immigrants are something of a special case, and probably always will be, given the necessary distinction between citizens and noncitizens.

Still, there remains substantial bias against some groups. In a 2012 Gallup poll, for example, while fewer than 10% of Americans admitted that they wouldn't vote for a candidate merely because the candidate was African American, Hispanic, a woman, Catholic, or Jewish, 30% said they would not vote for a gay or lesbian, 40% said they would not vote for a Muslim, and 43% said they would not vote for an atheist. And, though not included in the Gallup poll, anti-immigrant sentiments are plainly visible in the United States, as in many other countries. Of course, even in cases where group-based biases aren't routinely admitted, they can still operate in practice.

Of all the policy areas we discuss in this book, these kinds of group-based issues are among the most difficult. This difficulty doesn't arise because the nature of the underlying conflict is difficult to understand. The broad contours, in our view, are actually fairly simple, as we discuss below. However, the issues surrounding group-based discrimination are particularly vexing because our own peers are passionately convinced that there's a *right answer* here: Barrier-imposing, group-based discrimination is wrong, bad, evil. People who engage in it are deranged and corrupt. They are racists, sexists, xenophobes, homophobes. They are not rational actors but rather they are, at best, lost souls in need of enlightenment and, at worst, offenders to be judged and sentenced.

While we, your authors, have "liberal" policy preferences on these issues that are typical of our professorial demographic, our goal is not to advocate policies but rather to understand and explain why some people prefer group-based distinctions and others passionately oppose them. We're also trying to understand the frequently overlooked but common phenomena in which individuals favor group-based barriers for some groups while simultaneously opposing such barriers for others. And we don't think that a productive path to figuring these things out is to start off assuming that one side consists of diseased minds.

We understand that our agenda of explaining without advocacy will be unsatisfying to many, especially members of our own tribe, who might prefer us to frame these issues in terms of enlightenment and corruption, good guys and bad guys. Our argument, however, will be that *all* sides are generally trying to advance their own inclusive interests, and that the accompanying moral ferocity is unleashed to defend these competing interests.

Different Rules Create Different Winners and Losers

One could say that social advantages should not be based on race, religion, or other kinds of group-based categories, but such advantages will still be based on *something*—hardly anyone argues, for example, that university admissions or employee hiring and promotion should occur utterly at random. The *something* to use in place of group-based features could be any number of somethings. Many societies have based big chunks of social privilege on *inherited status* (aristocracies, caste-based systems, etc.). University "legacy" admissions—where children of alumni are preferentially admitted to top schools—are a kind of modern American example of inherited privilege. Another something is *seniority*, which labor unions have sometimes used as a major factor in determining who gets paid what and who survives layoffs. But, these days, the predominant background assumption is that the absence of group-based discrimination implies the presence of *meritocracy*, which largely comes down to survival of the smartest, advancing those who test well and have impressive educational pedigrees.

For these issues—the allocation of zero sum resources and opportunities—there's no such thing as a neutral set of rules. The main talk these days might be about "discrimination" versus "meritocracy," but these terms mask the complexity of the underlying conflict. All rule regimes *discriminate*, minimally, in the sense of drawing distinctions based on various features. Meritocracy, for example, "discriminates" against people with poor test-taking skills and mediocre educations.

Further, while the term "meritocracy" often carries the flavor of benefiting hard workers, in recent times it has become clearer that the real winners mostly have the kinds of intellectual skills and educational backgrounds that correlate with test-taking ability—a cluster of features closely related to what economists refer to as "human capital." Perhaps because "meritocracy" as it is currently implemented favors "good test-takers" rather than "hard workers," modern commentators have increasingly come to question its intuitive appeal.[1]

It might seem obvious to most of our readers that imposing group-based barriers is "unfair" and allowing meritocratic competition is "fair." But then some find meritocratic competition so "fair" that efforts to engage in affirmative action seem obviously "unfair." On the other hand, others find group-based barriers so "unfair" that efforts to affirmatively remedy past discrimination seem obviously "fair." Also, of course, lots of people still aren't sold on the notion that group-based barriers are all that "unfair" in the first place.

Our main concern is precisely with figuring out what drives these diverse perceptions of fairness. Our argument is that, as with the rules of sports, perceptions of fairness typically come down to the basic underlying fact that different policies have different winners and losers.

With group-based issues, often the conflict is over two competing rules: (1) maintain discriminatory barriers to members of a certain traditionally subordinate group, or (2) allow brain-based competition to proceed without the group-based barrier. Who wins under the first rule? People in the traditionally dominant group. Who wins in the second rule? People with lots of brains (i.e., human capital).

These ideas, taken all together, bring us to our central point: To identify the biggest winners and losers from the *competing rules*, one needs to *compare outcomes under the two regimes*. Who are the biggest winners from the group-based rule *relative to* the human-capital-based rule? The winners are not just the people in the traditionally dominant group, but more specifically they're the people in the traditionally dominant group *who also* don't *have lots of human capital*. These folks do well under the group-based rule and simultaneously do poorly under the human-capital-based rule. People who are in the traditionally dominant group and have lots of human capital, in contrast, do well under either rule—they're analogous to the talented white baseball players who wouldn't be affected much by integrating the sport.

Who, then, are the biggest winners from the human-capital-based rule *relative to* the group-based rule? The answer is that they're not just people with lots of human capital; specifically they are people with lots of human capital *who also are members of the traditionally subordinate group*. Such people do well under the human-capital-based rule and simultaneously do poorly under the group-based rule. People who are in the traditionally subordinate group and who do not have lots of human capital, in contrast, would struggle under either rule.

Further complicating matters is the simple reality that few people are members of only traditionally subordinate groups—there just aren't very many African immigrants who are lesbian atheists, for example. Most Americans are Christians, including most African Americans and Latinos. Most Jews and atheists are white. The large majority of people, regardless of other group identities, are heterosexual.

For people with mixed subordinate/dominant group identities, what are the best policies? For someone with both a subordinate group identity and lots of human capital, the answer is easy: The best regime is the one that prohibits group-based barriers in favor of human-capital-based distinctions across the board. This person's main concern would naturally be with group-based distinctions creating barriers to the person's own subordinate group(s), but the person has little incentive to impose barriers to human capital even when it comes to subordinate groups of which the person isn't a member. The person's high level of human capital makes the adoption of a general position in favor of human-capital-based distinctions attractive.

For a person with less human capital, however, matters are more complex. Policies that promote human-capital-based outcomes wouldn't, of course, maximize this person's position. Instead, the person would do better under pick-and-choose rules regarding groups, wanting a quilt of policies that protect and advance subordinate groups of which the person happens to be a member while allowing barriers to be placed in the paths of subordinate groups to which the person doesn't belong. For example, a white atheist with less human capital might do best under rules prohibiting barriers against atheists yet allowing barriers against racial minorities.

It can be tempting to see the kinds of group-based conflicts we're discussing as simply all the members of one group versus all the members of the other. But things aren't really that simple. Take opposing efforts with regard to same-sex marriage. One might expect gays and lesbians to be big supporters of same-sex marriage. But there's also a larger strategic matter at stake based on human capital: Is society going to have barriers of these kinds generally watering down human-capital-based competitions? So, one might expect gays and lesbians to be joined in substantial numbers by heterosexuals with lots of human capital. The key opponents of same-sex marriage, then, won't be heterosexuals generally, but heterosexuals with less human capital—that is, the heterosexuals who simultaneously gain ground from group-based dominance and lose ground under human-capital-advancing rules.

Summarizing Interests

As a simple empirical matter, in the context of modern American politics, whether a given group-based policy is labeled "conservative" or "liberal" depends on whether the group that stands to gain from the policy is dominant or subordinate. Policies that favor dominant groups at the expense of human capital (e.g., anti-gay policies) are generally "conservative" (and opposing such policies is "liberal") while policies that favor subordinate groups at the expense of human capital (e.g., affirmative action) are generally "liberal" (and opposing such policies is "conservative").

With this in mind, summarizing our views, when the battles involve group-based policies, and when the main alternative to using group-based distinctions is to use human-capital-based distinctions, we think people's interests turn out as follows:

- *People with lots of human capital and one or more traditionally subordinate group identities*: We have in mind here, for example, professionals who are racial minorities, immigrants, women, non-Christians, or homosexuals. Their primary strategic interest is in eliminating barriers to human-capital-based success mainly with regard to their own subordinate group or groups. For such people their views spill over into a wider pro-human-capital agenda of minimizing all group-based distinctions. This agenda might include opposing group-based policies that place barriers in the way of groups of which they are not themselves members, but might also include opposing affirmative efforts to assist other groups in ways that dilute human-capital-based competition. Thus, their views will look "liberal" in the sense that they seek to protect subordinate groups (especially their own subordinate groups) from the negative effects of barrier-imposing policies. Still, sometimes their views will look "conservative," particularly when they oppose (in the name of maintaining undiluted human-capital-based distinctions) affirmative measures that would advance specific subordinate groups.

- *People with lots of human capital who are members only of traditionally dominant groups*: This group consists of white, native-born, male, heterosexual Christians who are doctors, lawyers, graduates from better colleges, and so on—the analogues of the elite white baseball players. At very high levels of human capital, they might do better under pure human-capital-based policies, but most shouldn't be affected too strongly one way or the other. Perhaps the only consistent expectation is that they should be predicted to oppose efforts to affirmatively advance subordinate groups at the expense of human-capital-based rules. These people should be expected to have mixtures of centrist views on group-based policies, neither particularly "liberal" nor particularly "conservative" (except with regard to areas like affirmative action, where they should be more consistently "conservative").

- *People with less human capital and a mixture of traditionally dominant and subordinate group identities*: We have in mind here, for example, people with no college degrees and average or below average testing abilities who are white atheists, or African American heterosexuals, or immigrant Christians. Primarily their interests lie in opposing disadvantages and supporting advantages for their own groups. When it comes to policies that affect areas in which their own group identities are subordinate, their policy opinions would be "liberal" (e.g., atheists would have "liberal" views on school prayer; African Americans would have "liberal" views on race-based policies). But when it comes to policies that affect areas in which their own group identities are dominant, their policy opinions would be "conservative" (e.g., Christians would be "conservative" on school prayer; whites would be "conservative" on race-based policies).

- *People with less human capital who are members only of traditionally dominant groups*: These are white, native-born, male, heterosexual Christians with little in the way of educational attainment. Like other individuals with less human capital, they are best off in opposing disadvantages and supporting advantages for their own groups. All their positions would be "conservative" because all their own groups are traditionally dominant.

The people in the first category on the list—with lots of human capital and one or more traditionally subordinate group identities—are at the forefront of fights to remove barriers to traditionally subordinate groups. It's no coincidence that most efforts to impose "political correctness" come from these quarters, for example, from university professors who themselves are racial minorities, or immigrants, or women, or non-Christians, or homosexuals. And it's no wonder, after all, that the federal courts, containing probably the highest level of human capital on average of any federal or state government institution, have long been at the leading edge in striking down popular group-based barriers. And it's no wonder that on the Supreme Court—all individuals with very high levels of human capital—the "liberal" bloc consists of two Jewish women, a Jewish man, and a wise Latina, while the "conservative" bloc consists of four white, heterosexual, Christian men (plus Justice Clarence Thomas, who demonstrates the key additional point that all general observations have exceptions).

And it's similarly not a coincidence that the people in the last category on the list—with less human capital and who are members only of traditionally dominant groups—tend to be the most vocal opponents of political correctness and the federal courts. Other people with less human capital might oppose some aspects of political correctness and favor others—a white atheist, for example, might support the Supreme Court's decisions on school prayer but oppose them on race-based discrimination. However, for those who are members of only traditionally dominant groups, blanket opposition to interfering with group-based dominance in the name of human-capital-based dominance can become a larger cause. Simplifying, indeed, oversimplifying: pointy-headed liberals have a general opposition to group-based barriers (in the name of advancing human capital); good ol' boys have a general opposition to political correctness (in the name of advancing group-based dominance).

No Matter of Principle

Our basic argument is that, with respect to group-based policies, people typically take positions that align with their strategic inclusive interests. People's Boards of Directors are focused on rules that produce outcomes that help themselves, their families, their allies, and their social networks. People's Public Relations Departments then, to sell their positions, concoct public-friendly stories that often rely on lofty-sounding principles and values. People's mental Spokespersons then believe—really believe—that their views are in fact caused by their benign principles rather than by their own inclusive interests.

In contrast, political science has often taken the view that people really do derive policy particulars from higher-level values and ideologies.[2] But the psychological literature furnishes plenty of support for the idea that people's "higher-level" positions are flexible.

Some studies addressing this issue have looked at the degree to which people are in favor of "social dominance," roughly the idea that members of certain groups are superior to members of other groups and, therefore, ought to have advantages over them. A typical item on the scale used to measure this view is "Some groups of people are just more worthy than others." The key question here is this: Do people support particular policies because of their general commitments with regard to social dominance, or do they support general notions with regard to social dominance because their Boards of Directors are really thinking about the particular groups to which people belong?

One study surveyed Ashkenazi Jews and Mizrahi Jews, the latter of which are considered to be of lower ethnic status in Israeli society.[3] Some subjects were made to think of the relationship between these two groups of Jews, and other subjects were made to think about the relationship between Jews and Arabs. The subjects were then given the general survey items relating to social dominance. The results were that Ashkenazi Jews tended to endorse social dominance in either case—in both cases they are higher status, so this was to be expected. The interesting contrast is among the Mizrahi Jews, who are members of the *lower* status group in comparison with Ashkenazi Jews, but are members of the *higher* status group in comparison with Arabs. Indeed, Mizrahi Jews endorsed general notions of between-group discrimination to a greater degree when they were primed to think about Arab-Jewish relationships, while such ideas weren't so appealing when thinking about themselves in relation to Ashkenazi Jews.

In a similar study in Taiwan, survey-takers were first given either a long set of questions about gender or a long set of questions about Taiwan's different demographic groups, distinguished primarily by region, dialect, and how recently the groups immigrated to Taiwan.[4] When made to think about gender, men endorsed general notions of social dominance more than women, but the various demographic groups didn't differ. In contrast, when made to think about demographic groups, members of Taiwan's dominant group endorsed general notions of social dominance more than members of other groups, but men and women didn't differ.

Often political scientists are tempted to think that attitudes toward items like social dominance (and other similar "value" or political "personality" measures) represent fundamental causal factors that themselves lead to different political opinions. The results in relation to Taiwan and Israel, in contrast, illustrate that people have flexible views depending on the groups they are currently considering—depending, that is, on the practical, interest-based question of whose ox is being gored.

Issues Relating to Sexual Orientation and Religion

We now turn to data involving group-based issues from the U.S. General Social Survey. In this section, we look at items that relate to sexual orientation and religion; in the following section, we'll look at items relating to immigration, race, and gender.

Recall that a Gallup poll showed that few Americans admitted that they wouldn't vote for someone purely because of race or gender, but plenty still say they wouldn't vote for a homosexual, atheist, or Muslim. In a series of items, the GSS has asked related questions about whether these sorts of people should be allowed to give public speeches, teach in universities, and have their books in public libraries. These survey items include the following: (1) "a man who admits that he is a homosexual," (2) "somebody who is against all churches and religion," and (3) "a Muslim clergyman who preaches hatred of the United States." When it comes to these three groups, Americans over the past decade have been most tolerant of homosexuals, with only around two in ten opposing basic First Amendment rights of giving speeches, teaching, and having books in libraries. Tolerance of people against religion drops a bit—about three in ten oppose basic First Amendment rights for this group. Tolerance of anti-American Muslims, though, is low. Here, half of Americans oppose allowing their books in libraries, about six in ten oppose their right to give speeches, and about seven in ten oppose them teaching in universities.

The GSS has commonly asked two other questions about sexual orientation. One asks whether homosexual sex is immoral. The other asks about support for same-sex marriage. Over the past decade, about four in ten Americans believed that homosexuality is "not wrong at all" and that same-sex marriage should be allowed, while almost half viewed homosexuality as "always wrong" and thought same-sex marriage should not be allowed. Unlike most of the opinions we're looking at in this book, though, views on homosexuality have been shifting rapidly in recent years. In fact, by around 2010 public opinion on same-sex marriage had shifted from mostly opposed to mostly in favor.

Another GSS item asks about whether the subjects approve or disapprove of the Supreme Court's ban on school prayer. Overall, most people—almost six in ten over the past decade—would like to see the ban lifted. This is one of those cases in which the Supreme Court has overruled public will in the name of meritocracy (or rather, as their mental Spokespersons would say, in the name of constitutional principles). Allowing school prayer might not seem discriminatory, but the experience of nonpraying schoolchildren belies this view. Requiring or even allowing school prayer exposes nonpraying children to attacks of various sorts by their praying counterparts; nonreligious children are made perilously visible during times set aside for praying.[5] In addition, policies like these signal wider acceptance of imposing barriers against non-Christians in social life.

In total, then, almost half of Americans would deny homosexuals the right to marry, while around two in ten would deny them basic First Amendment rights. Almost six in ten oppose the school prayer ban that protects non-Christian children from discrimination, while around three in ten would deny basic First Amendment rights to people op-posed to religion.

What predicts people's views on these kinds of items? We tested many potential predictors, including the usual demographic suspects (age, gender, income, race, region, etc.), as well as all the religious and lifestyle items we discussed in chapter 4 (religion, church attendance, sexual history, marital status, etc.). Of special note for this chapter are two items measuring human capital. One was simply education level (whether people have high school diplomas, bachelor's degrees, etc.). The other was the subjects' performance on a ten-item vocabulary test and various true/false items testing basic scientific knowledge—to give three examples: whether the center of the earth is very hot (true; missed by 19%), whether the father's gene decides the baby's sex (true; missed by 38%), whether lasers work by focusing sound waves (false; missed by 54%). So, we used information not only on education level, but also on direct test performance, an important measure of modern meritocratic competence. In describing the views of different groups of Americans, we sometimes combine education and test performance into a single measure of human capital, splitting out, for example, those in the top 20% overall (which includes people with graduate degrees and top 60% test performance, people with bachelor's degrees and top 40% test per-formance, and people with some college education and top 20% test performance).

In testing this large range of potential predictors, when it comes to items relating to sexual orientation and religion, two broad patterns emerge (for these issues and the others described in this chapter, we give our full analyses in the Data Appendix for Chapter 5). First, people with more human capital (i.e., with more education and better test performance) tend to oppose these barrier-imposing efforts more than people with lower levels of human capital. If we just split the sample by whether people have bachelor's degrees or not, for example, the majority of the more highly educated group support same-sex marriage, the ban on school prayer, and the right of anti-American Muslims to give speeches, while the majority of the less educated group oppose these policies.

The second major pattern that emerges is that—unsurprisingly—people often support and oppose policies in line with their group identities. So, for example, while 70% of non-Christians approve of the ban on school prayer, only 35% of Christians share this view. Similarly, while over three-quarter of lesbians, gays, and bisexuals have supported same-sex marriage over the past decade, less than half of heterosexuals agreed (though, as we said, these numbers have been shifting in recent years).

On issues relating to sexual orientation, the religious and lifestyle variables we looked at in chapter 4 add further predictive punch. On the premarital sex item from chapter 4, the major predictors include church attendance, religion, and lifestyle features such as number of sex partners. But, interestingly, education and test performance don't add much predictive power, nor does sexual orientation. With respect to assigning a moral judgment to homosexual sex, though, sexual orientation and human capital play substantial roles, making predictive contributions essentially equivalent to church attendance and religion. The moral condemnation of homosexuality, indeed, looks like a direct hybrid of the kinds of issues we examined in chapter 4 (involving the connections among lifestyle politics, lived lifestyles, and religion) and the issues we're covering in this chapter (involving human capital and group-based identities).

The details of the GSS data show clearly how a group-identities-meets-human-capital perspective sheds light on why Americans differ when it comes to issues relating to sexual orientation and religion. What predicts whether people approve or disapprove of the Supreme Court's ban on school prayer? Well, who benefits most from drawing group-based distinctions with regard to Christianity that ultimately serve to interfere with social rules that would otherwise primarily favor people with lots of human capital? These should be Christians with less human capital. Who benefits most from removing barriers impeding non-Christians and letting human capital flourish? These should be non-Christians with higher levels of human capital.

When we look at the data, that's essentially what we find. For non-Christians with top 40% human capital, more than three out of four support the Supreme Court's ban on school prayer. For Christians with *bottom* 40% human capital, in contrast, around three out of four *oppose* the ban on school prayer. That is, *there's more than a 50-point gap between non-Christians with high levels of human capital and Christians with low levels of human capital.* Other groups fall in between these two on school prayer. For example, more than half of non-Christians with lower levels of human capital support the ban on school prayer, as do more than half of Christians with top 20% human capital.

On the question of whether an anti-religious person should be allowed to teach at universities, the key group-based distinction is not Christians versus non-Christians, but those with any religious affiliation (Christians, Jews, etc.) versus those with no religious affiliation. For those with no religious affiliation and top 60% human capital, almost nine in ten think an anti-religious person should be allowed to teach. For those with some religious affiliation and bottom 20% human capital, only around four in ten agree—around a 50-point gap. Again, other groups are in the middle.

On the question of whether an anti-American Muslim should be allowed to teach, the key distinction is between Christians and Jews on the one hand and everyone else on the other. For non-Christians and non-Jews with top 20% human capital (particularly those who were born and raised in the United States), around two-thirds think anti-American Muslims should be allowed to teach. For Christians and Jews with bottom 40% human capital, in contrast, fewer than one in five agree—another 50-point gap.

On issues of sexual orientation, there are similarities between lesbians/gays/bisexuals and people who are not Christians (mostly including those with no religious affiliation at all, but also including Jews, Buddhists, etc.). This is a combination that will pop up regularly throughout the remainder of the book, so we'll give them a name, "Heathens," just so we don't have to keep repeating the infelicitous construction, "people who are either lesbian/gay/bisexual or not Christian."*

Issues relating to sexual orientation, as we mentioned, are best predicted by group identities and human capital along with the religious and lifestyle features highlighted in chapter 4. Among heterosexual, weekly churchgoing Christians, for example, opposition to same-sex marriage is high, without major differences based on human capital—among these folks, more than half of Catholics and around three-quarters of non-Catholic Christians oppose same-sex marriage. But for other groups, human capital matters. Fewer than one in five Heathens with top 40% human capital oppose same-sex marriage, along with around one-third of Heathens with less human capital. Among heterosexual Christians who don't go to church weekly, groups vary from pretty liberal on same-sex marriage (e.g., women with top 40% human capital, where only around three in ten oppose same-sex marriage) to pretty conservative (e.g., non-Catholic Christians with bottom 60% human capital, where just over half oppose it).

As to whether a gay man should be allowed to teach at universities, the important splits involve human capital, primarily, along with church attendance. For those who have top 40% human capital and don't go to church weekly, more than nine in ten think gay men should be allowed to teach; for weekly churchgoers with top 40% human capital, this drops to around eight in ten. For those who have bottom 20% human capital and don't go to church weekly, around six in ten think gay men should be allowed to teach; for weekly churchgoers with bottom 20% human capital, this sinks to just four in ten.

Issues Relating to Immigration, Race, and Gender

As Republicans began to sort out the aftermath of the 2012 election, one idea that quickly moved to the front burner was the need to attract more

---

* "Heathens" might seem like a somewhat pejorative label, but both of your authors are non-Christians and thus are Heathens on this definition; we don't feel the need to bend over backwards to not offend ourselves.

Latino votes. The Republican elite, who had long favored immigration reform, saw the election debacle as an opportunity to move an otherwise intransigent Congress. But concerns grew that large chunks of the Republican base would be alienated, derailing this process. Group-based interests are helpful in explaining these dynamics: Latino immigrants are fundamentally supportive of immigration, highly educated folks are generally sympathetic, and less educated whites are generally opposed.

The GSS's main immigration item asks people whether they think immigration levels should be increased a lot, increased a little, left as is, reduced a little, or reduced a lot. Overall, during the past decade, more than four times as many Americans think levels should be reduced (52%) than think levels should be increased (12%).

Given that many immigrants are undocumented or not yet citizens, that many immigrants have family members who would like to come to the United States, and that views on this kind of immigration question express in large part one's orientation toward immigrants generally—whether American society will be a welcoming and supportive place for immigrants or not—it is unsurprising that the group that feels most strongly positive in their views on immigration is, well, immigrants. Only roughly one in five immigrants think that immigration levels should be reduced.

At the other end of the spectrum are whites who were born and raised in the United States, particularly those lower in human capital. Among born-and-raised whites with bottom 40% human capital, about two-thirds want less immigration. Born-and-raised whites with top 20% human capital land almost exactly in between immigrants and whites who have low levels of human capital—around four or five in ten want reduced immigration.

When it comes to racial issues, the GSS, as with other major surveys, rarely asks questions about views on overt, barrier-imposing policies (such as interracial marriage or white-only neighborhoods), and even when such questions are asked, there's no longer substantial disagreement. These days, most survey questions about policies directly related to race ask about support for or opposition to *benefits* for African Americans. The most commonly asked GSS items are about whether "the government has a special obligation to help improve [African American] living standards," about whether the government is spending too much or not enough on assistance to African Americans, and about affirmative action for African Americans.

For each of these items, the strongest demographic predictor, unsurprisingly, is race. African Americans on average most strongly favor government support for African Americans and raced-based affirmative action; whites on average are most opposed; Latino, Asian, and other Americans are in the middle, leaning somewhat closer to African Americans than to whites on average.

On government help for African Americans, the key contrast is between African Americans and a group that should sound familiar: born-and-raised, white, heterosexual Christians without lots of human capital (i.e., with bottom 80% human capital). Among these good ol' folk, roughly six in ten think the government should give no special treatment to African Americans; fewer than two in ten African Americans agree. Some of the most liberal-leaning whites on this issue are Heathens with top 20% human capital—of the people in this group, around four or five out of ten think the government should give no special treatment to African Americans, a position around 15 points to the left of the good ol' folk, but around 30 points to the right of African Americans.

Views on government spending tell a similar story. Among white, heterosexual Christians, only two in ten support increased spending for African Americans. This rises to four in ten for white, Heathen women with top 60% human capital (this figure is only three in ten for men). However, more than seven in ten African Americans think the government should be spending more specifically on African Americans.

We saw on barrier-imposing items (involving sexual orientation, religion, and immigration) that high levels of human capital are strongly associated with more liberal positions. But it isn't that folks with lots of human capital are generally liberal; instead, they seek to defend human-capital-favoring rules by opposing group-based barriers. With regard to government assistance for African Americans, the issues don't obviously relate to human-capital-based competitions, and, indeed, the extent of human-capital-based divisions diminishes.

From government assistance for African Americans, we now move to affirmative action. On affirmative action, the role of human capital in fact reverses; those with high levels of human capital are somewhat more conservative. Because affirmative action programs use group-based distinctions that weaken human-capital-based allocations, those with higher levels of human capital often oppose these programs.

We'll look at both race-based and gender-based affirmative action. Both are in the context of support for or opposition to businesses making special efforts to hire and promote African Americans, on the one hand, and women, on the other. In general, both race-based and gender-based affirmative action are unpopular when it comes to hiring and promotion. Overall, only 17% support race-based affirmative action and only 32% support gender-based affirmative action.

For race-based affirmative action, the strongest supporters, as with other issues of race-based support, are African Americans, 44% of whom support it. Among whites, those most likely to support it are white Heathens with top 20% human capital; in this group, 23% support race-based affirmative action. The biggest opponents aren't whites with the lowest human capital, however, but white, heterosexual Christians with top 80% human capital (only 8% support it) or white Heathens with middle levels of human capital (only 10% support it).

On the issue of gender-based affirmative action, higher levels of human capital more plainly predict opposition. The biggest opponents of gender-based affirmative action include white men with top 60% human capital—only 14% favor gender-based affirmative action. At the other end are minority women, 56% of whom favor gender-based affirmative action. White women with top 60% human capital are in fact only slightly more supportive than white men with top 60% human capital—only 19% favor it. Minority men are only slightly less supportive than minority women—49% support it.

Taking these patterns together, African American women are most likely to favor both race-based and gender-based affirmative action, though even in this group the overall support is limited to around half. The biggest opponents overall are white men with higher levels of human capital, who rarely support either race-based or gender-based affirmative action when it comes to workplace hiring and promotion.

Criminal justice issues typically don't explicitly relate to race, but nonetheless carry very strong racial overtones.[6] On the death penalty, for example, while around three-quarters of white Americans favor it, support among African Americans and Latinos drops to less than half. Among whites, native-born individuals without lots of human capital support it the most.

Another criminal justice issue involves police violence, a subject of passionate concern among members of many minority communities, but a topic that remains a non-issue for many whites. The GSS has included an item asking whether the person can imagine circumstances in which it is acceptable for police to strike an adult male citizen. Almost three-quarters of minorities with bottom 20% human capital say there are no circumstances in which it's OK for police to strike citizens. Among born-and-raised, white men with top 60% human capital, in contrast, only one in ten agree. Cases like this point clearly to the limits of white meritocrats' defense of minorities with lower socioeconomic status. From these results, it seems to us that when issues affect fundamental, everyday goals relating to their own safety, high-status whites tend to side with the police without regard to minority views.

Clear Interests and Jumbled Ideologies

Overall, solidly "liberal" and solidly "conservative" demographics on group-based issues aren't that common. A uniformly "liberal" demographic would involve something like African American Heathens with lots of human capital. A uniformly "conservative" demographic would involve the perfect storm of group identities that are all dominant (white, born-and-raised, heterosexual, Christian men) coupled with less human capital. But in both of these cases, we described how the "ideology" generally follows from interests. Outside of these limited demographic combinations, interests change accordingly, and liberal-conservative coherence breaks down.

White Heathens with lots of human capital are overall liberal on group-based issues, but with key exceptions. More specifically, these brainy, white lesbians/gays/bisexuals and/or non-Christians are most liberal when the issues relate to protecting lesbians, gays, and non-Christians from barrier-imposing efforts that would limit their ability to take full advantage of their human capital. When the issues relate to governmental support or affirmative action for African Americans, brainy white Heathens might be to the left of other whites, but they aren't nearly as liberal as African Americans. When the issues turn to gender-based affirmative action or police violence, their views are among the most conservative.

White, heterosexual Christians with lots of human capital—analogues of the talented white baseball players from our earlier sports examples—have no strong interests one way or the other and are in the middle. When the question is one of seeking group-based advantages based on their dominant categories, they split pretty evenly, often leaning slightly in a liberal direction (except when it comes to criminal justice issues, where they are among the most solidly conservative). When it comes to the other side of the coin—whether to have government funds for African Americans or affirmative action—they are solidly conservative.

At lower levels of human capital, opinions tend to be in line with seeking advantages for one's own groups. If we compare, at lower human capital levels, African American Christians with white atheists, we see differences that have everything to do with interests and very little to do with liberal/conservative labels. Most African American Christians with less human capital would prefer a world in which the anti-religious are not allowed to teach at universities, school prayer is allowed, and same-sex marriage is banned, but the government gives targeted help and more spending for African Americans, the death penalty is not used, and police do not strike citizens. Most white atheists with less human capital would prefer the opposite world, one in which anti-religious professors get to keep their jobs, school prayer is banned, and same-sex marriage is allowed, but the government gives no special treatment and no more than current spending to African Americans, the death penalty is permitted, and the police are allowed to strike citizens in some circumstances.

Political scientists have long noticed a lack of liberal-conservative coherence among those with less human capital.[7] This lack of ideological box-fitting, however, does not imply that people's views are not systematic. It's just that interests (rather than ideologies) provide the underlying structure.

Groups around the World

As in the prior chapter, we finish with a quick check of international data, using the World Values Survey. We focus on two broad areas involving group-based issues in the WVS: attitudes toward the nonreligious and attitudes toward immigrants (full details in the Data Appendix for Chapter 5).

In the United States, the GSS data show that people who are less religious and better educated hold the most favorable attitudes about the nonreligious, while people who are more religious and less educated hold the least favorable attitudes about the nonreligious. This pattern occurs in the WVS, not only for the United States, but also in other Western countries as well as in non-Western countries as a whole.

We've also seen in the United States that immigrants are most favorable about immigrants, native-born people with less education are least favorable, and native-born people with more education are in between. This pattern also occurs in the WVS data for the United States, other Western countries, and non-Western countries.

The most noticeable difference across these regions is that attitudes are generally more tolerant across groups in Western countries (other than the United States) and less tolerant across groups in non-Western countries. In the United States, however, opinions based on education and group identities typically span the full range—people in traditionally dominant groups who have less education in the United States disfavor those in traditionally subordinate groups almost as much as similar people in non-Western countries do; people in subordinate groups who have more education in the United States oppose discrimination against their own groups almost as much as similar people in other Western countries do. In general then, while the same overall pattern—involving group identities and human capital—holds worldwide, demographics point to heightened contrasts in policy preferences in the United States.

Adding Pieces to the Puzzle

When looking at issues relating to sexual and reproductive lifestyles in chapter 4, our basic point was simple: Figure out how these issues affect people's everyday lives, find demographic measures that track these effects, and one can understand the basic distribution of views among the public. These interests mostly related to Freewheeler versus Ring-Bearer lifestyles, signaled by such things as sexual histories, drinking, marital histories, and children. We saw that religion strongly intersected these lifestyle features, and that the best predictors of views on items like the moral condemnation of premarital sex, pornography, marijuana legalization, abortion, and birth control involved religious and lifestyle features—the most conservative people go to church a lot and have Ring-Bearer lifestyles while the most liberal people rarely attend church and have Freewheeler lifestyles. Race and education weren't major factors (except when it came to abortion, where individuals with more education have substantially more liberal views).

In contrast, when the issues relate to barriers on the basis of sexual orientation and religion, the dominant demographic predictors include sexual orientation, religion, and human capital. When the issues relate to immigration and race-based policies, the dominant demographic predictors become immigration status, race, and human capital. Different issues; different interests; different demographics.

These ideas help identify people who have different views across the lifestyle issues from chapter 4 and the group-based issues of this chapter. Want to find people who are conservative on lifestyle issues, conservative on LGB/religious issues, but liberal on racial issues? Go find people who have the right combination of interests—African American and Latino churchgoers with Ring-Bearer lifestyles and less human capital. Want to find people who are conservative across dominant-group-favoring issues but liberal on most lifestyle issues? Go find people who have the right combination of interests—native-born, white heterosexuals with less human capital and with Freewheeler lifestyles who are nominally Christians but who hardly ever go to church.

When one takes a closer look at lives and interests, the conventional wisdom that divides people broadly into liberals and conservatives (and maybe libertarians as well) begins to look plainly insufficient, even lazy. Forget red, blue, and purple—it's more like a 24-box of Crayons.

But very shortly, twenty-four won't be enough. In the next chapter, we move to our last set of political issues, those relating to tax-and-spend policies. One might imagine that people with more money would be more conservative on many of these issues, and, as we noted in chapter 2, one would be right. But notice something crucial. We saw that high levels of education often go with liberal abortion views because these folks tend to delay having children. We saw that high levels of education often go with liberal views that seek to eliminate group-based barriers because these folks usually do better under human-capital-advancing rules. But here's something else about people who have a lot of education: They also tend to have more money.

CHAPTER 6

Money Matters:
Redistribution and Hard-Times Programs

A TYPICAL AMERICAN WITH A GRADUATE DEGREE—MA, MBA, MD, JD, PhD, and so on—lives in a household with income greater than $100,000 a year (for everyone else, median household income is less than $60,000 a year). Yet recall from chapter 1 that the 2012 exit polls showed that Obama won among those with graduate degrees by 13 points while Romney won among those with incomes of $100,000 or more by 10 points. People with lots of education tend to have higher incomes, but the two have opposite influences on party votes.

The ways each side complains about the other side's "elites" highlight this contrast. From the right, the complaints are about educational elites whose big-city, Ivy League, cultural bubble makes them hopelessly out of touch with "real" Americans. Case in point: In 2008, Barack Obama appeared at a fund-raiser in San Francisco (of course, San Francisco!) and made his oft-repeated "bitter" comment:

> You go into some of these small towns in Pennsylvania, and like a lot of small towns in the Midwest, the jobs have been gone now for twenty-five years and nothing's replaced them. And they fell through the Clinton administration, and the Bush administration, and each successive administration has said that somehow these communities are gonna regenerate and they have not. So it's not surprising then that they get bitter, they cling to guns or religion or antipathy to people who aren't like them or anti-immigrant sentiment or anti-trade sentiment as a way to explain their frustrations.

From the left, the complaints are about wealthy elites whose country-club, Wall Street, economic bubble makes them hopelessly out of touch with the middle class. Case in point: At a 2012 fund-raiser hosted by a hedge fund manager (of course, a hedge fund manager!), Mitt Romney made his oft-repeated "47 percent" comment:

> There are 47 percent of the people who will vote for the president no matter what. All right, there are 47 percent who are with him, who are dependent upon government, who believe that they are victims, who believe that government has a responsibility to care for them, who believe that they are entitled to health care, to food, to housing, to you name it. That that's an entitlement. And the government should give it to them. And they will vote for this president no matter what. And I mean, the president starts off with 48, 49, 48—he starts off with a huge number. These are people who pay no income tax—47 percent of Americans pay no income tax. So our message of low taxes doesn't connect. And he'll be out there talking about tax cuts for the rich. I mean that's what they sell every four years. And so my job is not to worry about those people. I'll never convince them that they should take personal responsibility and care for their lives.

New York Times columnist Ross Douthat made the essential point when comparing Obama's "bitter" comments with Romney's "47 percent" dismissal:

> In both cases, a presidential candidate was speaking about poorer people to a room full of rich people; in both cases, he was pandering to those rich people's fearful stereotypes about a way of life that they don't understand or share.
>
> For rich Republicans, the stereotype is all about the money: They have it, other Americans don't, and those resentful, entitled others might just have enough votes to wage class warfare and redistribute the donors' hard-earned millions to the indolent and irresponsible.
>
> For rich Democrats, the stereotype is all about the culture wars: They think they've built an enlightened society, liberated from archaic beliefs and antique hang-ups, and yet these Jesus freaks in flyover country are mobilizing to restore the patriarchy.
>
> Both groups of donors seem to be haunted by dystopian scenarios in which the masses rise up and tear down everything the upper class has built. For Republicans, the dystopia is (inevitably) "Atlas Shrugged." For liberals, it's one part "Turner Diaries," one part "Handmaid's Tale."[1]

Douthat may have characterized both sides as "rich people," but the key to contrasting "elite" views in politics is the distinction between education on the one hand and income on the other. These are correlated, of course, but people's education (more broadly, human capital) and income have different influences on people's favored policies.[2] In the previous chapter, we explored how high levels of human capital lead to preferences that human capital be allowed to flourish unfettered by old-school group barriers, and, in chapter 4, we noted that higher education is associated with liberal views on abortion. These kinds of issues are what Douthat was referring to in contrasting "an enlightened society" with "archaic beliefs and antique hang-ups." Back in chapter 2, when we did some fact-checking of self-interest-denying claims, we found that richer people are more likely to oppose income redistribution and poorer people are more likely to support it. These sorts of issues underlie Douthat's comments about "class warfare" feared by Republican elites.

And so both sides complain about different sorts of "elites" who themselves complain about different downscale constituencies. Ivy League latte-sippers belittle uneducated hicks who want to retain all their group-based advantages. Mustache-twirling robber barons belittle poor, lazy moochers who want to redistribute—take—the nation's wealth.

In this chapter, we'll focus on issues about which the upper crust is particularly conservative, including tax-and-spend, social safety nets, entitlements, welfare, health care, and so on. As we've noted already, views on these issues relate to people's income levels. But there's more to it than just income.

We'll be talking a lot about "poorer" and "richer" people. People's views of income are often skewed. Recall how easy it is, for example, to overestimate how "wild" most college kids are (because the wilder kids are more visible) or to overestimate how many Americans have college degrees (because most of our readers probably hang out in circles in which most people are college educated). For similar reasons, it's easy to overestimate what counts as "richer" or "wealthier" in the United States. One would think, for example, that the top 10% of households surely count as "richer" or "wealthier" than most others; it would be weird to call people in the top 10% "middle class."

But the top 10% of American households includes those with more than $150,000 in total yearly income (combining the income from everyone in the household).[3] The top 5% of American households includes those with more than $192,000 in yearly income. For households with only one person, the middle 50% includes incomes around $14,000 to $49,000. For households with two people, the middle range is around $31,000 to $95,000. For households with three or more people, it's $38,000 to $115,000. The reality is pretty far removed from national political conversations that seem to agree that no family making less than $250,000 could plausibly count as wealthy.

In contrast, when we talk about "richer" or "wealthier" people in this book, we're not talking just about the top 1%. We're talking about people who are in the higher-but-not-necessarily-stratospheric percentiles (e.g., top 20%, top 10%)—even though most of those folks probably don't think of themselves as "rich" at all.

It's Not Just People Currently Submerged Who Want Flood Insurance

Government finances are, in a word, complex. The $2.5 *trillion* in federal revenue in 2012 came from an array of sources, about $1.1 trillion from individual income taxes, $845 billion from payroll taxes (Social Security and Medicare), and the rest from corporate income taxes, federal sales taxes on gasoline and other items, gift and estate taxes, and other sources. The other side of the equation, expenditures, are, of course, dizzying in their variety, ranging from the military to interest on the debt to the great ape enclosure at the National Zoo.

Some government programs are viewed as "public goods" that benefit everyone more or less equally, though it's difficult to identify satisfyingly pure examples of such programs in practice. Spending on highways might benefit everyone, but provide greater relative benefits to those whose livelihoods are more dependent on highway travel. Spending on mass transit follows the same logic. Defense is a typical example of a "public good," given that citizens are more or less equally protected by the armed forces. But defense firms and their employees particularly gain with larger military budgets, not to mention the fact that the military disproportionately hires middle-class males.

Other government programs are more clearly skewed, particularly those relating to safety nets. Welfare, Medicaid (health care for the poor), and food assistance, for example, are generally means-tested, directly helping the poor. Even programs that are not means-tested— unemployment insurance, Social Security, Medicare (health care for the elderly), etc.—help poorer people more, relative to income, than wealthier people.

Whether means-tested or not, safety-net programs are available in theory to citizens over the course of their lives, with some programs most likely to benefit poorer people at prime working and child-rearing ages, and others limited to benefiting the elderly. Such programs act, essentially, as insurance policies. If a person loses their job and doesn't have other income, the government will step in with temporary assistance. Even programs for the elderly work this way—the benefits are paid based primarily on simply being elderly, but act particularly as a buffer to prevent ill-prepared seniors from slipping into deep poverty or placing heavy burdens on family members.

A key point about insurance programs is that people tend to favor them not only when those programs would provide payouts *right now*, but also because the programs might benefit them *in the future*. Consider flood insurance. Suppose the federal government were to have a new program that used general tax revenue to compensate anyone who lost property in a flood. People whose homes were not currently underwater wouldn't receive any payments from the government today, but would stand to benefit if their homes were flooded in the future. People most at risk from flooding are the ones most likely to favor such a program. And if they can get the benefits while distributing the costs among taxpayers generally, without having to purchase private flood insurance, then all the better for them.

Some discussions in political science are presented as though it's something other than "self-interest" when people who are not poor today favor programs meant to help the poor, or when people who are not sick today favor programs subsidizing health care, or when people who are not old today support programs providing substantial benefits for the elderly. But this is equivalent to saying that only those underwater right now benefit from flood insurance. Most of the programs people think of as redistributive act as a kind of hard-times insurance. The question, then, isn't only who is experiencing hard times now, but who expects the possibility of hard times in the future.

These expectations depend on any number of factors. An educated reporter working in the print media might be well qualified and have many years of experience, but the nature of the industry might cause concern about long-term employment prospects.

Other factors that might reasonably affect expectations, however, are less idiosyncratic. Income obviously matters in deciding whether one might need hard-times programs in the future. Those who have extended periods with high incomes are more likely to save up money, a kind of self-insurance. Those with more modest incomes might not qualify for government assistance today, but probably have less savings, creating greater potential need for hard-times programs in the future. That is, when people with lots of savings and people with little savings experience a significant drop in income, both experience "hard times," but those with little savings have more need for gap-filling insurance to get them through it.

Education clearly relates to the likelihood of experiencing hard times. People with more education not only tend to have higher incomes, but also tend to have substantially lower unemployment rates. Less education, then, on average increases the potential need for hard-times programs in the future.

Gender is also a significant factor when it comes to hard times. Currently, most of the poorest American families are single women with young children. When married, of course, men and women by definition have identical family incomes. For single people, gender differences in income derive from a variety of sources. One source is that women are simply on average paid less than men, even for similar work. In addition, women are more likely than men to work part-time or not at all when they have young children, and women are more likely to be raising children as single parents than are men. These factors decrease women's average time in the labor force, which diminishes their long-term economic prospects. These effects have been widely studied, for example, in cases of divorce, which frequently substantially diminishes a woman's standard of living but not a man's.[4] Overall, then, women (including women currently married) have a greater potential need for hard-times programs in the future than do men on average.

Age introduces additional complexities. Before FDR's New Deal and LBJ's Great Society, the poorest Americans were often the elderly. This is no longer true. Today, both the elderly and young adults have lower work-based incomes than middle-aged individuals on average, but the elderly are subsidized by Social Security and Medicare while the young are not. Most programs helping non-elderly adults are either time-limited (unemployment benefits), means-tested (Medicaid and food assistance), or both (welfare benefits). And the benefits for the elderly far outpace the benefits for the poor. According to 2012 data, the average retired worker received over $1,200 per month from Social Security.[5] In contrast, the typical family with two children on welfare (these days known as Temporary Assistance for Needy Families or TANF) received only $412 a month.[6] Further, since the push for welfare reform in the Clinton years, TANF benefits have had significant strings attached and typically cannot be received for more than five years across an individual's lifetime. (Continued talk of lifetimes of dependency are mostly a myth, at least when it comes to federal TANF benefits.) If seniors and younger single mothers are asked a question about whether "government should be doing more for the poor," one should expect different answers if only because the status quo so heavily favors seniors.

Compounding the age issue is the fact that Social Security and Medicare are often seen—incorrectly—as earned benefits rather than redistribution programs. Most seniors collect substantially more in benefits from these programs than they ever paid in payroll taxes.[7] Further, the amount that seniors collect has much more to do with how long they live and the health problems they develop than it does with how much they paid in taxes. Nonetheless, the mistaken impression that these programs represent earned benefits has led to widely repeated, and surprisingly real, examples of seniors telling their government representatives to "keep your government hands off my Medicare."[8] This kind of thinking affects many seniors' views on government programs generally.

In sum, who has a greater and lesser potential need for hard-times programs in the future? Those with a greater need include poorer people, people with less education, women, and the elderly. Those with a lesser need include richer people, people with more education, men, and the middle-aged. The crucial caveat is that elderly people, though more in need, are largely having their essential needs met by existing government hard-times programs, even if many of them don't see it that way.

Public versus Private

Often the fight over safety nets is phrased in terms of liberals preferring government programs and conservatives preferring private charity. This captures something important. Some people might oppose taxpayer-funded hard-times programs because they don't see a need for hard-times insurance at all. Others, in contrast, might want such insurance to exist, but prefer it to be privately rather than publicly provided.

Private hard-times insurance typically means that individuals rely on family, communities, and charities for assistance. Many churches, for instance, provide hard-times assistance for their members, taking up collections and helping out in the event of a lost job or spousal death. In the 2012 campaign, Mitt Romney alluded to another source of private insurance for young people when he told supporters at an Ohio college: "We've always encouraged young people—take a shot, go for it, take a risk and get the education, borrow money if you have to from your parents, start a business." (There go those out-of-touch elites again, assuming that everyone's parents have piles of cash lying around.)

So, part of why someone might support taxpayer-funded, publicly provided hard-times programs is that a person needs or might need hard-times assistance. Another factor is that the person would get a better deal with public rather than private hard-times insurance. This relates to the relative costs and benefits of both. In some ways, the points about public versus private just reinforce the basic socioeconomic point that richer people with richer families and richer friends and richer communities have less need for hard-times insurance, and also less need for this to be public rather than private.

Beyond wealth, other demographic factors relate to the relative attractiveness of private versus public hard-times insurance. There's a lot more private money available in social networks and charities controlled by white Christians than among racial minorities and non-Christians. Based on the findings from earlier chapters, it is likely that these networks and charities often have some level of preference for beneficiaries that match their demographics. Federal programs, on the other hand, don't discriminate on the basis of race, religion, or sexual orientation. The result is that white, heterosexual Christians as compared with others at equivalent income levels will have similar average needs for hard-times insurance, but members of the two groups will have dissimilar average interests regarding the extent to which such insurance should be provided by the government.

Another complicating factor involves immigration status. Immigrants are, on average, poorer. But immigrants are also often excluded from public hard-times programs. Undocumented immigrants are excluded from practically all hard-times programs. And even legal immigrants face significant restrictions; sometimes they qualify for federal dollars, but often they do not. (The relevant rules are complex and involve factors like length of lawful residency and U.S. military service.) On the whole, then, some immigrants might be in the position of favoring redistribution, but not necessarily favoring specific programs from which they and their families are excluded.

Other People's Money, Other People's Programs

Finally, there is one more piece we'll add to the puzzle of economic policy interests: who is paying for whom. In one sense, the point is simple— richer people pay more but poorer people receive more benefits. The U.S. tax system is incredibly complex, but, generally speaking, though there are obviously exceptions, richer people are taxed at higher rates than poorer people (even taking into account payroll taxes and state and local taxes), and self-employed people are taxed at higher rates than those who are employed by others (mostly because the self-employed pay both the employer and employee halves of their payroll taxes).

In other times and places, class cut the contours of society, and the primary social divisions might have been between a wealthier, land-owning, legally privileged class and a poorer, wage-earning, legally re-stricted class. In these cases, the "us" paying for "them" would be summed up with income and class. In the contemporary United States, however, political divisions based on race, immigration, and religion are at least as important as those based on income, and certainly more im-portant than those based on Old World notions of class.

When Americans think of their chief political opponents, they don't always think in terms of income or class. Religious conservatives, for example, often consider their main opponents to be secular liberals with Freewheeler lifestyles. Such conservatives are particularly irked when they feel they are being asked to use tax money to subsidize their com-petitors' abortions or religion-mocking, homosexual-celebrating artists. Ivy League liberals usually take their main opponents to be those who want to erect the kinds of group-based barriers discussed in chapter 5. These high-human-capital liberals are particularly irked when asked to use tax money to subsidize the military, an institution they often see as a central proponent of sexist, homophobic, xenophobic, Islamophobic persons and policies.

In the 1960s, the United States sought both to expand public hard-times programs and to eliminate discrimination that in earlier times would have directed the benefits of public and private hard-times pro-grams disproportionately toward whites. The resistance of working-class whites formed the core of Republicans' subsequent Southern Strategy, which sought to peel them away from FDR's New Deal coalition.

In part because of these efforts, "welfare" has become associated with racial minorities and has been generally demonized, from Ronald Rea-gan's complaints about Chicago "welfare queens" in the 1970s to a 2013 contestant on the U.S. version of the reality show *Big Brother*, who re-ferred to welfare as "[n-word] insurance." These group-based dynamics contribute to odd-looking survey results: while 68% of Americans think government should spend more on "the poor," only 23% think government should spend more on "welfare."

The connection between welfare and race can be viewed from multiple perspectives. To take one point of view, a similar number of African American households and white households receive TANF benefits: in 2010, for example, 32% of TANF households were white, 32% were African American, and 30% were Latino American.[9] Looked at another way, though, African Americans and Latino Americans are overrepresented among TANF recipients—in 2010, only around 13% of U.S. households were African American and around the same percentage were Latino.

The racial element adds additional complexity to understanding Americans' economic policy positions, particularly with respect to race and human capital.[10] For racial minorities low in human capital, the major arrows point in the same direction, toward support for robust public hard-times programs. These are individuals who, on average, have greater need for hard-times insurance, have limited private support (which makes publicly provided programs more attractive), and favor programs that disproportionately help minority families. But for whites low in human capital, the arrows diverge. Greater need for hard-times insurance? Yes. Preference for public over private programs? Maybe, maybe not. Group-based reasons to *oppose* public hard-times programs? Yes.

The Complex Demography of American Economic Views

The following summarizes our points on economic interests:

- Income: Wealthier people generally have less need for hard-times insurance, disproportionately pay for public programs, and have better access to private help. Wealthier people, then, tend to show greater opposition than poorer people to redistributive policies and public hard-times programs.
- Race: Whites tend to be wealthier, have better access to private support networks, and are more likely to have group-based reasons

to oppose programs that disproportionately benefit minorities. Whites, then, tend to show greater opposition than minorities to public hard-times programs.[11]

- Immigration: Immigrants are often poorer and have diminished private support, but also are often explicitly excluded from public hard-times programs.

- Religion and sexual orientation: Religious groups often provide private support that makes public programs less needed.[12] Non-Christians and lesbians/gays/bisexuals (a combination we're referring to as "Heathens") are less likely to have access to reliable private support insofar as the greatest levels of nongovernmental support tend to come from Christian groups. Further, when they have higher levels of human capital, white Heathens are likely to adopt human-capital-based stances minimizing the relevance of group identities—they typically view their chief political opponents not as racial minorities, but as those who want to impose group-based barriers.

- Gender: Women potentially need hard-times programs more than men on average, and so tend to support these programs to a greater degree.

- Self-employment: The self-employed generally face higher tax burdens than those employed by others, and so tend to support public programs less.

- Education: Education is complex. Increased education decreases the need for hard-times insurance, but also decreases group-based racial objections to public programs among whites.

- Age: Age is also complex. Being older increases the need for hard-times insurance. But robust public programs already exist and are often viewed not as governmental assistance but as earned benefits. Many seniors may have "low income" in an important sense; at the same time, they have entitlement security that obscures the extent to which their lives depend on redistributive largesse.

We now turn to the data on economic issues from the U.S. General Social Survey. (We provide the details in the Data Appendix for Chapter 6.) Across a range of economic issues, the main story involves race and income. On most issues, the most liberal views tend to be held by lower income minorities and the most conservative by high-income whites.

But other factors add interesting side themes. Take religion. If one begins by looking at the tenets of the New Testament, with its emphasis on forgoing wealth and giving aid to the poor and the sick, one might predict that being Christian would lead to more support for programs that move wealth from rich to poor. If, however, one sees religion less for its dogmatic properties and more for its role in people's social lives (including religious groups' provision of private hard-times assistance), then religious involvement should, somewhat perversely, predict *less* support for public hard-times programs. Indeed, white, heterosexual Christians are generally the most conservative on economic issues; white Heathens are less conservative, but still well more conservative than racial minorities on average. This is not to say that being Christian makes one stingy; rather, it tends to lead to a degree of relative preference for private over public support.

White, heterosexual Christians with smaller incomes—especially when they are raising children—tend to express economic views that are almost as liberal as those of racial minorities. Such people, of course, are much more likely to be among those eligible for TANF and food-assistance programs, and it shows in their support for redistribution and hard-times programs. At higher income ranges, white, heterosexual Christians tend to be very conservative, particularly when (1) their income levels are especially high, (2) they're self-employed, and/or (3) they're seniors.

Latinos and Asians with less education and from immigrant families show the unusual pattern we addressed earlier: strong support for liberal policies on generally worded questions (e.g., whether there should be more support for the poor as a general matter), but very conservative views on whether government programs should receive more funding. In contrast, Latino and Asian Americans with native-born parents (who qualify for public programs to the same degree as other citizens, of course) tend to hold generally liberal economic views, and especially support government spending on specific areas.

We'll go through a few details of the GSS data. Of all the issue opinions discussed in this book, the one that correlates most strongly with people's political party affiliations is this one: "Some people think that the government in Washington ought to reduce the income differences between the rich and the poor, perhaps by raising the taxes of wealthy families or by giving income assistance to the poor. Others think that the government should not concern itself with reducing this income difference between the rich and the poor." Respondents are then asked to identify their own views on a scale that ranges from "the government ought to reduce the income differences between rich and poor" to "the government should not concern itself with reducing income differences."

The best single demographic predictor for this item is family income. Recall from chapter 2 that, comparing those in the bottom 20% of family income, the middle 20%, and the top 10%, 57% of the poorest group lean left of center in their responses, dropping to 49% of those in the middle, and dropping further to only 30% of those in the wealthiest group. The next best demographic predictor is race, with whites more opposed to redistribution than minorities on average, even after taking income into account.

But a range of other factors also predicts opinions on government redistribution. For example, other things being equal, people in union households are a bit more liberal than others on redistribution, and people in self-employed households are a bit more conservative than others.

An interesting bit of complexity involves religion and human capital. Other things being equal, non-Christians with high levels of human capital (e.g., graduate degrees) are unusually liberal when it comes to government redistribution. In contrast, Christians with upper-middle levels of human capital (e.g., bachelor's degrees but not graduate degrees) are unusually conservative. In both of these cases, the "other things being equal" is important because many highly educated non-Christians are wealthier whites, and their wealthy whiteness predicts substantially increased conservatism. The net result is that highly educated, white non-Christians typically wind up in the center on economic issues (influenced by both the left-leaning features of being non-Christians with high levels of human capital and the right-leaning features of being generally wealthier whites). But when it comes to wealthier, white Christians with bachelor's degrees, the conservative volume is dialed up to 10. Add self-employment, and—like Nigel's amp in *Spinal Tap*—these go to 11.

Across a range of redistribution and public hard-times policy views, other major factors show up as well. Lesbians, gays, and bisexuals tend to hold more liberal views than heterosexuals, particularly on government help for health care and the poor. Women, other things being equal, are a bit more liberal than men, particularly on government spending levels. In this case, "other things being equal" underestimates the differences between women and men because women also tend to have lower incomes (especially lower personal incomes) than men. Put another way, part of what makes women more liberal on economic issues than men is their lower average incomes, but another part is simply gender itself.

Seniors tend to hold more conservative views than younger people, particularly on government spending levels. Perhaps most oddly, other things being equal, seniors are more conservative on funding for Social Security. This requires some unpacking. The real difference is not that seniors favor cutting spending on Social Security—in fact, they're a bit less likely to favor cutting it than younger people. But when it comes to "keep it the same as is" versus "spend more," seniors are more likely to favor leaving it as is, while middle-aged people—people who typically do not yet receive any Social Security benefits—skew heavily toward wanting the government to spend more. One interpretation is that those currently excluded from the Promised Land feel its benefits are insufficiently generous, while those who have arrived often know firsthand that, hey, it's a pretty good deal as is.

Taking the various factors together, a reasonably clear picture emerges. Often the largest contrast is between, on the one hand, white, heterosexual Christians with family incomes in the top 10% and, on the other hand, African Americans. The former oppose rather than support government redistribution generally by 58% versus 25%; the latter support rather than oppose government redistribution generally by 59% versus 18%. Among African Americans, support for increased government spending is strong: 89% support increased spending on the poor (though only 38% on "welfare"), 84% support increased spending on education, 82% support increased spending on healthcare, 77% support increased spending on Social Security, and 71% support increased spending on child care. For white, heterosexual Christians with family incomes in the top 10%, in contrast, levels of support for increased spending are much lower, though not nearly as low as the congressional prototypes would suggest: 72% support increased spending on education, 59% support increased spending on health care, 53% support increased spending on the poor (though only 12% on "welfare"), 46% support increased spending on Social Security, and 43% support increased spending on child care. Indeed, the only case in which a majority of this demographic group generally prefers *less* spending is when support for the poor is phrased specifically as "welfare"—otherwise they tend to fall mostly in the "more" or "as is" categories.

Among white Heathens with top 10% incomes, views are generally less conservative than those of their heterosexual, Christian neighbors. The bigger differences tend to be on generally worded items rather than spending specifics. For example, should the government be *taking action* to help the poor? Among rich whites, only a bit over half of heterosexual Christians say yes but it's closer to three-quarters of Heathens. Consider, however, another item: Should the government be *spending more* on the poor? For this question there's very little difference between rich, white, heterosexual Christians, and rich, white Heathens—a bit over half say government should spend more. In general, on spending issues, the gap among rich whites between heterosexual Christians and Heathens runs from roughly 10 points (e.g., on health care spending) to basically 0 (e.g., on child care spending).

White, heterosexual Christians are sometimes about as liberal as minorities on economic issues, at least among those who have less income, who have children, and who are not seniors. Among people in this group, average views on redistribution and hard-times programs are almost as liberal as those of African Americans. Moving up the income ladder, white, heterosexual Christians with upper-middle incomes from the fortieth to ninetieth percentiles tend to have center-right economic views, and are often particularly conservative among seniors and the self-employed. Among these individuals who are not seniors and not self-employed, they split relatively evenly on the overall measure of support for government income redistribution and otherwise have views on spending areas very close to overall American averages.

Recall that Latinos and Asians with less education and from immigrant families have an unusual mix of views on economic issues. These individuals often support income redistribution the most, but support increased spending on education and health care the least (on these latter issues, to be clear, they are even to the right of rich whites on average). So are these immigrants liberal or conservative on economic issues? Does that question even make sense here? Instead of focusing on these kinds of labels, we're encouraging a more practical viewpoint, one that, in this particular case, points to the simple fact that many immigrants are poorer but nonetheless excluded from the benefits of specific public programs.

American Exceptionalism

As in previous chapters, we conclude by looking at data from the World Values Survey. The WVS has included items about general views on economic redistribution and government services, and we combined these into an overall measure of the kinds of economic views we have covered in this chapter. (More details can be found in the Data Appendix for Chapter 6.)

Overall, outside of Western countries, income and education both contribute substantially to general economic policy preferences. Those who are wealthier (relative to others in their respective countries) and have more education are more conservative on economic issues; those who are poorer and have less education are more liberal. In Western countries, however, while income is a substantial predictor of economic views, education is not—people with higher incomes and more education, for example, tend to be about as conservative on average as those who have higher incomes and less education. We saw this in our earlier analyses of U.S. views, in which income was a major contributor to economic opinions, but education mattered only weakly and in roundabout ways. It turns out that this is generally true of Western countries.

Views on economic policy are, on the whole, more conservative in Western countries than in non-Western countries. Nonetheless, opinions are actually quite similar at higher income and education levels around the world. The real differences emerge at lower socioeconomic ranges. Specifically, individuals with lower socioeconomic status hold substantially more liberal views on economic policies outside of the

West than in Western countries, and particularly more liberal than in the United States.

In sum, then, in relation to education and income:

- Very liberal: People outside the West with lower incomes and less education.
- Pretty liberal: Westerners outside of the United States with lower income; people outside the West with lower income but more education.
- Moderate: Those in the United States with lower income.
- Pretty conservative: People outside of the United States with higher income.
- Very conservative: Those in the United States with higher income.

Why is the United States exceptional in this respect? We saw hints of the answer in the GSS data earlier in the chapter. Not all Americans are especially conservative on economic issues. While there are income-based differences on these issues among Americans as with others worldwide, only certain Americans—specifically white, heterosexual Christians—are unusually conservative.

Indeed, in a major study of redistributive policies, Alberto Alesina and Edward Glaeser pointed to the fundamental fact that many countries that spend relatively little on social welfare are racially diverse (e.g., the United States and many countries in Latin America) while many that spend more on social welfare are relatively racially homogeneous (e.g., Japan and many countries in Europe).[13] They further note that, within the United States, welfare benefits are typically set at lower levels in states with higher proportions of African Americans (e.g., states in the Deep South), while many states with very low proportions of African Americans have substantially more generous welfare benefits (e.g., states in New England).

Overall our international comparisons have identified some broad similarities across the world. People high in religiosity and low in education tend to hold more conservative views on abortion and religious discrimination; people low in religiosity and high in education tend to hold more liberal views on abortion and religious discrimination.

Native-born people with less education tend to hold more conservative views on discrimination against immigrants; immigrants tend to hold more liberal views on discrimination against immigrants. People higher in socioeconomic status tend to hold more conservative views on redistribution; those lower in socioeconomic status tend to hold more liberal views on redistribution.

These similarities show that the patterns predicted by our basic argument—that individuals tend to match their policy preferences to their everyday interests—are not limited to the United States. However, idiosyncratic national features add texture to the picture.

The primary source of differences between the United States and the rest of the world—the primary source of American Exceptionalism in political views—rests in its greater diversity. The effects of this greater diversity are apparent for issues relating directly to group-based favoritism (as we saw in chapter 5), but American diversity affects other issues as well. The United States has a somewhat higher proportion of conservatives than other Western countries when it comes to abortion, but this relates to its greater religious and lifestyle diversity; on the whole, while in other Western countries Ring-Bearer churchgoers are a rather thin slice of the public, these folks maintain a larger (but by no means dominant) presence in the United States. On economic issues, group-based conflicts in the United States have a substantial effect on policy opinions. Income differences matter in relation to economic views in the Unities States to about the same degree as they do elsewhere, but there's an added layer of group-based diversity driving some groups unusually far to the right, something that tends to be true generally of nations with greater racial diversity.

From Issues to Coalitions

We've now seen three broad areas in which different interests imply different policy positions, related in each area through different demographic features. Different sexual and reproductive lifestyles create competing interests when it comes to moral and legal policies relating to areas like premarital sex, abortion, birth control, pornography, and marijuana legalization. Different group identities and human capital levels create competing interests about whether group dominance or human capital ought to reign when it comes to rules governing school prayer, same-sex marriage, immigration, affirmative action, and related areas. Income, race, and other factors create competing interests about the need for hard-times programs and whether those should be publicly or privately provided.

We now move into part III of the book, leaving the realm of political issues and entering the realm of political coalitions. Having seen the policy-specific connections among interests, demographics, and public opinion, we now use the tools we developed to create fuller pictures of groups and the policy-driven coalitions they form.

Political Coalitions

CHAPTER 7

The Many Shades of Red and Blue

OVER THE PAST DOZEN YEARS, we've been involved with an ongoing study of a group of people born in the mid-1950s. About 90% of the group are white, about two-thirds are men, and they have median family incomes in the top 1% or 2% of the country. They're likely to be married and they have pretty low divorce rates. Most have two or more kids, the men tend to work hard and spend most of their time off with their families, and the women were unusually likely to stop working full-time while they had young children.

Sounds like a bunch of Republicans, right? Actually, it's the Harvard/Radcliffe Class of 1977, and they skew about six to one Democrat versus Republican.

For the past twenty years, the U.S. president has been a baby boomer (born between 1946 and 1964) with a degree from Harvard or Yale (or even, in the case of George W. Bush, both). The 2012 election between Obama and Romney was a contest between two Harvard-educated baby boomers, just like the 2000 election a dozen years earlier between Bush and Gore. Bill Clinton ushered in the era of Ivy League baby boomer presidents with his victory over fellow Yale alumnus George H.W. Bush.

We've been able to get a close look at Ivy League baby boomer politics through the unusual efforts of the Harvard/Radcliffe Class of 1977. Starting with their ten-year reunion in 1987, this class has run a longitudinal study, collecting information on the lives and attitudes of its members every five years. One of us (Weeden) became involved with administering the study beginning with the twenty-fifth reunion in 2002, and has included a detailed set of political items ever since.

The Class of '77 includes some notable names. Bill Gates was in the entering class, though he dropped out midway to start Microsoft, and has in years since been one of Harvard's (and, really, the world's) most generous donors. Gates's successor at Microsoft, Steve Ballmer, graduated with the class, as did Staples CEO Ron Sargent. The class also includes Jim Cramer, the frenetic host of CNBC's *Mad Money*, who was the president of the *Harvard Crimson*, the school newspaper, during his tenure.

Mostly the Class of '77 is filled with the expected sorts of overachievers. Fully eight in ten have graduate degrees—JDs, MDs, PhDs, MBAs, MAs. Most members of the class are currently working in business, law, medicine, consulting, education, publishing, and other brainy elite fields.

What is perhaps most striking about individuals in the class is the enormous contrast between their everyday lives and their politics. The group has lots of rich, white guys (including Gates, arguably both the richest and the whitest guy ever) and family patterns that (since they were in their thirties, anyway) recall nostalgic visions of the 1950s. And yet self-identified liberals far outnumber self-identified conservatives. What gives?

The Harvard Paradox

In their 2008 book, *Red State, Blue State, Rich State, Poor State*, Andrew Gelman and colleagues examined what they have called the *red-blue paradox*: Wealthier *individuals* are more likely to vote for Republicans, but wealthier *states* (such as Connecticut, New Jersey, et al.) are more likely to vote for Democrats. The Harvard/Radcliffe Class of 1977 is like a (very) little (very) blue state, and the same "paradox"—we use quotes because it's more of a puzzle than a logical inconsistency—holds: Harvard graduates are very wealthy as a group and vote overwhelming for Democrats, but the wealthier *individuals* are less likely to be such strong Democratic supporters. The Harvard paradox is a powerfully distilled version of the red-blue paradox.

Most members of the Class of '77 are living enviable lives by typical American standards. The linchpin to their success, of course, relates to human capital—this is a group that succeeded beyond the dreams of avarice in the new test-based meritocracy. They got one of the best educations in the world and now typically work in jobs that directly translate brain power into cultural influence and economic success. Relative to less-brainy folks, the policies that would most directly threaten their positions are those that would seek to deflate the central role of human capital in modern social success, including policies that place group-based barriers in the way of brain-based competitions.

Most in the class, as we said, are white men (this was the last Harvard/Radcliffe class that came in before efforts to even out the gender ratio). But most are not Christian. At present, only 42% are Christian, 25% are Jewish, 22% have no religion, and 11% are something else (Unitarian, Buddhist, etc.). Among baby boomers in the wider American population, the contrast is plain: 83% are Christian, fewer than 2% are Jewish, 13% have no religion, and 3% are something else.

All told, only 22% of class members are white, male, heterosexual, and Christian. The other 78% are members of one or more traditionally subordinate groups. So are these individuals better off under old-style discrimination rules or meritocratic rules? The answer, clearly, is that these folks do better under meritocracy than practically any other group on the planet. For the 22% who are white, male, heterosexual Christians, maybe it's a closer call—they would do well under either set of rules—but while they're not usually whiter than other white people (Bill Gates notwithstanding) or straighter than other straight people, they are typically better at human-capital-based competitions even than most college-educated people. For the 78% of class members who *lack* some significant dominant group identity, it's not remotely a close call. For a successful doctor or lawyer who is not heterosexual or not Christian, for example, there is something that could pose a substantial threat to their success—a cultural shift making it more acceptable to discriminate against homosexuals or non-Christians.

Other kinds of policies are candidates for being "big deals" for a group like these Harvard graduates, but no deals as big as policies implicating meritocracy versus discrimination. Family planning has been a key aspect of most of the class members' lives. They had children late, the first coming, typically, when they were in their early or mid-thirties. Most had been sexually active at least since college, so this group was having sex for around ten to fifteen years before wanting kids. Those crucial years were filled with activities that laid the groundwork for their later economic success—graduate school, residencies, long hours doing the grunt work of law firms and investment banks. Today, their own children, many now in their teens and early twenties, are mostly traveling similar paths.

Like other Americans, many class members were promiscuous partyers in their younger years and many weren't. Today, of course, few are. We further suppose (but do not know) that their own kids are typical of most young people in being all over the map in their own lifestyles (though, from our surveys of college students, we know that white kids from less religious and wealthier homes tend to party and hook up a bit more than others). Divorce rates have been low for the class, in large part because they married so late without already having had children, and while there are hints that those with wilder college lives have had somewhat higher divorce rates, it's not a big effect. In any case, for members of this class, divorce isn't likely to lead to poverty.

For class members, rates of church attendance have been lower overall than for most Americans—we noted back in chapter 4 that about a third of baby boomers have attended church regularly as middle-aged adults, but for these Harvard baby boomers, that figure is less than one in four. The class members were most likely to seek out the family-supporting benefits of religious affiliation when they had more young children at home. For those who ended up with three or more children, for example, fewer than 20% were attending services regularly when they were in their early thirties, but this figure increased to around 40% when they were in their early forties before dropping back down to around 25% when they were in their late fifties. For those with no children or only one child, in contrast, no more than around 10% have attended services regularly at these ages. For class members, religious groups have not tended to play a substantial and persistent role in their lives.

On economic issues, while most of the class members are wealthy by national standards, higher taxes might not be very threatening. Higher taxes of course lead to lower take-home pay, but educated professionals typically have certain advantages that others lack when it comes to income.

Educated professionals tend to be paid more than others, of course, but there's something notable about brain-power work: Simply doing the work tends to increase one's asking price over time. For lawyers, for instance, every project they work on generally increases the value of their income-generating asset (i.e., their brains); that is, the more they know, the higher the price they can typically charge for their time and knowledge. Contrast this with owners of physical businesses. For owners of rental properties or factories or retail stores, every time they use their income-generating property, the property gets less rather than more valuable due to wear and tear. If the owners of a physical business want to grow their income down the road, they have to spend more money today to do it. Educated professionals don't typically have these same pressures of needing to spend a lot of additional money from year to year to grow their incomes.

For manual laborers, as well, though skills can develop over time increasing their labor-market value, the physical challenges of manual jobs increase over time. And so, generally speaking, the economic value of manual workers increases early but then diminishes when they're in their fifties and sixties. In contrast, the brain-power class is typically still experiencing increasing market values during this time.

Human-capital-based workers, then, feel the hit of taxes, but not as acutely. Losing some money this year stings, but they'll typically just make more money next year. For manual workers, income instability is higher, and a decent wage this year isn't as likely to imply an even higher wage next year. For those who make their money from physical capital, income growth typically requires putting substantial sums back into the business, creating additional pressures on the money left over for personal consumption. Some Harvard grads, to be sure, make more money from owning businesses (Mitt Romney and George W. Bush, among them), but most are lawyers, doctors, consultants, writers, and the like, who tend to get paid for renting out their time and brains.

Rich people come in many forms. Two broad stripes involve owners of physical businesses and highly educated professionals. Is it possible that the latter take perverse pleasure in higher taxes that affect business owners more than themselves? Would one group of rich people really go so far as to agree to take themselves down a peg through higher taxes just to see some other group of their rich neighbors get taken down two pegs?

Maybe. Consider what happens when researchers ask people to compare the following two worlds: (A) Your current yearly income is $50,000; others earn $25,000. (B) Your current yearly income is $100,000; others earn $200,000. Assume that a dollar in both scenarios translates into the same absolute level of purchasing power, so you really would be only half as rich in World A than in World B.

The scenario comes from a study of Harvard faculty, students, and staff, and, despite being only half as rich in World A, survey-takers generally split 50/50 in their preferences.[1] Across many domains—and not just with Harvard samples but more generally—people often prefer to have higher *relative* positions over higher *absolute* positions. That is, they'd often sacrifice some absolute purchasing power so long as others have to sacrifice even more.

In short, then, for the typical Harvard graduate, higher taxes might be a nuisance, but they are not a fundamental threat. On the one hand, Harvard grads tend to be richer, and so get hit by higher tax burdens. On the other hand, taxes don't diminish the income-generating capacity of their primary asset (i.e., their brain, their human capital). Further, taxes might actually have a kind of appeal for some to the extent that those taxes diminish some set of their social competitors more than themselves. If these factors are determining tax policy views, then wealthier graduates should be expected to dislike taxes more than their less wealthy classmates—and, indeed, this is true of the Class of '77.[2] But, on the whole, for super-educated people, something like taxes isn't going to loom as large as something affecting the role of human capital, which typically is the foundation on which their lives are built.

So what predicts being liberal and a Democrat rather than conservative and a Republican in the Harvard/Radcliffe Class of 1977? The strongest predictors are these:

- Being African American, or, somewhat less powerfully, being Latino or Asian American.
- Being lesbian, gay, or bisexual.
- Being a non-Christian (Jew, atheist, agnostic, etc.).

- Being female, or, somewhat less potently, being a male married to a working female.
- Having a something-less-than-massive income—say, having a yearly family income of less than around a half-million.

These features jointly predict who is more likely to go to the left versus the right among the class members. Among those with three or more of these five features, conservatives and Republicans are exceedingly rare—there are about forty-four liberals and Democrats for every conservative and Republican. So, think of Barack and Michelle Obama before running for office—heterosexual Christians, but then African American, Michelle worked, and they had secure but less-than-massive incomes.

Among class members with two of these five features, liberals and Democrats outnumber conservatives and Republicans by a still impressive ratio of about 6.5 to 1. Think of Bill and Hillary Clinton before running for office—white, heterosexual Christians, but, similar to the Obamas, Hillary worked and they had secure but less-than-massive incomes (though, to be sure, they have massive wealth now).

The only Ivy League baby boomers that Republicans have a real chance of attracting are those with none or one of those five features. Among such people, there are "only" 1.5 liberals and Democrats for every conservative and Republican. George W. Bush and Mitt Romney, before they ran for office, for example, were firing on all right-leaning cylinders—white, heterosexual, Christian males with stay-at-home wives and super-duper wealth driven as much by physical capital as human capital.

Crucially, even when identifying with Democrats, Ivy Leaguers are not usually far-left on economic issues. The Clinton administration, for example, was somewhere in the middle, increasing the earned income tax credit but cutting welfare, raising taxes a bit on the wealthy but engaging in pro-business trade efforts and financial deregulation. Among the Harvard/Radcliffe Class of 1977, opinions of Democrats are securely to the left on issues like same-sex marriage and immigration, but actually to the right of the public on items like Social Security. More than half of Democrats from the Class of '77 favor raising the Social Security retirement age, a policy favored by only a third or less of the general public.

Further, even when identifying with Republicans, Ivy Leaguers are not usually far-right on abortion or on group-based barriers, issues on which, as we have seen, educated people are especially likely to hold liberal views. Republicans from the Class of '77 are typically pro-choice and about evenly split on same-sex marriage. Elite Republicans also tend to be well to the left of their party on immigration, as in the case of George W. Bush's failed efforts at comprehensive reform, presumably stemming not just from pro-business motives but also from a generally meritocratic orientation on group-based issues.

Thomas Frank asked: What's the matter with Kansas? Kansans are poorer people who support Republicans. But we could also ask: What's the matter with Harvard? They're richer people who support Democrats.

Understanding the Harvard paradox requires considering the relevant interests across different issues. As we saw in chapter 5, super-high levels of human capital provide big incentives for favoring meritocratic rules, particularly among individuals lacking one or more of the dominant categories that win out under group-based rules. Further, people who are sexually active in early adulthood and delay childbearing—a pattern common among doctors, lawyers, professors, and so forth—have big incentives to favor the availability of family planning tools, including birth control and abortion. But on the other side of the coin, higher education is also typically associated with higher and more stable incomes, something that provides incentives against redistributive agendas.

On balance, then, it takes a lot to get someone from Harvard to support Republicans. What it takes, usually, is for someone's conservative positions on economic issues to outweigh their liberal positions on discrimination and family planning. In particular, it typically takes being a white, heterosexual, Christian man who has a very high family income despite not having a working spouse. And even when all of those conditions hold, it's often a close call between Democrats and Republicans. And even when such a person does split in favor of Republicans, Harvard grads are as likely to be essentially libertarian as they are to be true-red conservatives. And even among Harvard conservatives, one is still less likely to find group-based policy preferences typical of the less educated.

The Harvard paradox is no paradox. It's the straightforward result of individuals making a forced choice between two political parties and associated ideological labels based on a multidimensional policy landscape. For educational elites, issues relating to group-based versus human-capital-based allocation rules typically dominate the equation even when they're comfortably wealthy. On balance, then, they favor the party that opposes the old group-based policies. That's not a paradox; it's a reasonable compromise.

The American Quilt

The Harvard paradox, the red-blue paradox, and the Kansas paradox seem intriguing because of two often unstated assumptions: (1) People's political views tend to skew along a single dimension either to the left or to the right, and (2) socioeconomic status is especially important, even dominant, in determining this overall left-right skew. Under these assumptions, wealthier people should be expected to hold generally conservative views, and poorer people should be expected to hold generally liberal views.

Despite occasional statements to the contrary, most political scientists have long known—going back at least to Philip Converse's work in the 1960s, and probably farther to Walter Lippmann's in the 1910s/1920s—that many Americans do not in fact show substantial ideological consistency across policy views, except among limited groups.[3] And, indeed, back in chapter 1, we did some fact-checking on liberal-conservative coherence that illustrated the point. The 20% of the adult population who are white voters with bachelor's degrees show some degree of coherence when it comes to views on same-sex marriage and income redistribution. But, when it comes to the 40% of the adult public who have one or none of these characteristics—including, for example, African Americans and Latinos without bachelor's degrees and nonvoting whites without bachelor's degrees—there is no tendency whatsoever for people who lean in a given direction on one of these issues to lean in the same direction on the other. For the remaining 40% of the adult public, who have two but not three of these features (e.g., white voters without bachelor's degrees), ideological coherence is barely measurable.

Further, richer people aren't routinely "conservative" across the board, and poorer people aren't routinely "liberal"—one must go issue by issue to find the connections. As we saw in part II, people's views on sexual and reproductive policies relate primarily to their lifestyles and religiosity; people with more education tend to have more liberal views on abortion, but otherwise socioeconomic status isn't a major factor. Views relating to group-based issues primarily stem from group identities and human capital. The people who tend to be higher in socioeconomic status (i.e., those with more human capital) generally favor policies that reward high levels of human capital, which are often "liberal" policies (except when it comes to affirmative action and other minority-advancing policies). It's only on economic issues relating to redistribution and safety nets that one sees a major role for socioeconomic status, and particularly income, in driving increased policy conservatism, though even for these issues the role of income is supplemented by race, religion, gender, and other factors. Among the general public, there are different demographic predictors at work for different issue clusters, mostly in line with where the rubber of those particular issues meets the road of divergent interests.

So, the assumptions that make the red-blue paradox paradoxical—ideological coherence plus a pervasive role for socioeconomic status—do not generally hold. For most of the public, predicting political views requires attending to demographics rather than ideological labels. For the 40% of the adult population that includes less educated African Americans, Latinos, and nonvoting whites, for example, we've shown what matters for predicting views on same-sex marriage and income redistribution. Less educated populations of mostly heterosexual Christians? Should be mostly conservative on same-sex marriage. Less educated populations with lots of racial minorities? Should be mostly liberal on economic redistribution. And, indeed, the most common co-occurrence of views among this 40% of the population is in people who are against same-sex marriage but in favor of redistribution. Political elites haven't even bothered to agree on a name for this combination. Is it "communitarian," "populist," "statist," or what?

In contrast, highly educated, white voters—who comprise 20% of the adult population—are mostly either "conservative" (against redistribution and against same-sex marriage), "liberal" (in favor of redistribution and in favor of same-sex marriage), or "libertarian" (against redistribution but in favor of same-sex marriage) on these two issues. However, even among people in this group, views depend on demographics: church attendance, sexual orientation, and human capital all predict views on same-sex marriage, while income, gender, whether one is self-employed, and so forth predict views on redistribution. There are fewer "communitarians" (or "populists," or "statists," or whatever) among highly educated whites because there are fewer who fit the demographic—high levels of religiosity along with lower socioeconomic status.

Different segments of the population have different mixes of "ideological" combinations. Table 7.1 looks at four groups, splitting out the bottom 40% and top 40% in family income and the bottom 40% and top 40% in church attendance. It shows the percentages favoring same-sex marriage and favoring government income redistribution ("liberal"), favoring same-sex marriage and opposing government income redistribution ("libertarian"), opposing same-sex marriage and favoring government income redistribution ("communitarian"), and opposing same-sex marriage and opposing government income redistribution ("conservative"). (The boxes don't total to 100% because many people have neutral opinions on same-sex marriage and/or income redistribution.)

Table 7.1 shows, for example, that when a person hangs out with poorer people, they probably know many "communitarians" and a number of "liberals" and "conservatives," yet few "libertarians" (in the sense of knowing people with different combinations of views on the two issues, same-sex marriage and income redistribution). Among those who are wealthier and don't go to church very much (something that describes most top-tier social scientists and big-city journalists, even if they don't think that their well-above-average-but-below-obscene incomes count as "wealthier"), there are mostly "liberals" and "libertarians" and a number of "conservatives," yet "communitarians" are rarer. If ideological naming were controlled by poorer people, they might particularly highlight communitarianism and ignore libertarianism. Instead, the

Table 7.1. Views on Same-Sex Marriage and Income Redistribution, by Family Income and Church Attendance

	Church about Once a Year or Less	Church about Two or Three Times a Month or More
Family Income: Bottom 40%	28% "liberal" 19% "communitarian" 11% "libertarian" 10% "conservative"	29% "communitarian" 24% "conservative" 11% "liberal" 7% "libertarian"
Family Income: Top 40%	25% "liberal" 21% "libertarian" 16% "conservative" 11% "communitarian"	43% "conservative" 18% "communitarian" 9% "libertarian" 7% "liberal"

ideological labeling is controlled by social scientists and journalists, and so communitarianism gets ignored.

The Kansas paradox and the red-blue paradox aren't really paradoxes, or even particularly vexing puzzles. Find places in America with lots of heterosexual, Christian, native-born whites with less education, and you will find people who tend to hold conservative positions on group-based issues. On balance, if they also have higher incomes and frequently go to church (and live the Ring-Bearer lifestyles that typically accompany church attendance), they will usually have conservative views on both lifestyle and economic issues in addition to conservative group-based views. The result is that most such people will, reasonably, skew heavily Republican. When they have lower incomes and attend church infrequently (typically implying Freewheeler lifestyles), they will usually have left-leaning views on lifestyle and economic issues, and will be more likely to support Democrats *despite* their conservative group-based views (or perhaps they simply won't vote, unable to choose between parties that fail to reflect the totality of their views). When they find themselves one way on income and the other on church attendance, they will be more likely to land as Republicans with atypically liberal views specifically on either economic or lifestyle issues.

The importance of red and blue regions in contemporary politics mostly comes from the underlying fact that the central and southern regions of the United States and smaller American towns are home to many white people, but, more specifically, they have higher proportions of less educated, heterosexual, churchgoing Christians among their white populations. The coasts and larger cities have much greater numbers of minorities and immigrants, but also, among their white populations, higher education levels, higher proportions of lesbians and gays, higher proportions of non-Christians (Jews, atheists, etc.), and fewer Ring-Bearer churchgoers. Regional political differences derive primarily from these kinds of underlying demographic differences and the diverse interests to which they give rise. Put another way, less educated, white, heterosexual, churchgoing Christians look pretty similar politically these days whether they live in big cities or small towns, in Southern states or on the coasts—it's just that there are some places where such people are highly prevalent and other places where they are greatly outnumbered.

Patterns in Kansas, just as with Harvard alums, reflect individuals making the compromises required when trying to fit multidimensional policy preferences to a two-party system. Kansas and other Bible Belt areas, it turns out, have a relatively high percentage of people whose middle-class lives are not strongly affected by either taxing the rich or propping up the poor, but whose interests would be advanced by morally condemning promiscuity and by group-based allocation regimes that skew in their favor (i.e., against those who do not share their own race or country of origin or religion or sexual orientation). And so they tend to support the party that supports their policy agenda. Which ain't the Democrats.

America nurtures a tremendous hodgepodge of political views. It's just not the case that there exist two, or three, or four profiles. There are as many patterns as one is patient enough to find.

One can discover genuine liberals among highly educated whites—the best places to look are among people with some set of subordinate group identities (homosexual, non-Christian, female, foreign-born) along with stellar educations but (relatively) modest incomes. If conservatives want university professors to be less liberal, for example, they might pay them more (we say without any hint of self-interest, of course).

One can find Latino conservatives—the best places to look are among heterosexual, churchgoing Protestants with middle-of-the-road educations and high incomes, and whose families have not recently immigrated.

One can find libertarian women—the best places to look are among white, heterosexual Christians with low levels of church attendance, high education levels, and high incomes.

One can find people with mostly liberal views on both lifestyle and economic issues but conservative views on group-based issues—the best places to look are among white, heterosexual Christians with low levels of church attendance, low education levels, and low incomes.

One can find people with mostly conservative views on both lifestyle and economic issues but liberal-leaning views on barrier-imposing, group-based issues—the best places to look are among white, heterosexual, Christian men with high levels of church attendance, high education levels, and high incomes.

One can find people conservative on lifestyle issues and group-based items involving sexual orientation and religion but liberal on economic and racial issues—the best places to look are among Latino and African American heterosexual Christians with high levels of church attendance, low education levels, and low incomes.

The political positions of most of the public cannot be understood by focusing merely on who calls themselves "liberal" or "conservative," "Democrat" or "Republican." One has to zoom in issue by issue, feature by feature, interest by interest. It's complicated, but, as we've shown, it can be done systematically.

31 Flavors

In the next two chapters we'll present the results of some of our analyses of these sliced-and-diced demographic groups. To do this set of analyses, we took the sample from the U.S. General Social Survey and split it up based on demographic items that do a good job predicting people's political opinions. The items that fit the bill should at this point be familiar—race, sexual orientation, religion, church attendance, human capital, income, age, and gender.

We ended up with thirty-one mutually exclusive categories of Americans—a sort of Baskin Robbins menu of American political types. The Data Appendix for Chapter 8 and the Data Appendix for Chapter 9 give the full data on these groups. We discuss several of them at length in the next two chapters and skate over others.

There's nothing magical, of course, about thirty-one flavors. We could have kept going, introducing new splits for more fine-grained distinctions based on socioeconomic status or church attendance, or splitting out union members or the self-employed, or splitting out people from first-generation versus second-generation immigrant families, and so on, and so on. Really, there's no natural limit to what one might want to learn about individuals' everyday lives and interests. As we've shown, some features matter for certain policy opinions but not others. We've focused on the biggest of these demographic items here in the text, but the Data Appendixes present a wide range of demographic factors that bear on some issues but not others.

However, even this was a rather limited exercise, constrained by both the available data and our own tolerance for the level of complexity we were willing (and, true, able) to explore. In a perfect world, we might want to know a lot more about people's own lives, not to mention about the lives of their spouses, children, siblings, friends, and others. We might want to know more about individuals' life histories—the kinds of personal relationships they've had, the kinds of jobs they've had, and so on.

The fact that we've limited our breakdown of the American public primarily on the basis of a few big categories doesn't mean that this exhausts the ways in which an interest-based, demographically grounded perspective can shed light on political views. Yet the big categories really are big deals. We began in chapter 1 reviewing exit polls that mostly split the public on single dimensions—race, religion, education, gender, and so forth—but now we'll see the impressive power of looking at features in combinations to make more detailed splits. These analyses illustrate, we think, how the approach we've presented pays dividends, bringing into focus the political implications of diverse lives and interests.

CHAPTER 8

The Republican Coalition

JESSE HELMS WAS ABOUT AS CONSERVATIVE as any U.S. senator in the modern era. A Southern Baptist from North Carolina, he was conservative on both lifestyle and fiscal issues and, moreover, held views on group-based issues that, putting it mildly, couldn't exist anymore among national politicians. Helms began his political career working on the staff of a segregationist senator in the 1950s and was a persistent opponent of civil rights. In the 1990s, he opposed AIDS funding because, he said, it was homosexuals' "deliberate, disgusting, revolting conduct" that was to blame for the disease. The 1990s version of Helms draws clear contrasts with modern Democratic elites such as Hillary Rodham Clinton.

It's tempting to think of the current composition of America's political parties as reflecting some enduring reality about human nature. But here's a simple fact: In the 1960s, Hillary Rodham was a Republican and Jesse Helms was a Democrat. Both switched parties around 1970.

Much of political science, going back to the "Michigan model" from the 1950s, views enduring attachments to political parties as a central driving force in public voting patterns.[1] But political parties are coalitions of interests, and these change over time.[2]

Over the last century and a half, Democratic and Republican coalitions have undergone seismic shifts. After the Civil War, the parties were largely regional, with Democrats in the South and Republicans in the North.[3] In the 1930s and 1940s, Roosevelt assembled a broad "New Deal coalition" of farmers, laborers, Catholics, union members, and African Americans in the North and added these to the Dixiecrats of the segregationist South. Republicans were a smaller coalition primarily including upper-middle-class white Protestants outside of the South. This was the Republican party of a young Hillary Rodham, growing up in a Methodist household in Chicago, the daughter of a successful business-man and a stay-at-home mom.

But in the 1960s, after a couple of decades of relative stability, the par-ties again began to change rapidly, a process that continues to the pres-ent. In 1964, Democrat Lyndon Johnson championed the cornerstone of modern meritocracy, the Civil Rights Act. Johnson's advocacy solidified African American membership in the Democratic coalition, a pattern that has, if anything, strengthened in recent years.[4]

At the same time, an opportunity opened for Republicans, the so-called Southern Strategy used by Republicans such as Barry Goldwater (the first Republican presidential candidate in the twentieth century to win the Deep South) and Richard Nixon.[5] The idea was to emphasize "states' rights" and anti-crime policies to attract Southern whites. This gambit had the predictable effect of pushing the rising class of merito-crats more deeply into Democratic territory. Before the 1960s, Republi-cans had drawn their support from wealthy, educated Protestants in the North—it was, more generally, the party of old-school privilege.[6] But in the late 1960s, political coalitions shifted as more highly educated folks joined Democrats. These racial and educational shifts help explain why Helms and Rodham switched parties: he the unrepentant segregationist, she on the leading edge of a new highly educated elite.

Party alignments shifted again in the 1980s. Earlier in the twentieth century, American parties had something to do with religious identities (with Republicans attracting non-Southern Protestants and Democrats attracting Catholics and Southern Protestants), but almost nothing to do with overall church attendance or issues such as abortion.[7]

This began to change in the late 1970s as evangelicals organized to oppose both the sexual revolution and efforts to tear down group-based barriers.[8] Organizations including Jerry Falwell's Moral Majority led the charge by focusing on issues on which less educated, churchgoing Christians are especially conservative—abortion and other lifestyle is-sues, along with gay rights and school prayer.

In the 1980s, Republicans added white religious conservatives to their coalition, which had the further effect of pushing secular liberals into the Democratic party.[9] In the years since, church attendance has become a major predictor of party leaning among whites, and white Catholics have generally moved from the Democratic to Republican column.[10]

In the 1990s and continuing to the present, Democrats have further solidified their claim on the educated elite. Highly educated whites who don't go to church frequently have a mix of liberal views on group-based barriers, liberal lifestyle views, and centrist views on economic issues, racial issues, and criminal justice. Bill Clinton's "New Democrat," "third way" presidency was tailor-made for this demographic, stitching together social liberalism with economic centrism, highlighted with initiatives on race and crime, including welfare reform, mending-not-ending affirmative action, and get-tough-on-crime policies.[11]

By 2008 the Democratic party was an embarrassment of meritocratic riches, featuring a primary battle between two Ivy League lawyers, one a woman and the other an African American. The educated elite became even more solidly Democratic, further driving white Christians with less human capital but at least moderate incomes into the Republican camp, or out of the voting booth altogether.

Anchored against the changing party tides, however, has been the relatively consistent issue of economics. As in the days of Hoover versus Roosevelt, the Republican party remains the party of economic conservatism and the Democratic party remains the party of economic liberalism. Bound to their respective coalitions by this tether, wealthier individuals and business owners continue to favor Republicans while laborers and union members split Democratic. As the federal government built and reinforced the old-age safety net, however, the face of American poverty changed. With the rise in single-mother families, a new gender gap emerged as young and middle-aged women maintained support for Democrats by virtue of their views on attenuating the risks of economic uncertainty.

Race, education, and income are, to be sure, important for understanding party affiliations in the modern era. However, the interactions among these are complex. Whites tend to have both more education and more income. People with more education tend to have more income. Being white and having higher income are associated with economic conservatism. But high education levels are associated with group-based liberalism, particularly when it comes to removing barriers that get in the way of human-capital-based competition.

So, while it used to be that, outside of the South, Americans were organized primarily in something resembling class-based political co- alitions, the picture today is more complex.[12] To be sure, there remain fundamental differences between the parties on tax-and-spend issues, and these differences really matter because of America's stunning lev- els of economic inequality, which add fuel to the fires of fights over re- distribution. But America is a place of enormous diversity on several fronts, not just economic. Big-city secular liberals and small-town reli- gious conservatives, for instance, live lives that are almost unrecogniz- able to one another, with correspondingly mutually incomprehensible lifestyle policy preferences. The United States also has enormous racial, religious, and educational diversity, leading to high-stakes contests be- tween those seeking group-based advantages and those seeking human- capital-based advantages.

The balance of this chapter addresses how these factors shape the Republican coalition, deferring Democrats for the next chapter. The modern Republican coalition bundles wealthy individuals and business owners, people with dominant group identities (i.e., white, native-born, male, Christian, heterosexual), and Ring-Bearer religious worshipers. The party puts this bundling into effect with a hodgepodge of policies— against taxes and regulation, against income redistribution, against eco- nomic and social benefits disproportionately helping minorities, in favor of tougher immigration and law-enforcement policies, against same- sex marriage, for school prayer, against abortion and comprehensive sex education.

Our view is that this policy bundle isn't due to some preexisting philosophical coherence. It's not due to something fundamental about human nature. It's not due to any enduring historical legacy.[13] Instead, the policy bundles of parties come together and split apart and shift around as part of an ongoing chess match between motivated opponents forming coalitions within a continually evolving policy landscape.[14]

After the 2012 election, immigration reform became the poster child for efforts to introduce new shifts in the party coalitions, as Republi- cans have considered whether to soften their positions as a way to win

Labels Used in Chapter 8

Group	Description
Boehners	White, heterosexual, Christian men with weekly church attendance and upper-middle-and-higher levels of both human capital and income
Johnsons	White, heterosexual, Christian men with less than weekly church attendance and top 20% human capital
Church Ladies	White, heterosexual Christians with weekly church attendance, upper-middle levels of human capital (from the fortieth to eightieth percentiles), and income in the bottom 40%
Boehner Women	White, heterosexual, Christian women with weekly church attendance and upper-middle-and-higher levels of both human capital and income
Downscale Kansans	White, heterosexual Christians with weekly church attendance and both human capital and income in the bottom 40%
Freewheelers	(From chapter 4) People who sleep with more people, are sexually active outside of committed relationships, have more same-sex partners, party, drink, go to bars, and use recreational drugs more, live together outside of marriage, are less likely to marry at all, get divorced more when they do marry, and have fewer kids
Ring-Bearers	(From chapter 4) People who wait longer to have sex, tend to have sex only in committed relationships, go to bars and party less, don't cohabit outside of marriage, have long-lasting marriages, and have more kids

more Latino votes. The problem, however, is less educated whites, who frequently don't bother to exercise their franchise, stuck as they are between a party on the left that works against their group-based interests and a party on the right that works against their redistributive interests. A Republican tack to the left on immigration would further alienate these voters, who benefit from maintaining group-based advantages over foreign minorities and who often are on the losing side of introducing more competition for low-skill jobs.

It's easy enough to say that it would be a smart move for Republicans to woo Latinos, but there's no such thing as a free lunch. Most contentious political issues are, after all, contentious because they implicate competing interests. A move to win one demographic with targeted policy changes typically implies alienating some competing demographic on the issues in question.

The balance of this chapter looks at a few demographic subgroups that typically lean toward Republicans, with a focus on how different clusters of demographic features imply support for and opposition to different sets of policies, in line with divergent interests. We'll start with some people who are currently very likely to support Republicans, involving a strong alignment of conservative demographics on lifestyle and economic issues. But then we'll break things down by looking at groups that have some of these features and not others, and see how policy opinions move on select issues as a result. In each case, there are idiosyncratic collections of policy positions that might attract or repel these groups toward one or the other party.

Prototype Republicans

The prototypical modern Republican has conservative economic demographics (wealthy, white, male, etc.), conservative group-based demographics (white, native-born, Christian, and heterosexual, and lower levels of human capital), and conservative lifestyle demographics (frequent church attendance and Ring-Bearer lifestyle patterns).

This leads to an inevitable tension: people with low levels of human capital are less likely to be wealthy. Demographically, something has to give. Probably because wealthier constituents carry more sway than poorer constituents, the Republican party has been more tightly focused on advocating its economic positions than its majority-group-based ones—George W. Bush nominally supported a proposed anti-gay amendment to the U.S. Constitution as a way to attract voters of lower socioeconomic status, for example, but used his political capital on enormous tax cuts for the wealthy and spending increases helping defense, energy, and pharmaceutical industries. The result is that Republican support derives more from higher income than from lower human capital, though, indeed, the strongest support comes from those whose incomes exceed their human capital.

The most solidly Republican demographic cluster involves white, heterosexual, regularly churchgoing, Christian men who have upper-middle-and-higher levels of both income and human capital. This cluster includes the large majority of national Republican officeholders. It includes, for example, John Boehner (who became Speaker of the House of Representatives after Republicans won the majority in 2010) and Paul Ryan (Mitt Romney's 2012 running mate), both of whom are church-going Catholics with bachelor's degrees and high incomes. We'll name this cluster after the Speaker and call them "Boehners." Boehners, so defined, are about 3.5 times as likely to prefer Republicans as they are to prefer Democrats, more so to the extent that their income outpaces their human capital, less so to the extent that their human capital outpaces their income.

Here are the outlines of Boehners' political interests:

- *Lifestyle issues*: Boehners are heterosexual Christians with high levels of church attendance (and so, typically, have Ring-Bearer lifestyles). These features create interests in imposing higher moral and legal costs on Freewheeler lifestyles. As a result, one should expect conservative policy preferences on lifestyle issues. There are some mitigating factors. Boehners have more education, which liberalizes views on abortion—though high levels of church attendance tend to indicate pro-life views on the whole even with higher education levels. In addition, men are a bit more liberal than women, other things being equal, when it comes to pornography.

But still, on the whole, one can expect overall conservative views on lifestyle issues based on their demographics and interests.

- *Group-based issues*: Boehners have very high to moderately high levels of human capital and are white, male, heterosexual Christians. Their group-based interests are not strongly in one camp or the other. At the highest levels of human capital, one should expect overall opposition to group-based barriers, though very little support for affirmative efforts to advance traditionally subordinate groups. At more moderate levels of human capital, one should expect to see an increase in barrier-approving attitudes. We've noted that attitudes toward homosexuals, however, tend to be best predicted by looking at both group-based features and lifestyle features, and so Boehners' high levels of church attendance should point to more conservatism on same-sex marriage, despite their overall moderation on group-based barriers.

- *Economic issues*: Boehners are white men with higher incomes who are also heterosexual Christians. In terms of the economically relevant factors we discussed in chapter 6, Boehners have strong interests in opposing increased income redistribution. Thus, one should see robustly conservative opinions on economic issues.

Turning to the data, we find broad confirmation of these expectations (the full details are presented in the Data Appendix for Chapter 8). If they had their way, Boehners in the general public would live in a world in which: (1) premarital sex carries moral costs, marijuana and most abortions are illegal, and teens do not have access to birth control without parental consent, (2) homosexuality carries moral costs and same-sex marriage is outlawed, the government does not target benefits for African Americans, affirmative action programs are not available for African Americans or women, police are given latitude to be violent with detainees, and the death penalty is available for the worst offenses, and (3) the government does not redistribute wealth very much, though it plays something close to its current role in providing for the poor, providing health care, and funding Social Security and education.

Boehners are relatively evenly split on some key issues. One is school prayer. Boehners with top 20% levels of human capital lean ever so slightly in favor of the school prayer ban on the whole, but among those with merely upper-middle levels of human capital, a majority oppose the ban. On immigration, also, Boehners are generally split between wanting to reduce immigration, and not. In addition, as we noted, Boehners do not routinely support heavy cuts in current hard-times programs. They are far less likely to support *increases* in social spending than most Americans, but among the general public, their views are not typically extreme.

Democrats celebrated Republican hypocrisy on lifestyle issues when, for example, Republican senator David Vitter was identified as a client of a D.C. prostitution outfit, or when it came out that Republican representative Scott DesJarlais encouraged one of his mistresses to get an abortion, or when former Republican senator Larry Craig was charged with "lewd behavior" in a men's restroom. But, in fairness, this probably says more about the personalities of elected officials than it does about Boehners as a whole. In the general public, Boehners on average have Ring-Bearer lifestyles, with fewer sex partners, more children, and lower divorce rates than most men. Their support for policies reducing societal promiscuity is in line with their lives and interests.

On group-based issues, Boehners are not nearly so likely to favor group-based barriers as those with lower levels of human capital. When in the top 20% of human capital, for example, Boehners actually lean a bit to the left of the general public on school prayer and related issues, in addition to their centrist views on immigration. Like the talented white baseball players we discussed in chapter 5, Boehners overall don't have a strong set of interests one way or the other when it comes to group-based issues—on the whole, their lives would come out similarly either way. But they are spectacularly conservative on policies that would provide targeted assistance to African Americans or women.

On economic issues, however, their income, race, gender, and religion lead to tremendously conservative positions relative to other Americans (and also, as we saw in chapter 6, relative to most people on the planet). Nonetheless, Boehners generally acknowledge some role for government programs assisting the poor and elderly; they just aren't as eager to increase funding and do not support seeking out the wealthy for the bulk of the funds.

Overall, then, Boehners tend to have interests that call for policies advocated by the current configuration of the Republican party, and so they very often support that party. The only major aspect of the Republican coalition that might give them pause, on the whole, involves policies that threaten overt group-based barriers, something that is particularly true for those with very high levels of human capital (like the Harvard Republicans discussed earlier). Indeed, if Boehners with the highest levels of human capital continue to leak into the Democratic coalition, as they have in the past few decades, one can only wonder what other effects this might have. Would infusions of Boehners slowly moderate Democratic views on lifestyle issues? Would they continue to moderate Democratic views on economic redistribution? Would their absence from the Republican party lead to increased Republican conservatism on group-based barriers? Only time will tell.

Johnsons versus Church Ladies

We now compare two demographic groups that represent very different wings of the Republican coalition. One involves white, heterosexual, Christian men with top 20% human capital and something less than weekly church attendance. People in this group are like Boehners at similar levels of human capital, but they don't go to church as often (and, by the same token, aren't as likely to have Ring-Bearer lifestyles). We'll call people with these characteristics "Johnsons," after the former Republican governor Gary Johnson, who in 2012 ran for the Republican presidential nomination, lost to Mitt Romney, but then ran in the general election as the candidate for the Libertarian party.

The other group consists of white, heterosexual Christians with upper-middle levels of human capital (from the fortieth to eightieth percentiles, including many people with some college education but not bachelor's degrees), weekly church attendance, and family incomes in the bottom 40% (typically in the $20,000 to $40,000 range). They resemble Boehners at similar levels of human capital, but with lower incomes and including women. In part because this group consists of fewer men than women, we'll call these "Church Ladies," after Dana Carvey's late-1980s *Saturday Night Live* character, host of the fictional interview show, *Church Chat*. (For those too young to know what we're talking about, get off our lawn and look it up on the Internet machine.) About a third of Church Ladies (as we're using the term) are men, but then Carvey played his character in drag.

Both Johnsons and Church Ladies are a little over twice as likely to identify as Republicans than as Democrats. Johnsons typify what is often thought of as the libertarian wing of the party, while Church Ladies typify middle-class religious conservatives.

From previous chapters, one can guess how Johnsons and Church Ladies tend to differ from Boehners. Johnsons are like Boehners except with lower church attendance and more Freewheeler lifestyles—so, Johnsons should show more liberal attitudes specifically on lifestyle issues. Church Ladies are like Boehners except that they have lower incomes and include women—so, Church Ladies should show more liberal attitudes specifically on economic issues. Johnsons have very high levels of human capital, while Church Ladies go from middle ranges to moderately high ranges—so, Church Ladies should be more willing than Johnsons to subvert human capital by supporting barriers against subordinate groups.

Johnsons and Church Ladies have enough in common with Boehners to push them comfortably into the Republican coalition. Yet, crucially, Johnsons and Church Ladies have little enough in common with each other. They agree on only one broad set of issues—those involving race, immigration, and criminal justice. On these issues, Johnsons and Church Ladies match Boehners—they are against targeted benefits for African Americans, middle-of-the-road on immigration, and in favor of the death penalty and of police use of violence (in circumstances deemed appropriate).

However, when it comes to other kinds of issues, the contrasts are deep for these two Republican-leaning groups. On lifestyle issues and on group-based issues involving religion and sexual orientation, Johnsons have liberal views. After all, Johnsons have high levels of human capital and don't go to church frequently. In line with their Freewheeler and human-capital-advancing interests, most Johnsons are pro-choice, in favor of marijuana legalization, in favor of the ban on school prayer, and in favor of same-sex marriage. Church Ladies, in contrast, are among the most conservative on many of these issues. After all, Church Ladies have middle/upper levels of human capital and high levels of church attendance. For them, the preferred world would be one involving moral condemnation of premarital sex, making pornography illegal, outlawing most abortions, denying birth control to teens without parental consent, outlawing marijuana, allowing school prayer, and disallowing same-sex marriage.

On economic issues, the differences are similarly profound. After all, Johnsons typically have higher incomes while Church Ladies, by definition, have low incomes. And, indeed, while more Johnsons oppose income redistribution than support it, more Church Ladies support income redistribution than oppose it. Johnsons are like Boehners on government spending, mostly supporting existing spending but ambivalent about spending more. But Church Ladies mostly want higher spending on public hard-times programs—over two-thirds want to increase spending on health care and the poor. Relative to the general public, despite leaning Republican, Church Ladies are economic moderates on the whole, not as liberal as most minorities, for example, but not as conservative as Johnsons and Boehners.

What all these groups have in common is the tendency to support policies that advance the interests of people like themselves. It's of course not a perfect, one-to-one, no-noise-in-the-system kind of relationship. Far from it. People are complicated. Still, people with Ring-Bearer lifestyles tend to support policies advancing the interests of those with Ring-Bearer lifestyles; people with Freewheeler lifestyles tend to support policies advancing the interests of those with Freewheeler lifestyles. People with traditionally dominant group identities tend not to get too worked up about group-based barriers one way or the other when they have higher levels of human capital. Those with lower incomes and less economic security are more likely to support income redistribution and public spending on safety nets than those with higher incomes and economic security. And when people have "liberal" interests in one domain and "conservative" interests in another, then their opinion patterns typically diverge from a simple left-right framework.

These major differences between two key Republican subgroups, Johnsons and Church Ladies, illustrate how fragile these kinds of multidimensional coalitions can be. Johnsons and Church Ladies both play their role in supporting Republicans—on the conventional wisdom, Johnsons write checks and Church Ladies staff the phone banks. The Republican coalition couldn't afford major defections from either group. Yet the policies one would emphasize to further solidify support from these groups are by and large opposites. Enhanced emphasis on lifestyle conservatism would attract more Church Ladies but drive away more Johnsons. Enhanced emphasis on economic conservatism would attract more Johnsons but drive away more Church Ladies.

Boehner Women

A lot is made of the gender gap in voting, but the gap is actually not wide, especially set against factors such as race, religion, and sexual orientation, which loom much larger. Still, true, there is a gender gap. Earlier we looked at Boehners—white, heterosexual, regularly church-going, Christian men with upper-middle-and-higher levels of both income and human capital. They split around 70/20 Republican versus Democrat. Women who otherwise have this same cluster of characteristics (we'll call them "Boehner Women") split around 60/30—still a very solidly Republican-leaning group.

Popular discussions highlight a number of women's issues, primarily centered on reproductive rights. However, on the crucial issue of abortion, as we've mentioned, men and women don't really differ. Indeed, about three-quarters of Boehners are against legal abortion motivated by not wanting more children or by being poor or by being single; about the same percentage of Boehner Women (perhaps even a bit more) agree. Boehner Women are a bit less opposed than Boehners (though still generally opposed) to birth control for teens without parental consent. But on the other side, Boehner Women typically want to make pornography illegal, unlike the more accepting male Boehners. On balance, there is no consistent gender gap on lifestyle issues.

Boehners and Boehner Women also have very similar views on group-based issues. Again, there are differences—women are somewhat less likely to oppose same-sex marriage, for example—but the overall patterns are similar.

The main differences between Boehners and Boehner Women lie in economic issues and derive, we argue, from women's increased economic uncertainty relative to men. Women are more likely to need hard-times programs over the course of their lives, and so are more likely to want such programs publicly available and well funded.

Nonetheless, Boehner Women are white Christians with higher incomes and so lean conservative on economic issues compared to the population as a whole, just not as conservative as Boehners (or Johnsons). For Boehners, there are about twice as many opponents of income redistribution as supporters; for Boehner Women, it's a closer call, with the typical positions somewhere in the middle, leaning toward opposition. Boehners are about evenly split on the question of whether the government should spend more to help the poor and the sick; more than six in ten Boehner Women want to increase this spending. Even these differences, though, aren't terribly strong. There is about a 10-point difference between Boehners and Boehner Women on most economic issues, commensurate with the 10-point difference in party affiliations.

If Republicans wanted to attract more Boehner Women, they would take more moderate positions on safety-net issues. At the same time, taking such positions would risk party defections from Johnsons, who already tend to agree with Democrats on lifestyle issues.

Downscale Kansans[15]

Thomas Frank asked, *What's the Matter with Kansas?* His question translates, really, into: What's the matter with lower income whites? Part of the answer is to be found among Church Ladies, who are common in the Bible Belt. But Church Ladies don't represent the bottom of the socioeconomic ladder. They have middle/upper levels of human capital and lower incomes. Indeed, many in this group are either younger people who haven't yet reached their peak incomes or older people whose retirement incomes fail to reflect their true socioeconomic status.

We can take it deeper and look at white, heterosexual Christians with weekly church attendance and both incomes and human capital in the bottom 40%. These are typically people with no college attendance and yearly household incomes around the $15,000 to $35,000 range. We'll call them "Downscale Kansans."

As an initial matter, we note that this group isn't so solidly Republican as the others we've looked at, but merely leans Republican—around 45% versus 38%. And, sure enough, in line with their lower socioeconomic status, their economic views lean liberal relative to the population as a whole. They support income redistribution by almost two to one. They overwhelmingly support the notion that government should be helping the poor and the sick. Around 70% would like to see increased funding for the poor, health care, and Social Security. They're big-spending liberals, right?

Well, here are some other things Downscale Kansans would like to see happen: 84% oppose the ban on school prayer; 81% want to outlaw most abortions; 76% oppose same-sex marriage; 71% think immigration levels should be decreased; 70% want to make pornography illegal; 68% think a person who is against religion should not be allowed to teach at universities. Generously, only 46% would ban gay men from teaching at universities. Not so liberal after all, right?

When it comes to lifestyle issues and group-based issues, Downscale Kansans have interests solidly in line with imposing higher costs on Freewheeler lifestyles and with raising barriers to impede traditionally subordinate groups. That is, on the one hand, they are churchgoing Christians who generally have Ring-Bearer lifestyles, and, on the other hand, they have traditionally dominant group identities along with less human capital. In these areas, then, their policy views are routinely conservative. They are the earlier marrying, high fertility types from chapter 4; simultaneously, they are like the less talented white baseball players from chapter 5.

Frank acknowledges that Downscale Kansans tend to have these kinds of views, but he argues that it shouldn't rationally matter very much in their political calculus. He equates interests generally with redistributive economic interests in particular, and at any rate doesn't think that Republicans ever do much about religious and cultural issues.

Nonetheless, Downscale Kansans generally follow their interests when it comes to the particulars of their policy views. They tend to hold conservative views on lifestyle and group-based issues simultaneously with liberal views on economic issues because such a cluster of opinions is in their interests. They tend to have a hard time choosing between the current party coalitions because one set of interests is represented by one party and the other by the other. Many of Frank's readers, as supporters of Democrats, were very receptive to his message that, if only they were being rational, these Downscale Kansans would support Democrats in greater numbers. As Dana Carvey's Church Lady would say: *How convenient.*

There is an ideological label for Boehners: conservative. There is an ideological label for Johnsons: libertarian. But, as we've mentioned, there's no agreed ideological label for Church Ladies and Downscale Kansans, for people conservative on most things other than economic issues. But a lack of ideological labels doesn't mean that people like Church Ladies and Downscale Kansans have incoherent views. Like Boehners and Johnsons, they have views that generally fit their interests.

There are various other demographic groups that typically lean Republican (more detail can be found in the Data Appendix for Chapter 8). All are made up of white, heterosexual Christians, with varying (usually higher) levels of church attendance and socioeconomic status. We'll now move to Democrats, where white, heterosexual Christians are no longer the main story.

CHAPTER 9

The Democratic Coalition

THE MODERN REPUBLICAN COALITION IS LIKE A TREE. The trunk consists of white, heterosexual Christians on the wealthy/religious side whom we call Boehners and Boehner Women. The branches consist of groups of people who are like Boehners but with some important exceptions. Johnsons are like Boehners except they don't go to church regularly . . . and don't have conservative opinions on lifestyles. Church Ladies are like Boehners and Boehner Women except they have lower incomes . . . and typically lack conservative opinions on economic issues. Johnsons and Church Ladies might disagree with each other on a wide range of issues, but both groups agree with Boehners on enough issues to give the Republican party its treelike coherence.

The Democratic coalition, in contrast, has no trunk—it's more like a log pile. There is no demographic base providing the overall structure, no big influential group with solidly liberal views across a wide range of policy areas. Instead, what unites Democratic voter groups are powerful disagreements with Republican policy goals, though the specific disagreements differ for various Democratic groups. The Democratic party is in many ways an opposition party defined more by disagreements with Republicans than by broad-based within-party agreement.[1]

Labels Used in Chapter 9

Group	Description
Barneys	White, Heathen men with top 20% human capital
Steinems	White, Heathen women with top 20% human capital
Barney Steinems	White Heathens with top 20% human capital
Hillarys	White, heterosexual, Christian women with less than weekly church attendance and top 20% human capital
Springers	White, heterosexual Christians with less than weekly church attendance and both human capital and income in the bottom 40%
Boehners	(From chapter 8) White, heterosexual, Christian men with weekly church attendance and upper-middle-and-higher levels of both human capital and income
Johnsons	(From chapter 8) White, heterosexual, Christian men with less than weekly church attendance and top 20% human capital
Church Ladies	(From chapter 8) White, heterosexual Christians with weekly church attendance, upper-middle levels of human capital (from the fortieth to eightieth percentiles), and income in the bottom 40%
Boehner Women	(From chapter 8) White, heterosexual, Christian women with weekly church attendance and upper-middle-and-higher levels of both human capital and income
Downscale Kansans	(From chapter 8) White, heterosexual Christians with weekly church attendance and both human capital and income in the bottom 40%
Heathens	(From chapter 5) People who are either lesbian/gay/bisexual or not Christian
Freewheelers	(From chapter 4) People who sleep with more people, are sexually active outside of committed relationships, have more same-sex partners, party, drink, go to bars, and use recreational drugs more, live together outside of marriage, are less likely to marry at all, get divorced more when they do marry, and have fewer kids
Ring-Bearers	(From chapter 4) People who wait longer to have sex, tend to have sex only in committed relationships, go to bars and party less, don't cohabit outside of marriage, have long-lasting marriages, and have more kids

African Americans versus Barney Steinems

Two of the main logs in the Democratic pile are something of an odd couple of American politics. The first group is African Americans, who show remarkably consistent support for Democrats: African Americans favor Democrats by a ratio of more than ten to one.

Compared to whites, African Americans are, on average, more religious, less educated, and poorer. Christianity is slightly more common among African American adults (85%) compared to white adults (79%). But while the typical white adult goes to church a few times a year, the typical African American adult goes to church two or three times a *month*. In terms of education, about a third of white adults have bachelor's degrees, but only half as many African American adults do. The middle range of white adults live in households with annual incomes running from around $35,000 to $110,000; for African Americans, the middle 50% of adults live in households with incomes in the $19,000 to $73,000 range.

The other half of the Democratic odd couple consists of white Heathens with top 20% human capital—which is to say, whites who are either not Christian or not heterosexual and who are at-least-decent test-takers with graduate degrees, good test-takers with bachelor's degrees, and so forth. We'll call these folks "Barney Steinems." We take "Barney" from two sources. The first is former U.S. congressman Barney Frank, who is a gay, Jewish graduate of Harvard and Harvard Law School. A great line from Frank: "I'm used to being in the minority. I'm a left-handed gay Jew." The second Barney is Barney Stinson, the wealthy, womanizing character from *How I Met Your Mother*, played by gay actor Neil Patrick Harris. A great line from Stinson: "Discouraging premarital sex is against my religion." And we've picked "Steinem" from feminist icon Gloria Steinem. A great bit from Steinem: "There was one postcard I used to keep on my wall at *Ms*. It was like poetry; it had everything in it. It said, 'Now that I have read your magazine, I know for sure that you are a commie, lesbian, long-haired dyke, witch, slut, who dates negroids.' And then the finish: 'Isn't that just like a Jew.'"[2] We'll refer to the men here as "Barneys," the women as "Steinems," and both together as "Barney Steinems."

While African Americans are among the most religious and lowest socioeconomic Americans as a group, Barney Steinems are among the least religious and highest socioeconomic Americans. Most Barney Steinems do not attend religious services even once a year. Indeed, most of them indicate "none" as their religious affiliation. Their yearly household incomes typically run in the $55,000 to $170,000 range. They are mostly, that is, middle-income and wealthier whites. Yet their support for Democrats is solid. Steinems prefer Democrats over Republicans by about 5.5 to 1; Barneys run about three to one. Barneys, then, are almost as likely to favor Democrats as Boehners are to favor Republicans. A majority of the Harvard/Radcliffe Class of 1977 we examined earlier are Barney Steinems, as are both of your authors.

Though both of these groups are key parts of the Democratic coalition, Barney Steinems and African Americans have major policy differences. The differences are particularly noticeable when we compare Barneys with churchgoing African Americans (leaving aside, for a moment, Steinems and nonchurchgoing African Americans), echoing the earlier contrast on the Republican side between Johnsons and Church Ladies.

Barneys rarely attend religious services; they typically have Freewheeler lifestyles, spend a lot of time gaining education, and generally put off having kids. Churchgoing African Americans are typically less educated and, by definition, go to church weekly; they tend to have Ring-Bearer lifestyles and have kids earlier and in greater numbers than Barneys. These two solidly Democratic groups, therefore, have sharply conflicting views on lifestyle issues: Barneys are incredibly liberal on these issues while churchgoing African Americans are about as conservative as Church Ladies. Roughly eight in ten Barneys think premarital sex is not at all wrong, are pro-choice, and would legalize marijuana; less than a third of churchgoing African Americans agree. There is, then, almost a whopping 50-point gap on these major political issues separating these two important Democratic constituencies.

Barneys are, by definition, Heathens with lots of human capital. Churchgoing African Americans are overwhelmingly heterosexual Christians and typically have less human capital. Barneys should be expected to strongly favor eliminating barriers against non-Christians and homosexuals so that their high levels of human capital can pay off. The interests of churchgoing African Americans, in contrast, are not typically maximized by unlimited human-capital-based competition; their interests are often advanced by placing barriers in the way of traditionally subordinate groups to which they do not themselves belong. And, indeed, Barneys are tremendously liberal on group-based issues relating to sexual orientation and religion; churchgoing African Americans, like Church Ladies, are conservative on these issues. The large majority of Barneys support same-sex marriage while a solid majority of churchgoing African Americans oppose it. Almost nine in ten Barneys support both the school prayer ban and the right of anti-religious individuals to teach at universities; more than eight in ten churchgoing African Americans oppose the school prayer ban and only around half think that anti-religious professors should be allowed to keep their jobs. Looking just at this set of issues, Barneys look like good liberals while churchgoing African Americans look strikingly conservative.

In sharp contrast, on racial issues, these groups flip. On race, African Americans are tremendously liberal while Barneys occupy the middle of the road, occasionally veering toward the conservative lane. About three-quarters of churchgoing African Americans think the government should be supporting and spending more specifically on African Americans; fewer than half of Barneys agree. More than four in ten churchgoing African Americans favor race-based affirmative action and over half favor gender-based affirmative action when it comes to hiring and promotion decisions by businesses; only two in ten Barneys agree. Over half of churchgoing African Americans think the police are never justified in striking citizens; only one in ten Barneys agree.

Barneys are white men who are typically wealthier and embedded in wealthier social networks; but they are also Heathens with lots of human capital. Churchgoing African Americans are generally poorer, often embedded in poorer social networks. Barneys, then, have more apparently conflicting interests when it comes to economic issues, but their demographic features on balance indicate center-right views. Churchgoing African Americans typically have interests strongly in favor of robust public hard-times programs. For these reasons, on some economic issues, such as spending on the poor and Social Security, opinions sharply diverge between the two groups. Almost 90% of churchgoing African

Americans think the government should be spending more on the poor, but only 58% of Barneys agree (a level of support about equivalent to Boehner Women). Over three-quarters of churchgoing African Americans think the government should spend more on Social Security, but only 42% of Barneys agree (a level of support almost as low as Johnsons and Boehners).

On other economic items relating to redistribution, health care, and education, Barneys and churchgoing African Americans are more likely to agree, though African Americans typically occupy positions to the left of Barneys. Should the government reduce income differences? Churchgoing African Americans say "yes" by about 2.5 to 1; Barneys say "yes" by about 1.5 to 1. Over 90% of churchgoing African Americans and around 84% of Barneys think that the government has a role in subsidizing health care; over 80% of churchgoing African Americans and around two-thirds of Barneys think the government should spend more on health care. Around 80% of both churchgoing African Americans and Barneys think the government should spend more on education.

The foregoing illustrates that Barneys and churchgoing African Americans are divided on many important issues, sometimes sharply so. This raises the obvious question, *What are these two groups doing in the same party?* The answer is that they are united by a fundamental interest in opposing particular aspects of the Republican agenda. For many Barneys, the agenda is to minimize group-based barriers that undermine the competitive prospects of Heathens with lots of human capital. African Americans are more likely to be focused on race and poverty. Even when churchgoing African Americans hold lifestyle and religious views that line up with religious conservatives, their racial and redistributive interests tend to trump other interests, and so they overwhelmingly support the Democratic coalition against the Republican coalition.[3] While Barneys and churchgoing African Americans share little by way of specific policy agreements, they nonetheless share an interest in opposing the Republican coalition.

Steinems (the female equivalent of Barneys) are nearly indistinguishable from Barneys in terms of their (very liberal) views on lifestyle issues and group-based issues relating to sexual orientation and religion. But while Barneys have middle-of-the-road views on economic issues and on issues relating to race and criminal justice, Steinems run more liberal, falling somewhere between Barneys and African Americans.

Not all African Americans are regular churchgoers, of course. African Americans who are not weekly churchgoers are nearly indistinguishable from churchgoing African Americans on economic issues and issues relating to race and criminal justice. But while churchgoing African Americans typically have conservative views on lifestyle issues and on group-based issues relating to sexual orientation and religion, those not regularly attending church tend to have middle-of-the-road views (at lower levels of human capital) or liberal-leaning views (at higher levels of human capital) on these issues, landing somewhere in between churchgoing African Americans and Barney Steinems.

Latino/Asian/Other Americans

African Americans and Barney Steinems are not, of course, the only important groups in the Democratic coalition. We turn now to Latinos, Asians, and members of other nonwhite and non–African American ethnic groups, which for brevity we refer to as simply "others."

On most of the key demographic dimensions, Latinos, Asians, and others fall somewhere between African Americans and whites. Latino/Asian/other Americans attend religious services a bit more than whites on average, though substantially less than African Americans. The major difference is denominational—African Americans are primarily non-Catholic Christians; Latino Americans are primarily Catholic; Asian and other Americans are a mix of Catholics and non-Catholic Christians, Muslims, Hindus, Buddhists, and other non-Western religions. On socioeconomic measures, Latino/Asian/other Americans on average are also between African Americans and whites, though they lean closer to the lower education rates and incomes of African Americans.

The major demographic difference, of course, relates to immigration. Though it's difficult to know with precision, according to GSS data, over half of Latino/Asian/other adults living in the United States were born outside the United States, and close to three-quarters of their parents were born outside the United States. While many Latino/Asian/other Americans have families that have been in the United States for many generations, the 1990s and 2000s saw an unprecedented rise in Latino and Asian immigration, a tide that only began to ebb in the wake of the Great Recession. Among African American and white adults, in contrast, less than 10% of their parents were born outside of the United States, and many of these whites are seniors, having parents who came over in the great waves of European immigration of the early twentieth century.

Latino/Asian/other Americans, in large part because many are not citizens, are far less likely to vote. But those who do vote prefer Democrats over Republicans by about 2.5 to 1 over the past decade. In the 2012 election, for example, Latinos and Asians favored Obama over Romney by about 72% to 27%. While African Americans tend to favor Democrats independent of income or how often they attend church, Latino/Asian/other Americans tend to be less likely to favor Democrats at higher levels of income and church attendance (especially when they have both).

On lifestyle and religious group-based issues, Latino/Asian/other Americans don't differ much from other Americans on the whole—they are more conservative when they are more religious and have less human capital; they are more liberal when the reverse is true. On economic issues, Latino/Asian/other Americans hold center-left views similar to Barney Steinems, generally favoring economic redistribution and increased spending on the poor and health care—they are not as liberal as African Americans on average, but still to the left of most whites.

Perhaps the most interesting contrasts involve issues relating to race, immigration, and criminal justice. African Americans, as we saw, strongly support assistance for African Americans. Similarly, Latino/Asian/other Americans strongly support immigration. While about 58% of whites and 47% of African Americans would like immigration levels to be reduced, only about a quarter of Latino/Asian/other Americans do. When asked about support for African Americans, however, Latino/Asian/other Americans occupy the same center-left territory as Barney

Steinems, not as consistently conservative as Boehners and other white Republican-leaning groups, but not nearly as supportive as African Americans themselves. In the realm of criminal justice, African Americans and Latino/Asian/other Americans are about equally likely to oppose the death penalty and police violence, especially at lower socioeconomic levels, in contrast with the more conservative Barney Steinems with higher socioeconomic status.

Hillarys

Steinems, recall, are white, Heathen women with top 20% human capital. Boehner Women are white, heterosexual women who are churchgoing Christians and who have top 20% human capital (Boehner Women in chapter 8 also included those with middle/upper levels of human capital and higher incomes, but when we talk about Boehner Women in this section, we're limiting it to the branch of Boehner Women with top 20% human capital). Steinems prefer Democrats by around 5.5 to 1; Boehner Women prefer Republicans by around two to one.

Intermediate between these two groups are white, heterosexual women with top 20% human capital who are Christian but, importantly, aren't very: that is, they do *not* attend church weekly. We'll call this group Hillarys, after its best known member, Hillary Clinton. Hillarys are the female equivalents of Johnsons, but while Johnsons favor Republicans by over two to one, Hillarys favor Democrats by almost 1.5 to 1.

As we move from Boehner Women to Hillarys to Steinems, church attendance drops, of course, by definition. Boehner Women typically go to church once a week, Hillarys several times a year but not as often as once a month, and Steinems less than once a year. In a related manner, Ring-Bearer versus Freewheeler lifestyle features are different as well. For example, around three-quarters of Boehner Women are married, a bit under two-thirds of Hillarys are married, and just over half of Steinems are married. The median Boehner Woman or Hillary has two children while the median Steinem has one. Socioeconomically, the groups are very similar overall (with yearly family incomes typically between $55,000 and $145,000), but there's more variance among Steinems, who have higher numbers of households headed by single women, but also are more likely to have dual-income households when married or cohabiting.

Politically, Hillarys land between Steinems and Boehner Women on most issues. On lifestyle issues, Hillarys lean closer to the very liberal views of Steinems than the conservative views of Boehner Women. So, for example, while 78% of Steinems and 63% of Hillarys think premarital sex is not at all wrong, only 29% of Boehner Women agree. On group-based issues relating to sexual orientation and religion, Hillarys tend to land in liberal territory in between very liberal Steinems and merely left-leaning Boehner Women.

On issues relating to race, immigration, and criminal justice, Hillarys hold views that are basically the same on average as the right-leaning views of Boehner Women, in contrast with the left-leaning views of Steinems. On economic issues, Hillarys are middle-of-the-road in comparison with liberal Steinems and conservative Boehner Women. So, for example, Steinems are more likely to favor reduced income disparities by around 2.4 to 1, Boehner Women are a bit more likely to oppose government reducing income disparities by around 1.2 to 1, while Hillarys similarly lean slightly toward opposition at 1.1 to 1. Roughly 79% of Steinems think the government should be spending more on health care, compared to 74% of Hillarys and 61% of Boehner Women.

Summarizing the relative positions of whites with high levels of human capital, table 9.1 shows the approximate positions relative to the American public of Steinems, Barneys, Hillarys, Boehner Women, Johnsons, and Boehners.

While table 9.1 shows groups going from the one that leans most heavily Democratic (Steinems) to the one that leans most heavily Republican (Boehners), not all groups are homogenously liberal or conservative. Johnsons are the biggest outliers, with very conservative economic views but liberal views on group-based issues relating to religion and sexual orientation. In addition, whites with lots of human capital skew "more liberal" and "more conservative" within constrained ranges on many issues. None of these groups are conservative, relative to the general population, on group-based issues relating to religion and sexual orientation—the conservatives on these issues tend to be

Table 9.1. Overall Views of Whites with High Levels of Human Capital

	Lifestyle Policies	Religion and Sexual Orientation Policies	Race, Immigration, and Criminal Justice Policies	Economic Policies
Steinems	Very Liberal	Very Liberal	Lean Liberal	Liberal
Barneys	Very Liberal	Very Liberal	Moderate	Moderate
Hillarys	Liberal	Very Liberal	Lean Conservative	Moderate
Boehner Women	Conservative	Lean Liberal	Lean Conservative	Conservative
Johnsons	Lean Liberal	Liberal	Conservative	Very Conservative
Boehners	Conservative	Lean Liberal	Conservative	Very Conservative

heterosexual Christians with *low levels* of human capital. Also, none of these groups are among the most conservative on lifestyle issues, who tend to be religious people with less education. At the other end of the spectrum, none of these groups tend to be especially liberal on issues relating to race, immigration, and criminal justice—the genuine liberals tend to be African Americans and Latino immigrants. Similarly, the most liberal Americans on economic issues tend to be minorities with lower incomes.

Whites with high levels of human capital, then, have three broad flavors—liberal, conservative, and libertarian. Among these folks, however, "liberal" really means "very liberal on lifestyle issues and related group-based issues and center-left on economic issues and related group-based issues." "Conservative" really means "very conservative on economic issues, pretty conservative on lifestyle issues, pretty conservative on racial and related issues, but left-leaning on group-based issues relating to religion and sexual orientation."

Contrast these groups with, for instance, churchgoing African Americans, who tend to be very liberal on economics and race, but very conservative on lifestyle issues and related group-based issues. Recall as well Downscale Kansans—white, heterosexual, churchgoing Christians who are low in socioeconomic status—who have generally conservative views across lifestyle issues and the full range of group-based issues, but then generally left-leaning economic preferences. The views of whites with lots of human capital by no means exhaust the range of commonly occurring position clusters.

Springers

Another demographic group that defies easy labeling consists of those we'll call "Springers," a reference to stereotypical guests of *The Jerry Springer Show*. By our definition, Springers are like Downscale Kansans in most respects. They are white, heterosexual Christians who are not seniors and who have human capital levels and family incomes in the bottom 40% of the country. More than a third do not have high school diplomas, and typical yearly family incomes run in the $14,000 to $35,000 range. But, while Springers are Christians, they don't go to church weekly, unlike Downscale Kansans.

When writers cover the declining state of downscale whites, they're usually referring to something like the Springer demographic. Only a bit over a third of Springers are married at any given time; only a bit over a third of Springers vote in any given presidential election. Compare this with their churchgoing analogues, Downscale Kansans, among whom around 70% are married and over half vote.

When Springers are willing to express a party preference, they prefer Democrats over Republicans by about 1.4 to 1. Their policy opinions are a mix of liberal and conservative views, and make sense in light of their interests.[4] They are white, heterosexual Christians with low levels of human capital—and, indeed, they have overall conservative views on a range of group-based items. Roughly seven in ten disapprove of the ban on school prayer and half think that professors should lose their jobs when they express anti-religious views. Almost two-thirds think the government should reduce immigration. More than 80% oppose race-based affirmative action and think the government should not spend more to help African Americans.

But these are not regular churchgoers, nor do they typically have Ring-Bearer lifestyles. They are generally liberal on premarital sex and pornography. But they are nominally Christian and have low education levels—in line with this, about two-thirds oppose legal abortion in most cases.

On economic issues, though, Springers are solidly liberal. They favor government income redistribution by two to one. More than eight in ten think the government should be helping the poor, and nine in ten think the government should be helping with health care. Around 75% to 80% think the government should be spending more on the poor, health care, Social Security, and education.

If one were to ignore racial issues, Springers would look politically similar to African Americans with less human capital who don't go to church frequently. On racial issues, however, the two groups differ fundamentally.

In a related vein, Springers are also similar to downscale white Heathens, with Springers being just to the right of their Heathen counterparts on most issues. But when it comes to group-based items relating to religion and sexual orientation, the differences are pronounced—on these issues, Springers typically prefer conservative policies that advance their traditionally dominant groups, while their Heathen relatives typically prefer liberal policies that protect their traditionally subordinate groups.

Downscale folks who don't go to church much thus share a general description: They tend to be to the left on economics, left-leaning on lifestyles (though often not on abortion), but then hold group-based issue preferences that seek to help people in their own groups and hold back people not in their own groups. They are "liberals" overall except primarily when it comes to group-based views in areas in which their own groups are traditionally dominant.

Governing Coalitions

While only 25% to 30% of American adults have bachelor's degrees, almost all members of the U.S. Congress have them. Congressional members are also disproportionately wealthier, white, and male. The same is true of most presidents and their staffs. The same is true of the federal judiciary, practically all of whom have law degrees.

While the Democratic and Republican coalitions represent diverse interests, some interests are more equal than others. The Republican coalition includes those favoring Ring-Bearer policies, anti-meritocratic advantages for traditionally dominant groups, and limited economic redistribution. But among Republicans with high socioeconomic status (e.g., Boehners and Johnsons), the strongest consensus is on economics. On the other side of the aisle, the Democratic coalition includes those favoring Freewheeler-friendly policies, the elimination of anti-meritocratic barriers, and robust public hard-times support. But among Democrats with high socioeconomic status (e.g., Barney Steinems and Hillarys), the strongest consensus is on eliminating anti-meritocratic barriers and defending Freewheeling.

The compromises reached by the governing representatives reflect the fact that the bargaining is being done by the elites of the respective parties. The push on economics from elite Democrats is not as hard as it might be if the negotiators came from poorer minorities. The push on group-based policies and abortion regimes from elite Republicans is not as hard as it might be if the negotiators came from less educated white Christians. Elite negotiations result in more conservative economic policies and more liberal social and group-based policies because these positions are routinely strongly favored by the demographic groups grounding one coalition's elite representatives, but not routinely strongly opposed by the demographic groups from which the other coalition's elite representatives are drawn. Recall that Harvard Democrats hold less liberal views on Social Security than other Democrats and that Harvard Republicans hold less conservative views on abortion. More generally, Barney Steinems and Hillarys are not so strongly to the left on economic issues while Boehners and Johnsons at similarly high levels of human capital are not so strongly to the right on issues like school prayer and abortion.

What's the Matter with Kansas? pointed out that Republican elites often push their economic agenda but not the cultural and lifestyle views favored by downscale folks. Our view is that Democratic elites act similarly, but on different issues. So, for instance, as the Bush tax cuts expired on January 1, 2013, even though Democrats had powerful negotiating leverage given that Clinton-era rates automatically returned as the law of the land, and even though Obama had just won reelection campaigning on eliminating the Bush tax cuts for income higher than $250,000, and even though polls showed that at least two-thirds of Americans favored ending the tax cuts for income above $250,000—despite all this, Democratic negotiators (mostly including wealthy whites) agreed to lift the income target from $250,000 to $450,000, a significant and to many puzzling win for the top 1% given the circumstances.

Indeed, recently, pundits have had to invoke a different term—"populist"—for elected Democrats who appear to be serious about advancing liberal economic policies that are popular among the rank-and-file but not routinely taken seriously by the elite. High status, white Democratic leaders are often economic centrists relative to the general public and look economically "liberal" only in comparison to high status, white Republican leaders, who are far more conservative on economic matters than the population as a whole. And so, when it comes to Democrats such as New York mayor Bill de Blasio or U.S. senator Elizabeth Warren from Massachusetts, the need arises for a distinguishing label, one that calls attention to the fact that they're to the left of many, perhaps most, of their fellow highly educated, wealthier, white, Democratic colleagues.

Is it any wonder, then, that so many downscale whites don't vote? They typically favor robust income redistribution as well as group-based barriers. Democrats, on the one hand, favor income redistribution but oppose group-based barriers, and, worse, when push comes to shove, Democratic elites are more likely to protect human capital and cave on income redistribution. Republicans, on the other hand, oppose income redistribution and favor (some) group-based barriers; yet when push comes to shove, Republican elites are more likely to protect wealthy privilege and cave on group-based barriers.

Unlike many European countries, the United States has no nationalist populist party that prioritizes the positions of downscale whites. Instead, the third parties that performed best in the 2012 presidential election were the Libertarian party and the Green party, with the former organized around views typical of Johnsons and the latter organized around views typical of Steinems. Even Tea Party Republicans were organized around tax-and-spend issues and have spent much of their political capital opposing Obamacare (a redistribution program) rather than focusing on downscale issues like same-sex marriage or abortion.

Political science research has shown that national elected officials tend to vote in ways supported by those with higher socioeconomic status, largely ignoring the views of those at the bottom.[5] This in part derives, no doubt, from trying to please campaign contributors. But part of it surely derives from the demographics and interests of legislators themselves. Federal judges, after all, have long been advocates for positions especially favored by people with lots of education (e.g., striking down group-based barriers and ensuring legal abortion) . . . and they have lifetime appointments with no donors to please.

If the United States set policy simply by polling the resident population, the country would have a very different policy flavor.[6] There would be greater spending on the poor, health care, Social Security, and education. Anti-American Muslims would be forbidden to make public speeches. School prayer would be allowed. Immigration would be reduced. Abortion would be legal in cases of rape and fetal deformity, but illegal in cases where the abortion was motivated by not wanting more children, by being poor, or by being single.

Because their preferences are often unpopular, elites in both coalitions tend to endorse some degree of anti-democratic (with a small d) maneuvering to achieve their ends. Republicans' maneuvers include instituting voting restrictions (ID laws, felon bans, etc.) that attempt to suppress minority and poor votes as well as opposing campaign financing restrictions that would limit the wealthy from their disproportionate role in elections. Democrats' principal anti-democratic (again with a small d) maneuvers in the past sixty years have come from the federal courts overruling popular legislation. On abortion, indeed, it's about as dubiously creative for liberals to say that it's clear that the U.S. Constitution guarantees a right to abortion as it is for conservatives to say that it's clear that the Bible is against it. In both cases, the documents are silent; the words aren't there. People's Public Relations Departments (including those of Supreme Court justices and those of the Religious Right) are making stuff up to defend the policy preferences of their interest-driven Boards of Directors.

Part IV

Political Challenges

CHAPTER 10

An Uncomfortable Take on Political Positions

FROM COCKTAIL PARTIES TO CABLE NETWORKS to the halls of congress, people who disagree about politics nonetheless come together and agree on one point: Political differences exist because one side is fair, reasonable, and public-spirited while the other side is unfair, unreasonable, selfish, mean, and hypocritical. (They just don't agree on which side is which.)

As neighborhoods and media outlets become increasingly politically segregated, these kinds of explanations become more extreme, unfiltered by the usual demands of politeness that would otherwise temper one's impulses in mixed company. It's easy to describe one's political opponents as corrupt boobs and idiot saboteurs in a room full of allies. Even academic researchers occasionally make similar moves. In chapter 1 we discussed a study describing opposition to minority-advancing programs as "symbolic racism," which isn't exactly value-neutral, but also not likely to ruffle many feathers in a room full of social scientists.

In people's polite moments, they concede that both sides are fair, reasonable, and public-spirited—*Senator Soandso is a good family man who loves his country, but he and I simply have a fundamental disagreement about how to achieve prosperity and fairness for all Americans.* Some academic treatments take this tack. Moral psychologist Jon Haidt describes how liberals and conservatives are relying on different moral foundations—they're all good people, after all.[1] Libertarian economist Bryan Caplan describes how everyone is trying to do what's best for society, after all (it's just that, for Caplan, libertarian economists happen to know better what's best).[2]

Our take is neither partisan nor polite, and might make many uncomfortable. Our explanation for political disagreements begins with something obvious but often overlooked: The policies people fight over have real-life consequences that help some people and harm others. In our view, all sides typically seek to advance their interests and are hypocritical in the way they present their views. No side is particularly motivated by being fair or reasonable or public-spirited. Indeed, when it comes to policy disputes, we think that one's perceptions of what's "fair" or "reasonable" are themselves typically driven by one's interests. People are generally neither boobs nor saboteurs, but social animals competing over advantages for themselves, their families, and their social networks.

It doesn't take one very far to divide the country (much less the whole of humanity) into two or three ideological boxes. If one wants to understand the variety of public opinion, one needs to think about specifics. The key, we have argued, is to look at people's lives and interests, focusing on demographic features that provide clues to the particular outcomes that will help or harm them.

On sexual and reproductive issues, differences in Freewheeler and Ring-Bearer lifestyles help determine whether people gain or lose when higher costs are placed on Freewheeler lifestyles—when casual sex carries moral costs, when partying carries legal costs, and when family planning is restricted. These lifestyles influence people's decisions to affiliate with or avoid religious groups. People's religious and lifestyle patterns strongly predict their views on issues related to premarital sex, pornography, abortion, birth control, and marijuana legalization.

About group-based issues, we proposed that the two key factors in determining people's competing interests are, first, group identities (race, religion, etc.) and, second, accumulated human capital (education and related cognitive abilities). Analogous to talented African American baseball players in our allegory, people with lots of human capital who are also members of traditionally subordinate groups do better when the rules abolish group-based barriers and give advantages to those with lots of human capital. Analogous to less talented white baseball players in our allegory, people with less human capital do better when advantages are given to their own groups and other groups are held back. People's views on issues involving sexual orientation, religion, immigration, and race are well predicted by their group identities and levels of human capital.

Finally, on economic issues, people differ not only in how much they stand to benefit (or lose) when wealth is redistributed, but also in, first, how much they might need hard-times programs in the future and, second, how much they might rely on their own social groups and private charities when hard times hit. So, while income predicts people's economic views to a degree, race, age, gender, religion, sexual orientation, and human capital are also important for understanding and predicting preferences for public hard-times programs.

Because people generally adopt issue opinions that advance their multifaceted inclusive interests, they wind up frequently adopting, buffet-like, sets of particular views that fall outside of a simple left-right framework. When someone's interests point to "liberal" policy preferences on one set of issues and to "conservative" policy preferences on a different set of issues, that's usually how things turn out. Focusing on interests points the way to finding people who are typically liberal, typically conservative, typically libertarian, and typically whatever-we-should-call-the-opposite-of-libertarian, along with other nameless position profiles that are completely absent from the usual discussions of the political map.

We view it as a good sign that our efforts line up with certain aspects of political targeting by campaign professionals, the people who get paid to get such things right. We have tried to add to these perspectives by providing a psychological framework that can reveal interests in play in a wide range of issues (beyond the usual suspects involving economic redistribution). In particular, instead of viewing "social" or "cultural" or "religious" issues as symbolic and disconnected from the concrete concerns of real life, we've made the case that battles over sexual lifestyles and social status regimes have real-life effects as concrete as the results of fights over money. Without necessarily knowing the real reasons, across a range of policy areas, people are motivated to seek outcomes that advance the everyday goals of themselves, their families, their friends, and their wider circles of social allies.

On that point, we've also argued that human minds are designed for spin, to hide their strategic foundations behind socially attractive veneers. The Public Relations Departments of people's minds craft stories about the benevolent wisdom of their own views and the malevolent idiocy of their opponents' views, with Spokespersons almost wholly ignorant of the nature of the game. Public political discourse is frequently a battle between prickly Spokespersons fighting over made-up stories that have little to do with the underlying motives of people's mental Boards of Directors. Admitting that one's political opponents would often be worse off under one's own policy preferences interferes with the goal of advancing one's own agenda. People's desires to advance favorable policy outcomes typically trump any desire to express coherent views of themselves and others.

Observers can predict, with error, to be sure, other people's political positions and priorities by taking into account the other person's inclusive interests, considering their religion, lifestyle, sexual orientation, race, immigration status, education, intelligence, income, and so forth, *despite the fact that most people are themselves unaware that these interest-relevant features are important in shaping their own views.* In fact, most people, most of the time, will strongly deny, for example, that their opposition to abortion has anything to do with suppressing others' sexual promiscuity. Virtually no one says they favor meritocracy because it helps smart people like themselves beat less-smart people in social competitions. People's Public Relations Departments don't let their Spokespersons know such things, let alone say them out loud; they are the kinds of accounts, indeed, that people find insulting, regardless of how well the accounts explain the facts.

We think we've provided the basics to understand these kinds of political opinions, but we acknowledge the limits of the approach. We don't want to give the impression that we think our view explains the totality of the expanse of American political opinion. People are, in a word, complicated. We think we've given a foundation that is really useful, but it's obvious there's more to the story.

Issues We Haven't Addressed

Our approach has focused on people's everyday goals in social life, involving areas including safety and basic necessities, friendships and social status, romantic and sexual relationships, and parenting and other family relationships. In line with this focus, the political issues we have covered have largely been those with strong connections to competitive aspects of ordinary social life—fights over sexual and reproductive life-styles, fights over the rules determining social status, and fights over the redistribution of resources.

At the same time, we've largely ignored certain other issues that feature prominently in modern political battles. In some cases, our favored explanation offers little traction, leaving us with issues on which it's not clear (to us anyway) what, if any, the connections are to everyday social conflicts.

Two sets of issues in this category that loom large are fights over environmental policy and military matters. That's not to say that there aren't some real-life connections between some people's interests and the results of these conflicts. Those who work for oil companies or defense contractors, for example, have reasonably clear incentives to oppose policies that would diminish the profitability of their businesses. It's not mysterious why oil executives might view global warming with skepticism or why defense executives might think that strong military responses are crucial in meeting challenges overseas. Real-life interests could also help explain why people living close to a polluting factory favor regulating the factory. And it's not surprising to find that middle-class Americans with lots of friends and relatives who serve or have served in the military support the idea of a large, well-paid military.

These constituencies are too small, however, to explain the outsized role environmental and military issues play in political debates. Why, in short, do so many people only distally affected care so much about these issues? And why have they split out the way they have in terms of competing views? Fights over global warming, renewable energy, interventions in Middle Eastern conflicts, and related areas affect people's everyday lives, but the connections, it seems to us, are usually remote, and, further, it would have been hard to predict ex ante which people would have wound up on which side.

When it comes to spending on the environment, the correlations between people's positions and their demographic traits are modest in size, and don't lend themselves to easy interpretation. People who favor higher environmental spending tend to have more education, not to be regular churchgoers, to be younger and—perhaps most surprisingly—to have no children.[3] Less favorable attitudes toward environmental spending tend to come from white, Protestant churchgoers with less education, seniors, and—again surprisingly—those with children. The sorts of explanations we've emphasized wouldn't do much to illuminate these patterns.

On military spending, the demographic predictors make only marginally more sense. People in favor of greater amounts of military spending tend to be native-born Christians and Jews, particularly among whites and Asians with moderate and lower levels of human capital. Wanting to reduce military spending is especially common among the nonreligious, Muslims, and others who are neither Christian nor Jewish, among people from immigrant families, among people with top 20% human capital, and among African Americans and Latino Americans. The patterns recall the group-based issues we covered in chapter 5, pointing to the combination of human capital with religious, immigrant, and racial group identities. There are aspects that are sensible from an interest-based perspective. We can understand, for example, why many Muslim immigrants might particularly oppose widespread U.S. involvement in the Middle East—people's interests extend beyond themselves to family and friends, including those in foreign countries. But it's less clear how limited interests like these generalize into a very wide and very passionate ongoing debate over the U.S. military.

Along similar lines, while we can understand why news stories involving floods and storms, environmental catastrophes, or terrorist bombings are particularly attention grabbing for human minds—important parts of people's fundamental goals, after all, relate to health and safety—we don't see how this leads to widespread, passionate conflict within society. Generally it seems that people, more or less (putting aside people such as energy company executives and defense contractors), benefit to similar degrees, and endure similar costs, as policy shifts toward more defense spending (safer nation, perhaps, at the expense of national treasure) or more environmentally friendly regulation (cleaner nation at the expense, perhaps, of economic growth). In short, compared to the issues we've (not coincidentally) chosen to cover in this book, our approach, focusing on everyday interests, doesn't seem to do as good a job with these two sets of issues either in terms of their prominence or in terms of predicting what side people will be on.

We don't deny—at all—that other perspectives can be very helpful in unraveling these and other issues. For example, political science perspectives emphasizing interest groups and elite leadership could help in explaining military and environmental views. Perhaps the enormous dollars at stake for key defense and energy industries lead to powerful lobbies to encourage lawmakers to adopt pro-defense and anti-regulatory positions that few Americans would spontaneously find intuitively appealing. Perhaps, then, these lawmakers use their influence to broaden the view that supporting such positions is an important part of being a good member of their party coalition. And perhaps many ordinary citizens come along for the ride based on factors that don't clearly relate to their everyday interests. We find something like this plausible, but it's beyond the scope of our emphasis in this book, which has been on ordinary citizens' everyday interests.

Another issue we find puzzling is physician-assisted suicide or the right to die. Views on assisted suicide correlate with religiosity and with sexual and reproductive issues, but the right to die is not a sexual or reproductive issue. Our discussions in chapter 4 about Freewheelers and Ring-Bearers do little to explain suicide opinions. On this topic, we simply admit that our approach doesn't seem to provide any explanation. Note that biblical literalism doesn't do much work on this issue either. Just as the Bible doesn't actually say anything directly about abortion, it also doesn't explicitly condemn suicide, much less physician-assisted suicide.

We're confident that there are still other important issues on which our approach isn't particularly helpful. That's OK with us. We don't believe that our perspective must explain *everything* to explain *anything*. Our perspective, centered on everyday interests, should be expected to work best in the context of issues that widely affect everyday interests. For other kinds of issues, we are pleased to concede, there is a heightened need for other kinds of approaches.

Dynamics beyond Demographics

Predicting people's political positions is hard. Predicting how their positions will change over time is harder. In some ways our view provides general guidelines for thinking about policy opinion dynamics, but, again, it can't provide all the answers.

Take, for example, some of the big trends the United States has seen over the last sixty years. First, while no one is suggesting that the American educational system is without flaws, adults today are far better educated, on average, than their parents and grandparents. Second, the United States is experiencing a dramatic rise in racial and ethnic diversity. Third, Freewheeler lifestyles have been on the rise as Ring-Bearer lifestyles have declined, something that has been a big force in driving the slow decline in American church attendance and the rise in religiously unaffiliated people.[4]

These trends have had something to do with changes in attitudes on discriminatory issues (driven by higher numbers of racial and religious minorities along with higher educational attainment) and lifestyle issues such as premarital sex and marijuana legalization (driven by growth in Freewheeler lifestyles and declines in religiosity). But then there is the noticeably mysterious exception of abortion views, which haven't changed much over the past decades despite the big rise in less religious, Freewheeling folks with lots of education. In contrast, while issues like same-sex marriage and marijuana legalization have been changing in line with demographic changes, they've actually been moving more quickly in a liberal direction than simple demographics would predict.

In addition to long-term, demographic-driven directional shifts, there are also plenty of shifts in public mood from year to year, first in one direction, then in another.[5] Some of these changes probably have to do with the party in power, as the public tends to shift in a more conservative direction in response to Democratic administrations and in a more liberal direction in response to Republican administrations.

Social scientists have also focused on the short-term dynamics of individuals' political positions—how these positions can shift from moment to moment based on a variety of factors. Consider a survey in which the Danish government asked a large number of her citizens their political views on a number of issues, notably including the question of the government's role in transferring wealth from rich to poor. A team of political scientists, led by Michael Bang Petersen, took advantage of this survey to investigate an unusual question: Do hungry people favor such transfers more than less hungry people?

The researchers theorized that people's attitudes might depend in a systematic way on their current, transient state. Hungry people, the argument goes, are better off in a world in which people share. Less hungry people, in contrast, get no benefits from a strong sharing norm; they're doing just fine. Some people might be generally hungrier than others, having limited access to sufficient food from day to day. But everyone, even when generally well fed, is also hungrier and less hungry throughout any given day. Noting this, the researchers compared people who took the survey before lunchtime with people who took it after lunchtime. The results were that, indeed, hungrier people favored transfers more than their less hungry counterparts.[6] These results fit well with the broader literature in social science showing that people's attitudes and preferences can be surprisingly sensitive to context and present state.

In certain respects, our approach sits comfortably with such findings. Being hungry changes—according to this perspective, if only temporarily—one's interests, and policy views are tracking these temporary shifts. Still, if people's views are very sensitive to context or state in this way, then there is less conceptual work to be done by our favored demographic variables that point to more stable strategic interests, a point which we take seriously. Still, a lot more research is needed in order to understand how dynamics in the short term of the course of the day and long term of the course of history affect policy views. In the end, our expectation is that the sorts of variables we've pointed to will continue to predict people's views, on average, despite transient influences of context and state.

Nerd Fight: Contrasts and Connections with Political Science

Our impression of political scientists is that they appear in many different types when it comes to explaining issue opinions, broadly running from those who focus on policy content and demographics to those who focus on abstractions such as ideologies and values. We're obviously much more sympathetic to the former than the latter.

The key debate in these discussions, from our perspective, of course, is how much interests matter in driving political opinions. In chapter 2 we responded to claims that self-interest hardly matters: When we run simple tests of these simple claims, quite often the simple claims are simply untrue. We've focused on expanding the notion of interests and showing how interests express themselves in a wide range of issues, including ones where few researchers have thought to consider interest-based accounts at all.

Another related axis of debate is the extent to which it's useful to view people as primarily "top-down" or "bottom-up" thinkers when it comes to politics. Do people mostly take positions on particular issues by consulting their "higher-level" ideologies, values, and principles? Or do they care mostly about the real-life effects of policies, using those to determine what kinds of ideologies, values, and principles they express in a bottom-up fashion?

While many political scientists endorse the top-down view,[7] we believe people are mostly bottom-up thinkers—we think their mental Boards of Directors care primarily about the effects of policies on themselves, their families, and their wider social networks. This perspective doesn't exclude all top-down processes, however. A person might, for example, have strongly "liberal" views on abortion and related issues for interest-based reasons, and also have strongly "liberal" views on redistributive issues for interest-based reasons. This person might travel in social circles in which people often talk about their own views as "liberal" or "conservative," and would naturally call themselves "liberal" based on the average of their views. And, having identified themselves as a "liberal," the person might adopt more left-leaning positions on other kinds of issues on which their interests don't strongly point one way or another. Is this a top-down or a bottom-up situation? Both, but the dynamic starts with sets of issues on which the person has strong real-world interests and proceeds largely from the bottom up.

Unraveling causality is, of course, tremendously difficult.[8] Studies of political party identifications illustrate the problem. Many political scientists (but not all, of course)[9] view party identifications—thinking of oneself as either a Democrat or a Republican—as a big cause (rather than an effect) of one's positions on particular policy issues. Frequently, the key evidence in favor of such a view is that individuals' party identifications are pretty stable over time, particularly across adulthood.[10]

The problem with this line of reasoning is that a bottom-up, interest-driven view predicts party stability as well. Imagine a person who mostly has opinions that fit with the Democratic party and another person who mostly has opinions that fit with the Republican party. Now imagine that both people change their minds about one or two of their less important issue opinions. Do we expect them to change parties in a bottom-up world? No. If party identifications are essentially *averages* of one's important policy opinions, a number of key issue switches would be required to cause a big change in the overall average represented by a person's party identification.

So, stability of party identifications isn't good evidence in favor of parties-as-causes rather than parties-as-effects because both perspectives predict essentially the same thing. Still, one area where the two approaches do make different predictions involves party-issue realignments: cases in which a party that was once in favor of one policy that is central for some voters changes, adopting the competing policy. In such cases, the top-down, parties-as-causes view seems to predict that most people will change their *policy view* rather than change their *party*. In contrast, the bottom-up, parties-as-effects view predicts that the people who really care about the underlying issue in question should be relatively likely to switch parties (taking into account that party affiliations are driven by the various issue positions that really matter to a given person, and rarely by just one alone).

The recurring line from defenders of the parties-as-causes perspective, then, is problematic. Often they say, essentially: We know that parties are likely to be causes because party affiliations are really stable . . . unless the parties switch positions on issues.[11] Well, OK, which is it? Do people take positions because of party loyalty (in which case they wouldn't tend to switch parties because the party switched issue positions)? Or do they show party loyalty because the party reflects their positions on issues (in which case one *would* see certain population segments switch parties because of an issue realignment)?

One of the clearest modern examples of issue realignment, for example, was spurred by the civil rights acts of the 1960s. From 1876 to 1960, Republican presidential candidates *never* carried the Deep South. In July of 1964, Democrat Lyndon Johnson signed the first major civil rights act. It was opposed by the Republican nominee, Barry Goldwater. A mere four months later, in November, a Republican presidential candidate won the Deep South for the first time in a century, beating a former Texas governor who otherwise won forty-four of the fifty states. Over the next two decades, enormous numbers of Southern whites switched from identifying with the Democratic party to identifying with the Republican party. We take this as perhaps the signature example of how issues might drive people to parties, rather than the reverse.

When it comes to party identifications and ideological labels, we think they can exert substantial causal influence on a range of judgments, particularly in circumstances that are complex or ambiguous with respect to their impact on everyday interests. Even for the kinds of widely debated issues we focus on in this book, party identifications and ideological labels can still operate at the margins. Lots of people care deeply about some set of issues but don't care much about others. There is plenty of room for ideological positions and party preferences to have relatively big effects on issues on which a person otherwise doesn't have strong opinions.

Still, some individuals care deeply about some issues in a way that is basically unconstrained by ideologies and parties, something the 1964 election showed clearly. Does anyone seriously think, for another example, that there wouldn't be a big party shift among Ring-Bearers and Freewheelers if the modern parties switched positions on abortion and related lifestyle issues? Does anyone seriously think that *most* college-educated Freewheelers get their pro-choice positions from the fact that they (for unrelated reasons) started liking Democrats when they were in their twenties? Does anyone seriously think that if the modern parties switched their positions on safety nets that there wouldn't be a big party shift among Johnsons and African Americans? Does anyone seriously think that rich, white men tend to oppose redistribution *mostly because* they like Republicans (for reasons having little to do with their interests)? Does anyone seriously think that poorer African Americans tend to favor public hard-times programs *mostly because* they like Democrats? Or because they were raised to be "liberals"?

We're not taking an extreme position. We're not saying that people never shift their issue opinions based on allegiances to party-based coalitions. In fact, we think they often do shift to some degree, particularly among college-educated whites (who, as we noted in chapter 1, show greater issue coherence across opinion domains), and particularly when it comes to low cost behaviors like answering survey questions. But party affiliation is an implausible theory of the fundamentals—it's an implausible thing to posit as a singularly important Prime Mover.

The causality is even harder to sort through when it comes to "values" and political "personalities" as they relate to policy opinions.[12] This is particularly true given the DERP Syndrome tendencies we discussed in chapter 1. We don't know that it's possible to come up with sufficient strategies to figure out which way the causal arrows point when researchers use a set of survey items on discriminatory policy views to "explain" another set of survey items on discriminatory policy views, or when they use a set of generally worded views about income equality to "explain" another set of views about policies that advance income equality. At any rate, noting a big correlation between two sets of survey items with substantively equivalent content should never be the end point of a scientific inquiry. It's like tethering one hot-air balloon to another and hoping neither floats away.

Indeed, part of the attraction of approaches focused on demographics and interests is that they provide a way out of what are otherwise largely circular discussions. Reducing circularity has a lot to do with what attracts us to evolutionary psychology, economics, and related perspectives. Much of psychology, perhaps understandably, focuses on purely psychological motives. People conform out of a need for conformity. People seek approval out of a need for self-esteem. In contrast, evolutionary and economic approaches are more likely to focus on people's desires to achieve tangible outcomes in their lives. Evolutionary approaches, in particular, seek to tie these desires back to something authentically fundamental—the mechanical tendency within populations of replicators to replace over time less-replicating variants with more-replicating variants. This line of argument constitutes perhaps the only genuine proposal to tie off the "why" questions when it comes to goals and behaviors. At some point in the analysis, the train of "whys" ends with the ultimate (secular) Prime Mover.

Ask many political scientists who take an abstract approach what begins people's train of causality—what causes them to have different ideologies, different party identifications, different values, different political personalities—and the answer is quite often: Because people were raised that way. (Or, to use the fancy term, because of *socialization*.) We find that answer both intellectually unsatisfying and scientifically implausible.[13] Socialization—not to mention its even vaguer cousin, "learning"—is a kind of hypnotic curiosity anesthetic, an answer used to silence question-asking across the social sciences with a simple wave of the hand.

As to its scientific implausibility, the raised-that-way theory is very often undermined when actually tested. Important tests of such matters come from behavioral genetics, typically from studies involving twins. Twins come in two forms, identical and fraternal. In the case of the former, a sperm joins its genetic material with an egg to form a single zygote, and that zygote then splits into two genetically identical copies. Both of the identical zygotes then develop into genetically identical people. In the case of fraternal twins, two different eggs (with different versions of the mother's genes) combine with two different sperm (with different versions of the father's genes) to create two zygotes with the average degree of genetic overlap found in full siblings.

When raised together, twins have more or less all of their raised-that-way features in common—they typically have the same household, the same rearing parents and other family members, the same neighborhood, similar classrooms, similar friends, similar exposure to media, and so forth. When researchers compare identical twins with fraternal twins, then, to the extent that identical twins are more similar than fraternal twins, researchers can make inferences about how much of the variation in their attitudes and behaviors is driven by shared genes rather than shared environments.

A key insight is that children can resemble parents, but there are at least two reasons this might be so. Children might resemble (biological) parents in large part because they have genes in common—tall parents typically produce tall children. And children might resemble (rearing) parents in large part because of raised-that-way factors—English-speaking parents produce English-speaking children.

So what happens when researchers resist the hypnotic pull of raised-that-way stories and put the theory to a proper test? Summarizing a major set of twin studies, a team of political scientists noted, somewhat technically, that the studies "found that approximately half the population variance in a summative measure of political attitudes, the Wilson-Patterson Index, could be attributable to broad-scale heritability; only 11% was attributed to the twins' shared environment, with the rest owing to unshared environment."[14] In other words, genes account for about five times more variation than shared raised-that-way factors when it comes to political attitudes. The authors concluded with the polite but devastating line: "[T]he mainstream socialization paradigm for explaining attitudes and behaviors is not necessarily incorrect but is substantively incomplete."[15] Well, yeah.

Of course we're not saying—nor does anyone seriously believe— that there's a "pro-life gene" or a "health care subsidy gene" or a "school prayer gene." So what does it mean to say that lots of the variation in political views is a function of people's genetic variation? Political scientists have pointed out that perhaps people's genetic differences have to do with things like hormonal differences or perceptual differences, and that, perhaps, some combination of genetic factors influence the kinds of top-down "values" these researchers suppose are the foundations of political views.[16]

From our perspective, we would point out that we've found strong relationships between politics and various demographic items that are clearly related to genes—gender and sexual orientation, for example. In addition, it has long been known (though it is of course controversial) that differences in intellectual talents are in part due to differences in genetic inheritance.[17] Even the kinds of Freewheeler versus Ring-Bearer lifestyles we examined in chapter 4 show clear genetic influence. For example, research has suggested that the reason children of divorced parents are themselves more likely to divorce has a lot to do with genes.[18] In a related vein, people's differing levels of interest in casual sex have more to do with genetic than with raised-that-way factors.[19]

To the extent that many of the demographic features underlying strategic conflicts over policies are themselves substantially genetically influenced, this might help explain the high degree of heritability of many political opinions. This doesn't mean, of course, that a given genotype will reliably, in every place and time, produce an individual who opposes immigration, or supports abortion rights, or finds income redistribution appealing. Instead, it means that many of a person's features that might influence which policies are in their interests in a given place and time are themselves partly genetically influenced. And so, put two people with similar genetic codes into a similar environment, they'll both go through an ongoing process of figuring out the policies that advance their interests, and, to the extent that they started off this figuring-out process with similar interest-relevant features, the resulting political opinions will be similar as well.

Again, we don't view our approach in this book as exhausting the range of interesting factors that influence diverse political opinions. We think of it more as an attempt to adjust the direction of a large ship, even though we may not know the ship's ultimate destination. To the extent that researchers spend much of their efforts thinking that interests don't matter, that most things are driven by socialization, that the most interesting "determinants" of policy views are ideologies, parties, values, and so on, we're saying that they ought to be exploring different waters.

Can we all get along? (Well, you know, probably not.)

We've argued that people—Democrats and Republicans, political elite and the folk—are, in the final analysis, basically self-serving politicians in the worst sense of the word. They fight to advance their interests at others' expense and engage in blatant spin to hide their real motives, usually without even being aware that this is what they're doing. Our view is, almost by definition, a deeply cynical one.

Works that emphasize how both sides of the aisle are equally guilty of sin commonly conclude with a call for greater tolerance and understanding. *By shining additional light on the sources of our political divisions, we hope not to have fanned the flame of discord but rather to have lit the way forward on a path we can all walk together ... blah blah blah.* This general approach was taken (in a much more sophisticated manner, of course) by a number of excellent recent books, including *The Righteous Mind* by psychologist Jonathan Haidt, *The Three Languages of Politics* by economist Arnold Kling, and *Predisposed* by political scientists John Hibbing, Kevin Smith, and John Alford. All these authors express hope that their efforts to enhance mutual understanding might have positive effects, though with enough skepticism to avoid bland naiveté.

We find ourselves unable to follow suit. To borrow a country phrase, we have to dance with the one that brought us. While working together can produce lots of non-zero-sumness—ways we can all be better off— in the end, policies will be set one way or another, and the costs and benefits will be unequally felt. Either abortions will be widely available (in which case Ring-Bearers will have to cope with more Freewheeling neighbors) or they won't be (in which case Freewheelers trying to delay having children will have a tougher time of it). Universities will preferentially admit racial minorities (in which case some whites on the cusp will be denied admission) or they won't (in which case some minorities will be worse off than they otherwise would be). The transfers from some (richer, healthier, younger) to others (poorer, sicker, middle-aged) at the heart of Obamacare will be enhanced, left in place, diminished, or repealed, with each option affecting different people's wallets and well-being differently.

From this perspective, the sharp tone of people's disagreements is in large part a reflection of their different—very real—interests in policy outcomes.

Most people hope for lower volume but higher tones in political arguments; we're not holding our breath. Indeed, we suspect that people often make the case for political tolerance in situations in which their Boards have determined that their favored policies would benefit from tolerance: when, for instance, their favored policy is the status quo and they don't want it disturbed, or when their favored policy is some middle-of-the-road position that requires compromise from the extremes. In other cases, when it serves their policy objectives, people find angry protests, over-the-top accusations, and disruptive parliamentary tactics positively heroic.

A recent case in point: In June of 2013, Republicans in the Texas legislature sought to pass a bill imposing tight restrictions on abortion providers in the state. The Democratic response was a filibuster in the state senate led by Wendy Davis, and a series of disruptive protests. On the right, blogger Erick Erickson from redstate.com cried foul: "What we are seeing is, like in Wisconsin, if the left does not get its way it will hijack the process. The left will disrupt democracy to avoid defeat or ensure a win. The filibuster was not successful so the left caused a mob scene to run the clock out. . . . Last night in Austin, [left-wing activists] showed they'd be fine to [metaphorically burn to the ground] the democratic process."[20]

Erickson called on Texas governor Rick Perry to call a new session of the legislature to pass the anti-abortion law, which he did and it did. It was obvious all along that this would be the ultimate outcome. Does this mean that Wendy Davis had done something futile, something that merely wasted valuable time and resources?

To supporters of abortion rights, not at all. As *New York Times* columnist Gail Collins put it:

> [T]he now-famous 11-hour filibuster by State Senator Wendy Davis defeated a major anti-abortion bill. . . . The next day, however, Gov. Rick Perry announced that he was calling a new special session to take up the bill again. . . . Perhaps she can pull out her pink sneakers and filibuster for two or three weeks. . . . I wouldn't count on it. But that doesn't mean we didn't see something important happen in Austin. . . . [Attempts to limit abortion have] been going on all over the country, and if the high drama in the State Senate in Texas does nothing beyond making the story clear, it'll have done a lot.[21]

So far, we see two "principles" at work. From the right: It's bad to "hijack the process" and "disrupt democracy" to get one's way. From the left: It's good to disrupt the process if it calls attention to one's side.

A mere few months later, there was another dramatic political event, this time in the U.S. Congress. The central provisions of Obamacare were soon to go into effect, and at the same time, the federal budget was to run out. Democrats held the White House and the U.S. Senate, and it was obvious that Republicans did not have anything approaching enough votes to repeal or defund Obamacare.

But now Erickson—he who expressed principled outrage at the idea that anyone might "disrupt democracy to avoid defeat or ensure a win"— was singing an entirely different tune, urging Republican members of Congress to, well, hijack the process: "Our endgame is to leave the whole thing shut down until the President defunds Obamacare. And if he does not defund Obamacare, we leave the whole thing shut down. . . . Hold the line. Undermine Obamacare. Shut it down."[22]

And, of course, Collins now saw things differently as well: "[T]he big obstacle to any progress whatsoever is the small but mighty cadre of Tea Party Republicans in the House. The ones who are trying to tie funding the government to the death of Obamacare. They are egged on by people like Senator Ted Cruz of Texas, who kept his colleagues immobilized this week while he talked for 21 straight hours. . . . Cruz is basically a roadblock with a Princeton debate medal."[23]

It's clear what's going on in cases like these. The real "principle" at stake is that people's priorities usually involve policy substance rather than process or tone. When people are on the policy side that is winning, they want others to play nice and by the rules. They want the losing side to accept defeat gracefully and not cause trouble. But when people are on the policy side that is losing, then all's fair, disruptions and protests are laudable, and the most hard-headed characters refusing to give in despite the obviousness of their pending defeat are the heroes of the story.

Unsurprisingly, in fact, research has shown that different individuals' opposition to and support of lawmakers' filibusters is mostly the result of whether the individuals favor the policy being filibustered and the party doing the filibustering.[24]

In sum, our view suggests that people are mostly strategic beings who look out for their inclusive interests, but also that it will always be a terrible strategic move to admit that in public. The result is likely to be that, while our approach is useful and interesting in trying to understand one's own and other people's political positions, the approach is unlikely to change anything about how people argue publicly about their preferred policies.

In fact, our perspective sheds light on why political arguments typically fail to change people's positions. If we're right, then people with substantial interests at stake shouldn't be easily convinced about, say, basic levels of income redistribution, by logic or evidence. People's positions are often based on their interests, and you can't convince someone (easily) that they should give up their goal of having more rather than less money. Much of the public noise is people shouting post hoc rationalizations at each other, which we would expect to be singularly unimpressive in moving a motivated opponent.

If we're right, why do people even bother arguing? Mostly, we think, it's because there are always victories to be won at the margins. For all the issues we've looked at, there are opposing sides anchored by competing interests at both ends, but also people in the middle who don't have strong interests one way or the other. On sexual and reproductive policies, there are secular Freewheelers and churchgoing Ring-Bearers, but also people in the middle who aren't strongly affected by the competing policy alternatives. On group-based issues, there are people who do well both under meritocratic regimes and under rules allowing for group-based dominance, along with different people who don't do particularly well in either scenario—neither of these groups has strong interest-based reasons to defend one side or the other in these fights. On economic issues, there are people with sets of features that tend not to produce strong opinions—for instance, wealthy minorities, or upper-middle-class white Heathens, or middle-class white Christians.

Attempting to cast one's own strongly held positions in the best possible light helps to recruit to one's side those people without otherwise strong opinions. When political parties pretty evenly divide the population of strong partisans, for example, success in public perception at the margins can be the difference between gaining a bare majority and losing by a nose.

While campaigns may often focus on swing voters with conflicted or middle-of-the-road policy opinions, our efforts have been aimed at explaining the public's passionately held views, the kinds of views that are unlikely to change after watching a thirty-second commercial or scanning a glossy mailing. The tools we have provided are most useful when it comes to figuring out why different groups tend to produce individuals who are primarily driven by a particular set of positions— why Ring-Bearer churchgoers are especially focused on increasing the costs of promiscuity; why professionals and professors who are racial or religious minorities are especially focused on eliminating group-based barriers; why wealthy, white, heterosexual, Christian men are especially focused on reducing government redistribution of wealth; and so on.

Our analysis might not paint the rosiest picture of human nature, or offer the most optimistic view of what is likely to come. It might not provide comforting assurances to partisans that their own side had it right all along, or teach them satisfying new ways to feel superior to their opponents.

But our goal hasn't been to tell people what they want to hear about themselves. Instead, our goal has been to try to account for people's political views in a way that is consistent with psychological science and public opinion data. It would be impossible to achieve both goals simultaneously.

Because people can't be counted on to admit—or even know—the real reasons that underlie their particular positions, we have tried to pull back the veneer of convenient spin. What we find lying beneath—self-interest disguised through self-deception—isn't very pretty.

Which is, of course, why these agendas tend to remain hidden.

Acknowledgments

We owe a debt to several individuals whose comments and conversations helped us develop and improve the book, including, among others, Johnny Carter, Stan Kurzban, Gary Lewis, Justus Myers, Tanya Pazhitnykh, Michael Petersen, Tim Ryan, and Josh Tybur. We've also been very fortunate to have had such a capable and supportive team throughout the publishing process—our special thanks here go to our senior editor at Princeton University Press, Eric Schwartz, and to our copy editor, Marsha Kunin. All errors that remain are, of course, our responsibility alone.

Data Appendix for Chapter 2

A. Fact-Checking Kinder's Self-Interest Claims

1. Race-Based Affirmative Action

In 1994 the GSS asked whites whether they thought it was likely that they or anyone in their families would not get a job or promotion while an equally or less qualified African American receives one instead. Conversely, the GSS asked African Americans whether they thought it was likely that they or anyone in their families would not get a job or promotion while an equally or less qualified white receives one instead. The item is labeled RDISCAFF in the datafile. Respondents were also asked one or both of two substantially similarly worded items (labeled AFFRMACT and JOBAFF in the datafile) recording their support for or opposition to preferences in hiring and promotion of African Americans. We combined these two items into a single measure of opinion on affirmative action.

For the sample of whites and African Americans answering both the RDISCAFF and one or both of the AFFRMACT and JOBAFF items, the correlation between being a white and opposing race-based affirmative action was .51 ($p < .001$; N = 1244). Among whites, the correlation between viewing one's self/family as unlikely to lose a job/promotion to an African American and opposing race-based affirmative action was $-.12$ ($p < .001$; N = 1073). Among African Americans, the correlation between viewing one's self/family as unlikely to lose a job/promotion to a white and opposing race-based affirmative action was .18 ($p = .016$; N = 171).

Table 2A.1 summarizes the results.

Table 2A.1. Summary of Results on Race-Based Affirmative Action

Group	% supporting affirmative action for African Americans	% strongly opposing affirmative action for African Americans
Whites who indicate that it is likely that they or a family member will lose a job or promotion to an African American	8%	77%
Whites who indicate that it is unlikely that they or a family member will lose a job or promotion to an African American	8%	65%
African Americans who indicate that it is unlikely that they or a family member will lose a job or promotion to a white	47%	29%
African Americans who indicate that it is likely that they or a family member will lose a job or promotion to a white	62%	22%

2. Unemployment Benefits

The GSS's primary employment variable (labeled WRKSTAT in the datafile) includes response options for working full-time, working part-time, temporarily not at work (because of illness, vacation, strike), unemployed/laid off/looking for work, retired, in school, keeping house, and other. For these analyses, we compared those working full-time with those unemployed/laid off/looking for work.

In 1985, 1989, 1990, 1996, and 2006, the GSS asked respondents whether they thought that it is the government's responsibility to provide a decent standard of living for the unemployed (labeled AIDUNEMP in the datafile). Among those working full-time and those unemployed, the correlation between being unemployed and believing the government should not provide for the unemployed was $-.14$ (p < .001; N = 3226).

Table 2A.2. Summary of Results on Unemployment Benefits

	Full-time	Unemployed
Government responsibility		
Definitely should be	11%	34%
Probably should be	35%	40%
Probably should not be	35%	20%
Definitely should not be	18%	6%
Spend more or less		
Much more	7%	23%
More	20%	34%
Same as now	50%	32%
Less	17%	11%
Much less	5%	1%

In 1985, 1990, 1996, and 2006, the GSS asked respondents whether they would like more, the same as now, or less government spending on unemployment benefits (labeled SPUNEMP in the datafile). Among those working full-time and those unemployed, the correlation between being unemployed and desiring reduced spending on unemployment benefits was −.13 (p < .001; N = 2604).

Table 2A.2 summarizes the results.

3. Government Health Insurance

In 1998 and 2002 the GSS asked respondents both whether they were covered by health insurance and whether they believed the government has a responsibility to help pay for doctors and hospital bills or whether they believed that people should take care of themselves (labeled HELPSICK in the datafile). The health insurance items (labeled HLTHINSR and HLTHPLAN in the datafile) did not distinguish between those on private or government plans.

To test Kinder's claim about the "medically indigent," we regressed HELPSICK simultaneously on (1) lacking health insurance and (2) family income (gathered from the GSS's INCOME98 variable, recoding the

Table 2A.3. Summary of Results on Government Health Insurance

	Inc. > $50k; Covered (N = 751)	Inc. > $50k; Not covered (N = 50)	Inc. < $50k; Covered (N = 663)	Inc. < $50k; Not covered (N = 164)
1 Responsibility of government to help	23%	44%	33%	43%
2	23%	14%	19%	22%
3 Both	35%	30%	34%	22%
4	10%	10%	6%	9%
5 People should take care of themselves	9%	2%	9%	4%

categories into middle income values per category and adjusting for inflation). In this regression (N = 1628), the standardized coefficient for lacking health insurance was −.09 (p < .001) and for family income was .10 (p < .001).

Table 2A.3 summarizes the results. We split the sample at its median family income of $50,000 as well as whether the respondent had or did not have health coverage.

4. Public School Funding

In 1998 and 2000, the GSS asked respondents whether they have any children older than age five (labeled KID5UP in the datafile) and, if so, whether all their children attend/attended public school for all their elementary and high school education (labeled PUBSCH in the datafile). Over this time period, the GSS asked two substantially similar items about whether "we're spending" too little, too much, or about the right amount of money on education (labeled NATEDUC and NATEDUCY in the datafile).

The GSS PUBSCH variable does not track whether the children are currently enrolled in school, so, to test an approximation of Kinder's claim, we regressed opinions on education spending simultaneously on (1) having or having had children attending exclusively public schools

Table 2A.4. Summary of Results on Public School Funding

	Age < 50; Yes Public (N = 1100)	Age < 50; No Public (N = 1526)	Age 50+; Yes Public (N = 997)	Age 50+; No Public (N = 495)
Spending too little	79%	74%	67%	68%
About right	18%	22%	27%	24%
Spending too much	3%	4%	6%	8%

(as against both those without older children and those whose children did not attend public schools) and (2) age. In this regression predicting opposition to higher funding (N = 4118), having or having had children educated exclusively in public school had a standardized beta of −.06 (p < .001) and age had a standardized beta of .14 (p < .001).

Table 2A.4 summarizes the results, splitting the sample into those above and below age fifty and those whose children exclusively attend/attended public school and those either without school-aged children or whose children did not attend public schools.

5. Working Women

The GSS's primary employment variable (labeled WRKSTAT in the datafile) includes, as described above, categories for full-time employment as well as keeping house. The GSS also contains similar information for the respondents' spouses' employment (labeled SPWRKSTA in the datafile). Along with gender (labeled SEX in the datafile), we used this information to create a variable contrasting (1) women working full-time with (2) women who are married to full-time workers and are keeping house.

We examined three dependent variables. Two of the variables examined opposition to and support for employers hiring and promoting women (labeled FEJOBAFF [asked in 1996 and 2000 through 2010] and FEHIRE [asked in 1996 and 2000 through 2010] in the datafile). The third variable asked about opposition and support for the proposition that women should receive paid maternity leave when they have a baby (labeled MAPAID in the datafile [asked in 1994 and 2002]).

For women, the correlation between opposition to hiring and promoting women and keeping house (versus working full-time) was .03 (p = .193; N = 1388) for FEJOBAFF and .04 (p = .162; N = 1553) for FEHIRE. The correlation between opposition to paid maternity leave and keeping house (versus working full-time) was .01 (p = .840; N = 771).

6. Bilingual Education

In 2000 the GSS included items about speaking languages other than English (labeled OTHLANG, OTHLANG1, and OTHLANG2 in the datafile) as well as an item gauging agreement or disagreement with the statement "Bilingual education programs should be eliminated in American public schools" (labeled NOBILING in the datafile). We used the language items to create two variables, one indicating that the respondent speaks Spanish (in addition to English) and the second indicating that the respondent speaks any language other than Spanish (in addition to English).

We regressed to two language variables on support for bilingual education (N = 1335), resulting in the Spanish-speaking variable having a standardized coefficient of .13 (p < .001) and the other-speaking variable having a standardized coefficient of .04 (p = .123).

Table 2A.5 summarizes the results.

Table 2A.5. Summary of Results on Bilingual Education

	No Spanish; No other (N = 986)	No Spanish; Other (N = 146)	Spanish; Other (N = 56)	Spanish; No other (N = 147)
Strongly agree with eliminating	7%	5%	11%	1%
Agree	17%	15%	11%	12%
Disagree	52%	44%	30%	43%
Strongly disagree with eliminating	24%	36%	48%	45%

7. Gun Control

We used the GSS's primary gun ownership variables (labeled OWNGUN and ROWNGUN in the datafile) to create a variable indicating whether the respondent owned a gun. From 1980 to 2010, the GSS also included an item asking whether the respondent favors or opposes a law requiring a police permit before buying a gun (labeled GUNLAW in the datafile). In 2004, the GSS also included an item asking about agreement or disagreement that there should be more legal restrictions on handguns (labeled HGUNLAW in the datafile). In 2006, the GSS also included four additional gun control items concerning: (1) whether the respondent favors or opposes a law requiring background checks for private gun sales in addition to sales by licensed dealers (labeled GUNSALES in the datafile); (2) whether sales of semiautomatic, assault weapons should be sold to the public or be limited to military and police (labeled SEMIGUNS in the datafile); (3) whether gun control laws should be stricter or less strict as a result of the 9/11 terrorist attacks (labeled GUNS911 in the datafile); and (4) whether high power, 50-caliber rifles should be available to civilians or restricted to police and military (labeled RIFLES50 in the datafile).

Correlations between gun ownership and gun control variables were as follows: (1) for GUNLAW, .26 ($p < .001$; N = 26287); (2) for HGUNLAW, .34 ($p < .001$; N = 860); (3) for GUNSALES, .25 ($p < .001$; N = 858); (4) for SEMIGUNS, −.29 ($p < .001$; N = 852); (5) for GUNS911, .31 ($p < .001$; N = 807); and (6) for RIFLES50, .28 ($p < .001$; N = 862). All correlations were in a direction such that gun ownership signaled increased opposition to gun control.

Table 2A.6 summarizes the results.

8. Socioeconomic Differences

We examined the GSS data from 2002 to 2012. We used the GSS's measure of family income adjusted for inflation (labeled REALINC in the datafile). We looked at two issue items: (1) a recurring item measuring opposition or support for government reduction of income differences (labeled EQWLTH in the datafile), and (2) a recurring item measuring

Table 2A.6. Summary of Results on Gun Control

	Gun owner	Non-owner
GUNLAW: Gun permits		
Favor	60%	85%
Oppose	40%	15%
HGUNLAW: More restrictions on handguns		
Agree	48%	83%
Disagree	52%	17%
GUNSALES: Background checks for private sales		
Strongly favor	45%	68%
Favor	21%	17%
Neither	8%	8%
Oppose	14%	4%
Strongly oppose	12%	3%
SEMIGUNS: Sales of semiautomatic, assault weapons		
Public	32%	9%
Military/police only	68%	91%
GUNS911: Stricter or less strict gun control		
Stricter	61%	89%
Less strict	39%	11%
RIFLES50: Sales of high power, 50-caliber rifles		
Police/Military only	70%	92%
Civilians	30%	8%

whether the respondent thinks the government should be helping the poor or whether they should help themselves (labeled HELPPOOR in the datafile). The correlation between family income and opposition to government reduction of income differences was .21 (p < .001; N = 6866). The correlation between family income and opposition to government helping the poor was .17 (p < .001; N = 6790).

Table 2A.7 summarizes the results, splitting out the sample into family income percentiles.

Table 2A.7. Summary of Results on Income Differences

	Family Income Percentiles					
	Bottom 20%	Next 20%	Middle 20%	Next 20%	Next 10%	Top 10%
EQWLTH						
1 Government should reduce differences	32%	25%	21%	15%	11%	8%
2	9%	10%	9%	9%	10%	6%
3	16%	17%	19%	19%	18%	16%
4	19%	21%	20%	19%	18%	16%
5	11%	12%	13%	15%	17%	16%
6	4%	5%	7%	8%	9%	14%
7 No government action	9%	10%	11%	15%	17%	24%
HELPPOOR						
1 Government action	29%	23%	14%	11%	8%	5%
2	11%	12%	13%	12%	13%	12%
3 Agree with both	43%	46%	48%	44%	46%	44%
4	8%	9%	14%	20%	21%	25%
5 People help selves	9%	10%	11%	13%	12%	14%

B. Regression Exercise with a Constructed Dataset

One of the more common procedures used in studies that seek to draw conclusions about the causes (or origins, determinants, bases, influences, and equivalent terms) of political or moral issue opinions involves regressing a number of predictors simultaneously on the opinion under investigation. The predictors typically include demographic variables like sex, age, race, education, and income along with items often referred to as "symbolic" predictors, including self-placement on general liberal-conservative ideology measures, political party identification, and religiosity. In addition, the predictor sets often include further measures meant to track various interest-based or situational features and more specialized symbolic or value-based scales tracking egalitarianism, authoritarianism, social dominance orientation, racial prejudice, and others.

However, these regression procedures are plainly incapable of differentiating causes from effects. No one denies that correlation does not equate with causation, but the situation is more serious with multiple regressions than with simple correlations, because the entry of substantial effects or noncausal "siblings" of predicted variables as predictors in multiple regressions can wreak havoc on the interpretability of coefficients for other predictor variables in one's model. In political studies claiming on the basis of such regressions to determine which predictors are causally important and which are not, then, not only might the coefficients for symbolic and value predictors be suspect because of direct arguments against their causal role, but the appropriate interpretation of other predictors in the model (like demographic or interest-based predictors) will be savaged if it turns out that the causal assumptions driving the entry of the values and symbolic predictors were untrue.

In what follows, we present results from a constructed dataset intended to mimic some possible features of political studies, but where "causation" is known with certainty. These results provide a straightforward demonstration of the ways in which studies in politics and elsewhere may lead to seriously misleading interpretations in cases where the causal assumptions regarding the variables in question are substantially flawed.

Construction of Dataset

To run the regression exercise, we first created a set of nineteen randomly generated, approximately normally distributed columns of 10,000 numbers each. These initial variables (labeled A1 to A19) were created by averaging in each case a different set of five random number columns using Excel's RAND feature. The result was, as expected, nineteen approximately normally distributed variables that were uncorrelated except for very small, chance correlations.

We then created two variables using only the initial randomly generated variables, with one (labeled B1) being the simple sum of A_1, A_2, A_3, A_4, A_5, A_6, A_7, A_8, A_9, and A_{10}, and the other (labeled B2) being the simple sum of A_1, A_2, A_3, A_4, A_5, A_{11}, A_{12}, A_{13}, A_{14}, A_{15}. Thus, the variables B_1 and B_2 are intended to represent two variables that have half of their causal influences in common (variables A_1 through A_5), but have no direct causal relationship with each other.

In political studies, there are many possible examples of variables with relationships like B_1 and B_2. An example may be opinions on two closely related political issues, like positions on the question of whether the government ought to expand spending on welfare programs and positions on the question of whether the government ought to do more generally to raise standards of living among poor people. Whatever one's views on the causal influences of such policy opinions, they surely share substantial influences. One expects them to correlate highly, then, regardless of whether they have direct causal influence on one another.

Finally, we created an additional variable, labeled C_1, by summing standardized versions of variables A_{16}, A_{17}, A_{18}, A_{19}, and B_1. A real-world example of variables that have similar relationships might be political party identifications as C_1, opinions on governmental redistribution of wealth as B_1, and opinions on abortion legality as A_{16} (and other factors, including error in measuring C_1, as A_{17} through A_{19}). This assumes, of course, a controversial view of the role of political party identifications, but what we mean to show here, in part, is how badly regressions can miss the mark if one's causal assumptions do not hold.

For these regression exercises, we used only variables A_1, A_6, A_{11}, A_{16}, B_1, B_2, and C_1. The idea is to imagine a typical situation in which the researcher has identified and measured an incomplete set of variables that have various direct and indirect relationships—the difference here being that we have a God's-eye view of the underling causal truth. As a summary: A_1 is a 10% cause of both B_1 and B_2; A_6 is a 10% cause of B_1; A_{11} is a 10% cause of B_2; and B_1 and A_{16} are both 20% causes of C_1.

Results for Exercise Focused on Variable C1

We begin with the intuitively simple case where the researcher has focused on explaining C_1, and has measured A_1, A_6, A_{11}, A_{16}, B_1, and B_2 as predictor variables. Table 2B.1 presents the results. The "Direct Causal Role" column is the God's-eye view, which we know here only because this is a constructed dataset—in most studies, of course, this is essentially unknowable in any direct way, and is the situation about

Table 2B.1. Summary of Relationships with Variable C_1

Predictor Variable	Direct Causal Role	Correlation	Multiple Regression	
			Std. Beta	VIF
A1	0%	.15***	.01	1.17
A6	0%	.14***	.00	1.16
A11	0%	.01	.01	1.17
A16	20%	.45***	.45***	1.00
B1	20%	.45***	.46***	1.68
B2	0%	.22***	−.02*	1.68

Note: * p < .05; ** p < .01; *** p < .001.

which we are trying to make useful inferences based on our statistical operations.

The correlations between the predictor variables and C_1 reveal mathematically clear effects of the procedures used to construct the variables. A_{16} and B_1 were among the five essentially uncorrelated variables that were summed to create C_1, and so both should share about 20% of their variance with C_1. Correlations are squared to determine the applicable percentage of variance, and here the correlations between A_1 and B_1 on the one hand and C_1 on the other are indeed around .45, the approximate square root of .20.

C1 also has smaller correlations with A_1 and A_6, because A_1 and A_6 were among the ten essentially uncorrelated variables summed to create B_1, and B_1 was among the five essentially uncorrelated variables summed to create C_1. Each of A_1 and A_6 should share about 10% of their variance with B_1, and B_1 should share about 20% of its variance with C_1, so each of A_1 and A_6 should share about 10% times 20% of their variance with C_1, or about 2% of their variance. The square root of .02 is approximately .14, and, indeed, the correlations between C_1 and both A_1 and A_6 are around .14.

The correlation between C_1 and B_2 is derived from the fact that B_1 and B_2 have half of their causes in common, and so themselves share

25% of their variance (50% times 50%), along with the fact that B_1 and C_1 share 20% of their variance. Thus, the percentage of variance shared between C_1 and B_2 should be around 25% times 20%, or 5%, resulting in a correlation between C_1 and B_2 approximating the square root of .05, or around .22.

While the correlations are somewhat complex, the multiple regression is refreshingly clear and accurate with respect to the underlying causal story. This is the sort of result that multiple regressions are paradigmatically thought of as producing. The regression reveals that once A_{16} and B_1 are taken into account in predicting C_1, the other correlated predictors add essentially no variance. Further, the standardized coefficients for A_{16} and B_1 are commensurate with their actual, direct causal influence. The only wrinkle in the model is that the small negative coefficient for B_2 in the regression reaches the commonly accepted significance level of .05, but this is noise and should urge caution over the extent to which one should press interpretations of marginally significant findings.

We have also presented variance inflation factors (VIFs) for the regression coefficients. VIFs are a commonly used diagnostic statistic that can reveal problematic colinearity among predictor variables. VIFs closer to 1.00 show minimal colinearity problems, while VIFs above about 10.00 reveal problematic colinearity. The VIF statistics in the regression in table 2B.1 show that the correlations among the predictors have not resulted in problematic colinearity.

In a typical report of data of the kind presented here, the researcher might say something like this:

> In our study of C_1, we found a number of significant correlates among our predictors, but a multiple regression analysis revealed that only A_{16} and B_1 were substantial independent contributors. When controlling for A_{16} and B_1, we found that A_1, A_6, A_{11}, and B_2 play little or no direct role in accounting for C_1.

Given our God's-eye view, we know that this interpretation is indeed accurate. The multiple regression performed a useful service in eliminating correlates that were not direct contributors to C_1 and further highlighting the appropriate interpretation of the data.

Results for Exercise Focused on Variable B_1

We now present a case where the researcher has focused on explaining B_1, and has measured A_1, A_6, A_{11}, A_{16}, B_2, and C_1 as predictor variables. Table 2B.2 presents the results.

The correlations with B_1 are mathematically simple to understand given our God's-eye view. A_1 and A_6 are among the ten essentially uncorrelated items summed to create B_1, and indeed both share about 10% of their variance with B_1, resulting in correlations around .32. B_1 and B_2 share no direct relationship, but each shares with the other half of its causal variables, resulting in their sharing 25% of their variance (50% times 50%), which is marked by a correlation around .50. Lastly, B_1 is among the five essentially uncorrelated items summed to create C_1, and so B_1 and C_1 share about 20% of their variance, resulting in a correlation of approximately .45.

Unlike the regression of the selected variables on C_1, the regression of these items on B_1 shown in table 2B.2 reveals not causal accuracy or clarity but produces starkly misleading complexity given typical assumptions about what regressions show. Variables that we know to be related to B_1 but not causal (B_2 and C_1) carry the largest coefficients, variables that we know to be causal (A_1 and A_6) are deflated in impor-

Table 2B.2. Summary of Relationships with Variable B_1

Predictor Variable	Direct Causal Role	Correlation	Multiple Regression Std. Beta	VIF
A1	10%	.32***	.13***	1.13
A6	10%	.31***	.25***	1.03
A11	0%	.00	−.14***	1.13
A16	0%	.00	−.17***	1.27
B2	0%	.51***	.43***	1.31
C1	0%	.45***	.37***	1.38

Note: * p < .05; ** p < .01; *** p < .001.

tance (especially A_1, which shares substantial variance with B_2), and two variables we know to be utterly unrelated to B_1 (A_{11} and A_{16}) carry significant coefficients.

There is nothing technically wrong with the regression formula that produced table 2B.2. It is not bothered by problematic colinearity and is mathematically sound. It shows, simply, the most efficient way to predict values for B_1 using the predictor set. For example, one of the most potentially confusing aspects of the regression—the significant coefficients for A_{11} and A_{16}—results from ordinary algebra. Recall that C_1 was constructed by summing B_1, A_{16}, A_{17}, A_{18}, and A_{19}. So, $C_1 = B_1 + A_{16} + A_{17} + A_{18} + A_{19}$. Solve for B_1 and the equation becomes: $B_1 = C_1 - A_{16} - A_{17} - A_{18} - A_{19}$. Thus, when we regress variables on B_1 that include C_1, the regression formula is enhanced to the extent it backs out those aspects of C_1 not related to B_1 to highlight the shared variance between C_1 and B_1. The story is similar with respect to A_{11}. Recall that B_1 and B_2 have causes in common (A_1 through A_5), but that B_1 also includes separate causes (A_6 through A_{10}), as does B_2 (A_{11} through A_{15}). Thus, when B_2 is used to help build a formula to predict B_1, that formula is enhanced to the extent that, once B_2 is in the model, the independent elements in B_2 (like A_{11}) are backed out through offsetting coefficients.

Another plainly problematic aspect of the model from the point of view of interpretation is the low regression coefficient for A_1 despite our God's-eye knowledge that it was in fact one of the elements used to build B_1. But the low coefficient is a clear mathematical outcome given the presence of B_2 in the predictor set. Basically, B_2 necessarily achieves a large coefficient in this predictor set because it shares much variance with B_1 through their common causes in A_1 through A_5. When B_2 is allocated a coefficient, that coefficient simultaneously highlights the roles of A_1 through A_5, and therefore the need to allocate an independent coefficient to A_1 is diminished. The coefficient for A_6 is much less diminished than that of A_1, even though A_1 and A_6, we know from our God's-eye perspective, played equal roles in producing B_1. This is because, unlike for A_1, there are no variables like B_2 in the model with respect to A_6 that would serve to draw variance so directly away from A_6 (though C_1, being in part a direct product of B_1, will draw some predictive variance away simultaneously from smaller causes of B_1).

Without the benefit of our God's-eye view, a typical report of the multiple regression for B_1 might read as follows:

> In a multiple regression analysis, we found that the primary determinants of B_1 are B_2 and C_1. A_6 also plays a role in determining B_1, as do A_{16}, A_{11}, and A_1, though their effects are small. While other studies have not been consistent in finding effects for A_{16} and A_{11} in explaining B_1, our regression shows the importance of appropriate controls in highlighting their significant effects.

Given our God's-eye view, we know that such a report is riddled with serious problems to the point, indeed, of *having done more harm than good in understanding the "origins" of B_1*, which included A_1 and A_6 but none of the other variables discussed.

Lessons from the Regression Exercise

It has been common practice in political studies to acknowledge to some extent that differing causal interpretations exist, but to let some form of multiple regression help to justify conclusions as to which interpretations are more plausible. Nonetheless, we have provided regression exercises from a constructed dataset to demonstrate clearly that such conclusions are not likely justified. Despite the sophistication of multiple regressions, one cannot be assured that the coefficients they produce accurately pick out direct causes from noncausal correlates where realistic levels of causal complexity are involved.

One caution from the constructed exercise is this: *The biggest predictors in a multiple regression are not necessarily the ones that indicate direct causal influence.* We provided two examples of large but noncausal predictors in the regression predicting B_1 (table 2B.2 above), one of which was in fact an effect rather than a cause of B_1 and the other of which was a variable that shared substantial causes with B_1 but played no role in causing it (a kind of "sibling" variable).

A second caution is in large part the reverse of the first: *When a predictor variable fails to account for substantial variance in a multiple regression, especially if it has a larger bivariate relationship with the predicted variable, one does not necessarily know that the predictor variable has not played a substantial direct causal role in producing the predicted variable.* In particular, the regression exercise in table 2B.2 presents an example (involving B_2 and A_1 simultaneously predicting B_1) in which a causal variable appeared to have been "mediated" by a noncausal one when used simultaneously in a regression.

The regressions also contained at least one additional caution. We demonstrated cases with the constructed dataset (in table 2B.2 involving C_1 and A_{16} simultaneously predicting B_1 as well as B_2 and A_{11} simultaneously predicting B_1) in which predictors that were utterly unrelated to and rightly uncorrelated with the predicted variable nonetheless had solidly significant coefficients in a multiple regression.

Such demonstrations are likely to be highly relevant to studies in which researchers use strongly related scales, one as the predicted variable and the other as a predictor variable, in multiple regressions containing several demographic and other variables. Often in such studies the demographic variables have reduced significance and the related scales have substantial significance in multiple regressions, even when the demographic variables seemed somewhat promising when viewed as bivariate correlates. As our constructed demonstration has shown, however, the outcome that is supposedly demonstrated by such studies is actually the very thing one must *assume* to justify the interpretation in the first place. It may be that many such cases are uninteresting examples of predictor variables that share much causal origin with the predicted variable, and so soak up variance from the smaller causes the two share in multiple regressions. In extreme examples, indeed, the predicting scales contain items virtually indistinguishable from the predicted item—they're more than "siblings," they're "twins."

Data Appendix for Part II

A. U.S. General Social Survey

For Part II of the book, our primary data source for the United States was the U.S. General Social Survey, combining years 2002 to 2012. Overall, there were 16,128 individuals in this dataset.

1. Predictor Variables

For our predictor variables, we created sets of categories, each coded from 0 to 1. Our names for the variables indicate the direction of the coding—e.g., when we refer to "Born outside the U.S.," the coding is such that 1 indicates born outside the U.S. and 0 indicates *not* born outside the U.S. Missing data generally received a "0" code; e.g., in our series regarding family income, a contrast between "Family income in top 20%" and others is between those in the top 20% and both those in the bottom 80% and those with missing data.

The following table provides a description of the GSS variables we used to create our predictor variables, the procedures we used to transform the GSS variables, and the resulting variable names used in the part II data analyses.

2. Issue Variables

We examine a number of issue opinions. The GSS variables are as follows:

- In chapter 4: views on premarital sex (PREMARSX); views on the legality of pornography (PORNLAW); views on the legality of abortion (ABDEFECT, ABNOMORE, ABHLTH, ABPOOR, ABRAPE, ABSINGLE, ABANY); views on birth control for teenagers without parents' consent (PILLOK, PILLOKY); views on the legality of marijuana (GRASS).
- In chapter 5: views on speeches, teaching, and books by those against religion (SPKATH, COLATH, LIBATH); views on speeches,

GSS Variables	Procedure	Resulting Variables
PARBORN	Information on whether parents were born in the U.S. recoded to indicate whether both parents (or only parent known) were foreign-born (1), whether only one parent was foreign-born (.5), or whether neither parent (or only parent known) was foreign-born (0).	Parents born outside the U.S.
BORN	Recoded to indicate foreign birth.	Born outside the U.S.
REG16	Information on place of residence at age 16 was used to create a categorical variable indicating foreign residency in childhood.	Raised outside the U.S.
RACE; HISPANIC; RACECEN1; RACECEN2; RACECEN3; ETHNIC; ETH1; ETH2; ETH3; HHRACE	Each set of race/ethnicity variables was coded to indicate either African, Asian, white/European, Latin American, or other ancestry, with 1 meaning the source variable indicated 100% inclusion in that category, 0 meaning the source variable indicated no inclusion in that category, and intermediate values meaning mixed responses. E.g., in response to the RACE source variable, a person coded as "White" would receive 1 for White with regard to the RACE variable and 0 for all other categories with regard to the RACE variable. E.g., if a person indicated in the ethnicity source variables (ETHNIC, ETH1, et al.) that their ancestors were from both Asia and Africa, the person would receive .5 for Asian with respect to the ethnicity variables, .5 for African with respect to the ethnicity variables, and 0 for all other categories with respect to the ethnicity variables. Lastly, measures from the categories resulting from each source variable were averaged, leaving a set of variables for each individual indicating, roughly, the proportion (from 0 to 1) of ancestry for the different regions.	African American; Asian American; Latino American; Other American; White
SEX	Information regarding sex was recoded into a variable with 1 indicating female and 0 indicating male.	Female

(continues)

GSS Variables	Procedure	Resulting Variables
AGE	Information regarding age was recoded into overlapping categories.	Age 18 to 29; Age 18 to 39; Age 50+; Age 65+
EDUC; DEGREE	Information regarding years of schooling and degrees was combined to create overlapping categories.	High school diploma or more; Some college or more; Bachelor's degree or more; Graduate degree
ODDS1; ODDS2; HOTCORE; RADIOACT; BOYORGRL; LASERS; ELECTRON; VIRUSES; EARTHSUN; SOLARREV; WORDA; WORDB; WORDC; WORDD; WORDE; WORDF; WORDG; WORDH; WORDI; WORDJ	The GSS has included tests of scientific knowledge and general vocabulary. Each item was recoded such that correct answers were coded 1 and incorrect answers and "don't know" responses were coded 0. Each item was standardized and the full set was averaged to create a single measure of test performance. Four overlapping variables were created from the overall average.	Test performance in bottom 20%; Test performance in bottom 40%; Test performance in top 40%; Test performance in top 20%
RELIG	Information regarding religious preference was recoded into mutually exclusive categorical variables indicating no religious affiliation, Catholic, non-Catholic Christian (including Protestant, Orthodox Christian, Christian, and inter- or nondenominational), Jewish, and other ("Other religion" includes, e.g., Muslims, Hindus, Buddhists, etc.).	No religion; Catholic; Non-Catholic Christian; Jewish; Other religion
	From the religion variables, No religion, Jewish, and Other religion were combined into a single category for non-Christians.	Not Christian
ATTEND	Information regarding attendance at religious services was recoded into overlapping categories.	Church several times a year or more; Church about once a month or more; Church 2 to 3 times a month or more; Church about once a week or more; Church more than once a week

Variable	Description	Categories
SEX; SEXSEX18; SEXSEX; NUMWOMEN; NUMMEN; SEXSEX5; SEXORNT	Each set of sexual activity/preference variables was coded to indicate same-sex activity/preference, with 1 indicating only same-sex activity/preference, 0 indicating only opposite-sex activity/preference, and intermediate values indicating bisexual activity/preference. The resulting variables were then averaged into a single measure of same-sex activity/preference.	Lesbian/gay/bisexual
PARTOPN5; PARTNRS5	Information regarding number of sex partners in the past five years was recoded into three variables.	No sex partners in past five years; 1 sex partner in past five years; 2 or more sex partners in past five years
NUMWOMEN; NUMMEN	Information regarding number of sex partners since age 18 was recoded into four overlapping variables.	No sex partners since age 18; 1 sex partner since age 18; 2 or more sex partners since age 18; 5 or more sex partners since age 18
SOCBAR	Information on how often the respondent goes to a bar or tavern was recoded into two variables.	Has not been to a bar in the past year; Went to bars about once a month or more in the past year
REALINC	Information regarding family income (adjusted for inflation) was recoded into five overlapping variables.	Family income in bottom 20%; Family income in bottom 40%; Family income in top 40%; Family income in top 20%; Family income in top 10%
REALRINC	Information regarding the respondents' personal income (adjusted for inflation) was recoded into five overlapping variables.	Personal income in bottom 20%; Personal income in bottom 40%; Personal income in top 40%; Personal income in top 20%; Personal income in top 10%

(continues)

GSS Variables	Procedure	Resulting Variables
MARITAL; DIVORCED; WIDOWED; POSSLQ; POSSLQY; HHTYPE1	Information regarding marriage, divorce, widowhood, and cohabitation was combined to create a series of overlapping variables.	Never married (the opposite of which is "Ever married"); Married; Ever divorced or separated; Ever married and never divorced; Ever widowed; Nonmarital cohabitation (limited to those currently cohabiting)
CHILDS	Information on number of children ever born to respondent was used to create overlapping categories.	No children; 1 or more children; 2 or more children; 3 or more children
REGION	Information on the region in which the interview took place was recoded into three variables: New England and Middle Atlantic; South Atlantic, East South Central, West South Central; and Pacific.	Northeast region; South region; Pacific region
XNORCSIZ; SRCBELT; SIZE	Three measures of population density or urban/rural residence were standardized and averaged into a single measure used to create four overlapping categories.	Population density in bottom 20%; Population density in bottom 40%; Population density in top 40%; Population density in top 20%
WRKSTAT; HRS2	Information on work status used to create variable indicating whether respondent is currently employed (including self-employed) or not.	Employed
SPWRKSTA; SPHRS2	Information on spouse work status used to create two variables: whether respondent is married and spouse works and whether respondent is married and spouse does not work.	Married to a person who is employed; Married to a person who is not employed
WRKSTAT; SPWRKSTAT	Information on respondent and spouse was used to create a variable indicating that either the respondent or their spouse is unemployed and looking for work.	Unemployed
UNION; MEMUNION	Information on union membership was used to create a variable indicating that either the respondent or their spouse is a union member.	Union household
WRKSELF; SPWRKSLF	Information on self-employment was used to create a variable indicating that either the respondent or their spouse is self-employed.	Self-employed household

teaching, and books by homosexuals (SPKHOMO, COLHOMO, LIBHOMO); views on speeches, teaching, and books by anti-American Muslims (SPKMSLM, COLMSLM, LIBMSLM); views on school prayer (PRAYER); views on same-sex marriage (MARHOMO); views on the morality of homosexuality (HOMOSEX); views on immigration levels (LETIN1); views on gender-based affirmative action (FEJOBAFF, FEHIRE); views on race-based affirmative action (AFFRMACT); views on government assistance for African Americans (HELPBLK); views on government spending on African Americans (NATRACE, NATRACEY); views on the death penalty (CAPPUN); views on police striking citizens (POLHITOK, POLHITOY).

- In chapter 6: views on government reduction of income differences (EQWLTH); views on government help for the poor (HELPPOOR); views on government spending on welfare and the poor (NATFARE, NATFAREY); views on government help for medical care (HELPSICK); views on government spending on health care (NATHEAL, NATHEALY); views on government spending on Social Security (NATSOC); views on government spending on education (NATEDUC, NATEDUCY); views on government spending on child care (NATCHLD).

3. Multiple Regressions

For each issue variable, we used the full predictor set (except as otherwise noted) to create a regression equation to predict the issue variable.

We recoded the issue variables as response percentiles such that higher values closer to 100 indicate "liberal" responses and lower values closer to 0 indicate "conservative" responses. We'll go through one example in detail. In chapter 4 we examine views toward premarital sex. The weighted (using the WTSSALL variable) response percentages for PREMARSX are as follows: 24.1% say premarital sex is "always wrong," 7.8% say "almost always wrong," 17.9% say "sometimes wrong," and 50.2% say "not wrong at all." We recoded these responses as 12.05 for "always wrong," 28 for "almost always wrong," 40.85 for "sometimes wrong," and 74.9 for "not wrong at all." In other words, the resulting re-codes indicate the liberal percentile of the respondent on the item. E.g., the most conservative response was "always wrong," 24.1% gave this response, and thus these respondents are at the 12.05 percentile (on a 100-point percentile scale) in their liberalness.

For issue variables including more than one GSS item (e.g., our overall abortion variable, which combined seven specific abortion attitude measures), we standardized the base variables, averaged them, and used the single average to create percentile scores.

Thus, each issue variable involved in the multiple regressions in part II is coded consistently (on the same percentile scale and in the same liberal/conservative direction). The benefits of this continuity are primarily that, because all predictors are simple categories running from 0 to 1, and because we report unstandardized coefficients, it is a simple matter to compare effect sizes across predictor variables and across different issues. If a predictor has a coefficient of (positive) 5.0 in a particular regression model, for example, it simply means that, taking into account the other predictors in the model, the presence of this predictor category is associated with a 5-percentile increase in the liberalness of responses.

For the "Top 5" model for a particular issue, we used stepwise regression procedures to identify the top five predictors in terms of the absolute values of their unstandardized coefficients (without considering any interactions). This generally involved running forward stepwise procedures including all predictors with p-values < .001, and then eliminating those with the smallest unstandardized coefficients in stepwise fashion until only five were left.

For the "Full" model for a particular issue, we engaged in stepwise regression procedures across the predictor batch, first identifying substantial predictors from among the set, then testing interactions among the major initial predictors, then running a final procedure including the major interaction terms along with the full set of potential predictors again. We used cutoffs both in terms of p-values (generally excluding predictor variables with p > .001) and in terms of absolute values of the unstandardized coefficients, discarding subpar predictor variables through stepwise procedures. The resulting full regression models, then, provide equations for predicting the given issue variables limited to the most substantial set of predictors.

The initial value presented in each model is the intercept (and so applies to everyone in the sample); each subsequent value is the unstandardized coefficient for the adjacent predictor variable (and so applies in full to those who are members of the relevant category and not at all to those who are not members of the relevant category, given that each predictor variable is coded from 0 to 1). In the "Full" models, interaction terms are also included when applicable. These are marked by an "&" between two variables. With interactions, the coefficient applies to those possessing both features, and does not apply otherwise.

4. Interpreting the Models

Estimating outcomes for groups with varying characteristics is straightforward using the regression models in the appendixes for chapters 4, 5, and 6. We'll go through one example here, the full model estimating views on government redistribution of income from the chapter 6 appendix, reproduced here:

Government Equalize Incomes—Full Model

56.8

13.2 Age 65+ & Personal income in top 40%

7.3 Not Christian & Bachelor's degree or more

7.1 Graduate degree

6.4 Bachelor's degree or more & Test in top 20%

5.8 African American

5.0 White & Family income in bottom 40%

4.2 Union household

3.7 Family income in bottom 20%

3.4 Not Christian

2.2 Personal income in bottom 40%

−0.6 Family income in bottom 40%

−1.9 Personal income in top 40%

−4.9 Personal income in top 20%

−4.9 Self-employed household

−6.4 Bachelor's degree or more

−6.8 Age 65+

−7.4 Test in top 20%

−7.7 African American & Personal income in bottom 40%

−8.7 White

−9.4 Family income in top 10%

Let's say one wanted to know the typical views on income redistribution among people matching the demographic characteristics of Paul Ryan (the Republican nominee for vice president in 2012 and current U.S. representative). To do so, one would simply add (or subtract) the values that apply in this case. Based on our information and assumptions about Paul Ryan, the highlighted terms apply to him:

Government Equalize Incomes—Full Model

56.8

13.2 Age 65+ & Personal income in top 40%

7.3 Not Christian & Bachelor's degree or more

7.1 Graduate degree

6.4 Bachelor's degree or more & Test in top 20%

5.8 African American

5.0 White & Family income in bottom 40%

4.2 Union household

3.7 Family income in bottom 20%

3.4 Not Christian

2.2 Personal income in bottom 40%

−0.6 Family income in bottom 40%

−1.9 Personal income in top 40%

−4.9 Personal income in top 20%

−4.9 Self-employed household

−6.4 Bachelor's degree or more

−6.8 Age 65+

−7.4 Test in top 20%

−7.7 African American & Personal income in bottom 40%

−8.7 White

−9.4 Family income in top 10%

So, the result for Paul Ryan's demographic features: 56.8 + 6.4 − 1.9 − 4.9 − 6.4 − 7.4 − 8.7 − 9.4 = 24.5. This doesn't mean that Paul Ryan himself is expected to have this exact outcome, only that this value approximates the average result for people who shared his demographic features in the GSS sample.

Note a couple of interpretive features of the model. First, to figure out interaction terms, one must focus on the interaction term (e.g., "Bachelor's degree or more & Test in top 20%") as well as on its two separate components (in this example, both "Bachelor's degree or more" alone and "Test in top 20%" alone). It would be tempting to conclude that people with both bachelor's degrees and top 20% test performance are more liberal on this item (given the positive coefficient on the interaction term "Bachelor's degree or more & Test in top 20%"), but here one has to keep in mind that both bachelor's degrees and high test performance carry individual negative coefficients. In this case, what the interaction term should be thought of as saying is something like: Having a bachelor's degree is associated with being more conservative on income redistribution, and having top 20% test performance is associated with being more conservative on income redistribution, but having both simultaneously isn't associated with being doubly conservative.

Second, as we mentioned earlier, many of our predictor variables are nonexclusive categories. So, for example, in this case, we assumed that Paul Ryan's personal income is in the top 20%. Incomes in the top 20% are also in the top 40%. Therefore, in calculating the results for his demographic, one needs to include the coefficient for "Personal income in top 20%" as well as the coefficient for "Personal income in top 40%" to take into account the full effect of his personal income.

As a general matter, one can know that the result for the Paul Ryan demographic of 24.5 indicates substantially conservative views on average relative to the full sample. As we described, each issue variable has been recoded on a 100-point liberalness percentile scale (such that the middle of the sample is by definition 50, lower numbers are more conservative, and higher numbers are more liberal). One can look at the "Groups" tables below the regression model to figure out exactly what a number like 24.5 implies about a given issue. In this case, here's the relevant table from the chapter 6 appendix:

The most conservative response shown involves "No government action" and contains 21% of the full sample. Thus, people answering at this end were coded around 10.5 on our recoded scale (i.e., the midpoint of this 21%). People answering at the center point of this item received 43.5, given that 34% were more conservative and 19% landed in the middle—so, 34 plus half of 19 is 43.5. This means, then, that the Paul Ryan group's result of 24.5 indicates that these individuals typically lean toward responses preferring no government action to reduce income differences.

An easier way to cut to the chase, of course, is simply to refer to the "Groups" table independently of the regression models. Here, if we were thinking of Paul Ryan's demographic, our best guess is that he resides in

Government Equalize Incomes—Groups

Group	Gov. reduce diff.	3	4	5	No gov. action
All	30%	17%	**19%**	13%	21%
Latino/Asian/other American; Parent(s) born outside the U.S.; No high school diploma	47%	**15%**	20%	8%	10%
African American	44%	**15%**	22%	9%	10%
White; Family income in bottom 40%; Heterosexual; Christian; Age 18–64; Has children	37%	**18%**	19%	14%	12%
Latino/Asian/other American; Parent(s) born outside the U.S.; High school diploma or more	31%	**23%**	21%	12%	13%
White; Income in bottom 90%; Not heterosexual and/or not Christian	36%	**19%**	18%	12%	15%
White; Family income in bottom 40%; Heterosexual; Christian; Age 18–64; No children	26%	**25%**	18%	12%	19%
Latino/Asian/other American; Parents born in the U.S.	33%	**17%**	**22%**	12%	16%
White; Family income in bottom 40%; Heterosexual; Christian; Age 65+	28%	10%	**22%**	15%	25%
White; Income in upper-middle 50%; Heterosexual; Christian; Age 18–64; Not self-employed household	24%	18%	**18%**	16%	24%
White; Income in top 10%; Not heterosexual and/or not Christian	22%	18%	**14%**	10%	36%
White; Income in upper-middle 50%; Heterosexual; Christian; Age 65+	19%	13%	**21%**	15%	32%
White; Income in upper-middle 50%; Heterosexual; Christian; Age 18–64; Self-employed household	17%	12%	20%	**14%**	37%
White; Income in top 10%; Heterosexual; Christian	11%	14%	17%	**18%**	40%

the bottom group (White; Income in top 10%; Heterosexual; Christian), and we can see directly the actual (not estimated, but actual) percentage responses from the GSS sample. In this case, 58% of the Paul Ryan demographic group leans toward wanting no government action to reduce income disparities, 17% are in the middle, and 25% lean toward wanting government action. In these tables, we have often **bolded** the median outcome for the different groups. Note that the percentages in the "Groups" tables throughout (as well as in the tables in the appendixes for chapter 8 and chapter 9) are weighted using the WTSSALL variable in the GSS datafile.

In the text of the book we mostly limit our discussions to the information in the "Groups" tables, because these tables provide easy-to-understand information that, in an important sense, is what it is—there's no complex model with various assumptions underlying the result, but instead just a simple statement of fact: When we isolate different subgroups in the GSS data, we get the described response percentages. The regression models are included for those who want to go deeper and understand how individual predictor variables are collectively driving the group outcomes.

B. World Values Survey

For international comparisons in part II of the book, used the World Values Survey (WVS), combining years 1994 to 2008. Overall, there were 262,842 individuals in the dataset.

1. Predictor Variables

For our predictor variables, we created sets of categories, each coded from 0 to 1. Our names for the variables indicate the direction of the coding—e.g., when we refer to "Education in bottom 20%," the coding is such that 1 indicated education levels in the bottom 20% of the sample and 0 indicated education levels not in the bottom 20% (i.e., those in the top 80%).

The following table provides a description of the WVS variables we used to create our predictor variable set, the procedures we used to transform the WVS variables, and the resulting variable names used in the part II data analyses.

WVS Variables	Procedure	Resulting Variables
S003; S003a	Information on country in which the survey was given was used to code those in Western countries, including (1) those in Europe outside of the former Eastern Bloc, (2) those in the United States and Canada, and (3) those in Australia and New Zealand.	Western
S003; S003a	Information on country in which the survey was given was used to code those in the United States.	United States
A006; A060; A065; A098; F024; F028; F034; F050; F063; F065; F067	Measures of religiosity were standardized and averaged into a single measure used to create four overlapping categories.	Religiosity in bottom 20%; Religiosity in bottom 40%; Religiosity in top 40%; Religiosity in top 20%
X023; X024; X025	Measures of education level were standardized and averaged into a single measure used to create four overlapping categories.	Education in bottom 20%; Education in bottom 40%; Education in top 40%; Education in top 20%
G005; G017; G026; G027	Information on immigration, citizenship, and parental immigration was combined into a single measure of immigrant/noncitizen status. Respondents were given a 1 if any of the following applied: (1) they indicated they were an immigrant, (2) they indicated they were not a citizen of their country of residence, (3) they indicated that both of their parents were immigrants.	Immigrant

WVS Variables	Procedure	Resulting Variables
C006; X047	Measures of satisfaction with financial situation and scale of income were standardized and averaged into a single measure used to create four overlapping categories.	Income in bottom 20%; Income in bottom 40%; Income in top 40%; Income in top 20%

2. Issue Variables

For the WVS sample, we combined multiple items into single-issue variables. In each case individual WVS items were standardized and averaged into a single measure; the issue variable was then recoded as response percentiles such that higher values closer to 100 indicate "liberal" responses and lower values closer to 0 indicate "conservative" responses.

WVS Variables	Resulting Variables
A048; A049; F120	Abortion views
F102; F107; F112	Tolerance of the nonreligious
C002; E143; G032	Tolerance of immigrants
E035; E037	Economic views

3. Multiple Regressions

Our demographic predictor sets were limited based on the issue variable. For abortion views, we included only religiosity and education measures as potential predictors. For tolerance of the nonreligious, we included only religiosity and education measures as potential predictors. For tolerance of immigrants, we included only immigration and education measures as potential predictors. For economic views, we included only income and education as potential predictors.

We also included our categorical variables for Western and United States in each regression, as well as the interactions between these and each of the demographic variables specified above.

We engaged in stepwise procedures across the predictor batch. We used cutoffs both in terms of p-values (generally excluding predictor variables with p > .001) and in terms of absolute values of the unstandardized coefficients, discarding subpar predictor variables. The resulting full regression models, then, provide equations for predicting the given issue variables limited to the most substantial set of predictors.

Data Appendix for Chapter 4

SEE THE DATA APPENDIX FOR PART II for general comments about variables and methods.

A. U.S. General Social Survey

Freewheeler and Ring-Bearer Categories

For some of the group-based tables below, we use simple categories, determined as follows:

- Add one point for: 5+ sex partners since age 18; Went to bars about once a month or more in the past year; Lesbian/gay/bisexual; Nonmarital cohabitation
- Subtract one point for: None or 1 sex partner since age 18; Has not been to a bar in the past year

1 or more = Freewheeler lifestyle
0 = Middle lifestyle
−1 or below = Ring-Bearer lifestyle

	% of weighted sample	Age (middle 50%)	Female
Freewheeler lifestyle	39%	30 to 51	44%
Middle lifestyle	27%	33 to 58	55%
Ring-Bearer lifestyle	34%	34 to 64	66%

Issue Models and Groups (Excluding Religious Variables)

Premarital Sex—Top 5 Model (excluding religious variables)

53.4

7.9 Nonmarital cohabitation

7.8 5+ sex partners since age 18

−6.3 1 sex partner since age 18

−7.1 No sex partners since age 18

−11.6 Has not been to a bar in the past year

Premarital Sex—Full Model (excluding religious variables)

60.1

10.1 1 sex partner since age 18 & Never married

7.5 Female & Graduate degree

7.4 Nonmarital cohabitation & Has not been to a bar in the past year

6.3 5+ sex partners since age 18

4.7 Family income in top 10%

4.5 Northeast region

2.8 Nonmarital cohabitation

−0.5 Never married

−1.9 Graduate degree

−3.5 Female

−3.8 Ever married and never divorced

−4.4 Ever widowed

−4.8 Population density in bottom 20%

−5.1 African American

−5.4 Married to person who is not employed

−5.7 South region

−6.9 1 sex partner since age 18

−8.9 No sex partners since age 18

−9.2 Has not been to a bar in the past year

Table 4A.2. Premarital Sex—Groups (excluding religious variables)

Group	Not wrong at all	Sometimes wrong	Almost always wrong	Always wrong
All	**50%**	**18%**	8%	24%
Freewheeler lifestyle	**67%**	18%	5%	10%
Middle lifestyle	**52%**	20%	7%	21%
Ring-Bearer lifestyle	34%	**17%**	10%	39%

Pornography—Top 5 Model (excluding religious variables)

55.5

  7.5 2+ sex partners in past five years

  7.2 Lesbian/gay/bisexual

−7.2 Has not been to a bar in the past year

−8.2 Female

−8.8 Age 65+

Pornography—Full Model (excluding religious variables)

55.7

  8.1 Age 18–29

  6.3 5+ sex partners since age 18

  5.6 Lesbian/gay/bisexual

  5.0 Graduate degree

  4.5 2+ sex partners in past five years

  3.8 Went to bars about once a month or more in the past year

  3.0 Age 65+

−3.0 White

−3.6 3+ children

−4.0 South region

−5.3 Age 18–29 & 5+ sex partners since age 18

−5.8 Has not been to a bar in the past year

−7.2 Age 18–29 & Went to bars about once a month or more in the past year

−7.2 Female

−10.1 Age 65+ & White

Table 4A.3. Pornography—Groups
(excluding religious variables)

Group	Legal for adults
All	65%
Freewheeler lifestyle	80%
Middle lifestyle	64%
Ring-Bearer lifestyle	49%

Abortion—Top 5 Model (excluding religious variables)

36.8	9.4 High school diploma or more
12.3 Graduate degree	7.8 Pacific region
11.7 5+ sex partners since age 18	−8.5 Latino American

Abortion—Full Model (excluding religious variables)

42.5

10.2 Northeast region & Population density in bottom 20%

7.8 Pacific region

7.4 Graduate degree

7.2 5+ sex partners since age 18

6.9 High school diploma or more

5.7 White

5.0 Northeast region

4.7 Bachelor's degree or more

3.8 Family income in top 20%

0.5 Age 18–39

−0.6 1 sex partner since age 18

−3.2 3+ children

−4.8 Married

−5.4 Age 18–39 & White

−6.1 Population density in bottom 20%

−6.2 3+ children & Bachelor's degree or more

−6.3 No sex partners since age 18

−6.4 1 sex partner since age 18 & White

−6.5 Latino American

−6.6 Has not been to a bar in the past year

Table 4A.4. Abortion—Groups (excluding religious variables)*

Group	(1)	(2)	(3)	(4)	(5)	(6)	(7)
All	87%	77%	74%	44%	43%	41%	41%
Freewheeler lifestyle; Bachelor's degree or more	94%	91%	87%	69%	68%	69%	68%
Middle lifestyle; Bachelor's degree or more	91%	82%	79%	56%	54%	54%	54%
Freewheeler lifestyle; No bachelor's degree	92%	85%	80%	50%	49%	46%	48%

Table 4A.4. (*continued*)

Group	(1)	(2)	(3)	(4)	(5)	(6)	(7)
Ring-Bearer lifestyle; Bachelor's degree or more	86%	69%	66%	39%	37%	36%	36%
Middle lifestyle; No bachelor's degree	87%	75%	73%	39%	36%	34%	35%
Ring-Bearer lifestyle; No bachelor's degree	80%	66%	62%	28%	29%	25%	25%

*Allow abortion in cases of: (1) mother's health; (2) rape; (3) fetal defect; (4) wants no more children; (5) poor; (6) single; (7) any reason.

Birth Control for Teens without Parental Consent—Top 5 Model (excluding religious variables)

53.5
  6.0 2+ sex partners in past five years
  4.4 Female
−5.3 Age 50+

−5.6 Ever married and never divorced
−5.7 Has not been to a bar in the past year

Birth Control for Teens without Parental Consent—Full Model (excluding religious variables)

56.6
  5.5 Female
  4.7 5+ sex partners since age 18
  4.3 2+ sex partners in past five years
  4.2 Family income in top 10%
−3.7 2+ children

−4.4 Ever married and never divorced
−4.7 Age 50+
−4.8 High school diploma or more
−5.1 Has not been to a bar in the past year

Table 4A.5. Birth Control for Teens without Parental Consent—Groups (excluding religious variables)

Group	Strongly agree	Agree	Disagree	Strongly disagree
All	25%	**31%**	24%	20%
Freewheeler lifestyle	33%	**35%**	19%	13%
Middle lifestyle	23%	**33%**	25%	19%
Ring-Bearer lifestyle	19%	26%	**27%**	27%

Marijuana Legalization—Top 5 Model (excluding religious variables)

49.8

10.0 Lesbian/gay/bisexual

 9.4 5+ sex partners since age 18

−5.3 Age 65+

−5.5 Has not been to a bar in the past year

−9.1 Latino American

Marijuana Legalization—Full Model (excluding religious variables)

47.4

11.3 Latino American & Some college or more

 7.8 Lesbian/gay/bisexual

 7.4 5+ sex partners since age 18

 6.5 Age 50+ & Some college or more

 4.7 Test in top 40%

 4.7 White

 4.5 Ever divorced

 3.6 Pacific region

 3.2 2+ sex partners since age 18

−2.9 Some college or more

−4.0 Age 50+

−4.5 Has not been to a bar in the past year

−5.2 Age 65+

−5.5 Married

−6.8 2+ sex partners since age 18 & Ever divorced

−11.0 Latino American

Table 4A.6. Marijuana Legalization—Groups (excluding religious variables)

Group	Legal
All	41%
Freewheeler lifestyle	56%
Middle lifestyle	37%
Ring-Bearer lifestyle	26%

Church Attendance per Year—Top 5 Model

21.8

11.0 African American

7.3 Ever married and never divorced

−6.2 Went to bars about once a month or more in the past year

−8.1 5+ sex partners since age 18

−8.5 Nonmarital cohabitation

Church Attendance per Year—Full Model

13.7

9.1 Latino American & Pacific region

8.7 No sex partners since age 18

7.4 African American

6.9 Nonmarital cohabitation & Went to bars about once a month or more in the past year

6.6 1 sex partner since age 18

5.7 Latino American

5.5 African American & Female

4.3 3+ children

4.2 Has not been to a bar in the past year

4.1 High school diploma or more

3.7 South region

3.6 Bachelor's degree or more

3.6 2+ children

2.4 Female

−2.4 Ever divorced

−3.5 Northeast region

−4.1 Went to bars about once a month or more in the past year

−4.2 5+ sex partners since age 18

−4.3 Ever divorced & 3+ children

−4.4 Pacific region

−4.5 Never married

−4.9 Never married & 2+ children

−6.1 Latino American & High school diploma or more

−7.1 Never married & 1 sex partner since age 18

−7.9 Nonmarital cohabitation

Table 4A.7. Church Attendance per Year—Groups

Group	About once a year or less	In between	About once a week or more
All	42%	**27%**	31%
Freewheeler lifestyle; Not African American	**55%**	29%	16%
Middle lifestyle; Not African American	42%	**27%**	31%
Freewheeler lifestyle; African American	34%	**38%**	28%
Ring-Bearer lifestyle; Not African American	32%	**24%**	44%
Middle lifestyle; African American	24%	**36%**	40%
Ring-Bearer lifestyle; African American	18%	26%	**56%**

Issue Models and Groups (Including Religious Variables)

The following groups are used for the GSS-based tables in the remainder of this chapter 4 appendix:

Group	Description	% of weighted sample
1	Church less than about once a week; High school diploma or more; Not Christian; 5+ sex partners since age 18	8%
2	Church less than about once a week; High school diploma or more; Not Christian; 0 to 4 sex partners since age 18	9%
3	Church less than about once a week; Bachelor's degree or more; Christian; Age 18–64	10%
4	Church less than about once a week; High school diploma but no bachelor's degree; Christian; Age 18–64	27%
5	Church less than about once a week; No high school diploma	10%
6	Church less than about once a week; High school diploma or more; Christian; Age 65+	5%
7	Church about once a week; Never married	4%
8	Church about once a week; Ever married; 5+ sex partners since age 18	5%

(*continued*)

Group	Description	% of weighted sample
9	Church about once a week; Ever married; 0 to 4 sex partners since age 18	15%
10	Church more than once a week	7%

Premarital Sex—Top 5 Model

57.4

8.9 2+ sex partners since age 18

−9.3 Church two or three times a month or more

−9.6 Church about once a week or more

−9.6 Non-Catholic Christian

−11.6 Church more than once a week

Premarital Sex—Full Model

59.6

15.3 Church more than once a week & Went to bars about once a month or more in the past year

14.7 Other religion & White

8.7 Church about once a week or more & Family income in bottom 20%

4.6 Family income in top 10%

4.4 2+ sex partners since age 18

3.7 White

3.5 5+ sex partners since age 18

1.9 Went to bars about once a month or more in the past year

−1.2 Non-Catholic Christian

−2.5 Church two or three times a month or more

−3.7 Population density in bottom 20%

−4.0 Married to person who is not employed

−4.4 Has not been to a bar in the past year

−4.5 No sex partners in past five years

−4.6 Family income in bottom 20%

−5.2 Church two or three times a month or more & Non-Catholic Christian

−5.9 Church several times a year or more

−6.6 Non-Catholic Christian & White

−9.8 Church about once a week or more

−10.2 Other religion

−10.9 Church more than once a week

Table 4A.9. Premarital Sex—Groups

Group	Not wrong at all	Sometimes wrong	Almost always wrong	Always wrong
All	**50%**	**18%**	8%	24%
Church less than about once a week; High school diploma or more; Not Christian; 5+ sex partners since age 18	**82%**	14%	2%	3%
Church less than about once a week; High school diploma or more; Not Christian; 0 to 4 sex partners since age 18	**68%**	20%	4%	8%
Church less than about once a week; Bachelor's degree or more; Christian; Age 18–64	**64%**	20%	5%	11%
Church less than about once a week; High school diploma but no bachelor's degree; Christian; Age 18–64	**60%**	21%	6%	13%
Church less than about once a week; No high school diploma	**52%**	16%	8%	24%
Church less than about once a week; High school diploma or more; Christian; Age 65+	47%	**20%**	13%	20%
Church about once a week; Ever married; 5+ sex partners since age 18	37%	**21%**	11%	31%
Church about once a week; Never married	31%	**25%**	13%	31%
Church about once a week; Ever married; 0 to 4 sex partners since age 18	23%	16%	**14%**	47%
Church more than once a week	11%	6%	10%	**72%**

Pornography—Top 5 Model

56.8		−7.5	Female
10.0	Jewish	−8.8	Age 65+
7.4	2+ sex partners in the past five years	−11.3	Church about once a week or more

Pornography—Full Model

54.0

7.7 Age 18–29

6.0 Jewish

5.4 Graduate degree

5.1 Lesbian/gay/bisexual

5.0 5+ sex partners since age 18

4.3 African American

3.7 2+ sex partners in the past five years

2.9 White

2.9 Went to bars about once a month or more in the past year

2.5 Age 65+

−0.9 Non-Catholic Christian

−5.1 Has not been to a bar in the past year

−5.2 5+ sex partners since age 18 & Age 18–29

−5.9 Non-Catholic Christian & White

−6.0 Church more than once a week

−6.5 Female

−6.8 Went to bars about once a month or more in the past year & Age 18–29

−8.0 Church about once a week or more

−9.4 Age 65+ & White

Table 4A.10. Pornography—Groups

Group	Legal for adults
All	65%
Church less than about once a week; High school diploma or more; Not Christian; 5+ sex partners since age 18	91%
Church less than about once a week; High school diploma or more; Not Christian; 0 to 4 sex partners since age 18	81%
Church less than about once a week; Bachelor's degree or more; Christian; Age 18–64	76%
Church less than about once a week; High school diploma but no bachelor's degree; Christian; Age 18–64	75%
Church less than about once a week; No high school diploma	66%
Church about once a week; Never married	66%
Church about once a week; Ever married; 5+ sex partners since age 18	59%
Church less than about once a week; High school diploma or more; Christian; Age 65+	51%
Church about once a week; Ever married; 0 to 4 sex partners since age 18	39%
Church more than once a week	31%

Abortion—Top 5 Model

43.9

11.4 Graduate degree

11.4 High school diploma or more

11.0 Not Christian

−12.6 Church more than once a week

−16.1 Church about once a week or more

Abortion—Full Model

49.3

8.9 Not Christian

8.5 African American & Church about once a week or more

6.9 High school diploma or more

6.2 Graduate degree

5.9 Some college or more

5.7 African American & Age 18–39

5.7 5+ sex partners since age 18

5.5 Age 65+ & Church about once a week or more

4.1 Bachelor's degree or more

1.2 Catholic

0.9 Age 65+

−2.0 African American

−3.9 Raised outside the U.S.

−4.1 Church one a month or more

−4.7 Church several times a year or more

−4.8 Has not been to a bar in the past year

−5.5 Population density in bottom 20%

−6.3 Age 18–39

−6.7 Catholic & Age 65+

−7.6 Church about once a week or more & Some college or more

−8.2 Church about once a week or more

−8.7 African American & Not Christian

−12.2 Church more than once a week

Table 4A.11. Abortion—Groups*

Group	(1)	(2)	(3)	(4)	(5)	(6)	(7)
All	87%	77%	74%	44%	43%	41%	41%
Church less than about once a week; High school diploma or more; Not Christian; 5+ sex partners since age 18	97%	96%	93%	78%	77%	75%	75%
Church less than about once a week; High school diploma or more; Not Christian; 0 to 4 sex partners since age 18	95%	91%	87%	67%	64%	63%	62%
Church less than about once a week; Bachelor's degree or more; Christian; Age 18–64	96%	90%	88%	61%	59%	59%	62%
Church less than about once a week; High school diploma but no bachelor's degree; Christian; Age 18–64	92%	85%	79%	46%	45%	42%	44%
Church less than about once a week; High school diploma or more; Christian; Age 65+	93%	87%	89%	48%	48%	46%	42%
Church less than about once a week; No high school diploma	84%	70%	70%	35%	33%	29%	30%
Church about once a week; Ever married; 5+ sex partners since age 18	84%	73%	66%	34%	30%	28%	31%
Church about once a week; Never married	82%	63%	53%	29%	29%	26%	31%
Church about once a week; Ever married; 0 to 4 sex partners since age 18	79%	60%	58%	23%	22%	22%	21%
Church more than once a week	62%	39%	38%	14%	13%	12%	11%

*Allow abortion in cases of: (1) mother's health; (2) rape; (3) fetal defect; (4) wants no more children; (5) poor; (6) single; (7) any reason.

Birth Control for Teens without Parental Consent—Top 5 Model

46.4	5.9 Female
9.0 Not Christian	−8.4 Church more than once a week
8.5 2+ sex partners in past five years	−9.8 Church about once a week or more

Birth Control for Teens without Parental Consent—Full Model

53.4	−3.9 Has not been to a bar in the past year
8.6 Not Christian & White	−3.9 Church several times a year or more
5.7 Female	
5.2 Lesbian/gay/bisexual	−4.4 Age 50+
5.3 2+ sex partners in past five years	−4.7 Church about once a week or more
4.5 Church once a month or more	−8.4 Church more than once a week
0.0 Not Christian	−9.8 Church once a month or more & White
−0.3 White	

Table 4A.12. Birth Control for Teens without Parental Consent—Groups

Group	Strongly agree	Agree	Disagree	Strongly disagree
All	25%	31%	24%	20%
Church less than about once a week; High school diploma or more; Not Christian; 5+ sex partners since age 18	39%	38%	16%	7%
Church less than about once a week; High school diploma or more; Not Christian; 0 to 4 sex partners since age 18	35%	37%	17%	11%
Church less than about once a week; Bachelor's degree or more; Christian; Age 18–64	29%	34%	24%	13%
Church less than about once a week; No high school diploma	31%	31%	22%	16%
Church less than about once a week; High school diploma but no bachelor's degree; Christian; Age 18–64	26%	36%	22%	16%

Table 4A.12. (*continued*)

Group	Strongly agree	Agree	Disagree	Strongly disagree
Church about once a week; Never married	27%	**29%**	25%	19%
Church less than about once a week; High school diploma or more; Christian; Age 65+	18%	26%	**35%**	21%
Church about once a week; Ever married; 5+ sex partners since age 18	18%	28%	**27%**	27%
Church about once a week; Ever married; 0 to 4 sex partners since age 18	14%	23%	**32%**	31%
Church more than once a week	12%	17%	**28%**	43%

Marijuana Legalization—Top 5 Model

54.4

  8.9 Lesbian/gay/bisexual

  8.3 5+ sex partners since age 18

−5.4 Has not been to a bar in the past year

−6.3 Church about once a week or more

−6.4 Church several times a year or more

Marijuana Legalization—Full Model

50.1

  9.4 Not Christian

  6.9 Lesbian/gay/bisexual

  5.9 5+ sex partners since age 18

  4.2 2+ sex partners in past five years

  3.9 Test in top 40%

  0.6 Test in bottom 40%

−2.0 Born outside the U.S.

−4.0 Church several times a year or more

−4.3 Has not been to a bar in the past year

−4.4 Church more than one a week

−4.8 Church about once a week or more

−5.0 Latino American

−6.9 Not Christian & Test in bottom 40%

−7.5 Not Christian & Born outside the U.S.

Table 4A.13. Marijuana Legalization—Groups

Group	Legal
All	41%
Church less than about once a week; High school diploma or more; Not Christian; 5+ sex partners since age 18	75%
Church less than about once a week; High school diploma or more; Not Christian; 0 to 4 sex partners since age 18	52%
Church less than about once a week; High school diploma but no bachelor's degree; Christian; Age 18–64	47%
Church less than about once a week; Bachelor's degree or more; Christian; Age 18–64	45%
Church less than about once a week; No high school diploma	37%
Church about once a week; Ever married; 5+ sex partners since age 18	37%
Church less than about once a week; High school diploma or more; Christian; Age 65+	34%
Church about once a week; Never married	33%
Church about once a week; Ever married; 0 to 4 sex partners since age 18	20%
Church more than once a week	14%

B. World Values Survey

Abortion—Full Model

47.5	1.2 Education in top 40%
13.1 Western	−4.4 Western & Religiosity in top 20%
8.2 Religiosity in bottom 20%	
7.0 Religiosity in bottom 40%	−4.9 Education in bottom 40%
3.5 Western & Education in top 40%	−5.2 Religiosity in top 20%
	−7.3 Religiosity in top 40%

Table 4A.14. Summary of Regression Model

	Education in top 40%	Education in middle 20%	Education in bottom 40%
Religiosity in bottom 20%	Western: 80.6 Other: 64.0	Western: 75.8 Other: 62.7	Western: 70.9 Other: 57.8
Religiosity in next 20%	Western: 72.3 Other: 55.7	Western: 67.6 Other: 54.5	Western: 62.7 Other: 49.6
Religiosity in middle 20%	Western: 65.3 Other: 48.7	Western: 60.6 Other: 47.5	Western: 55.7 Other: 42.6
Religiosity in next 20%	Western: 58.0 Other: 41.4	Western: 53.3 Other: 40.2	Western: 48.4 Other: 35.3
Religiosity in top 20%	Western: 48.5 Other: 36.3	Western: 43.7 Other: 35.1	Western: 38.8 Other: 30.2

Data Appendix for Chapter 5

SEE THE DATA APPENDIX FOR PART II for general comments on variables and methods.

A. U.S. General Social Survey

In addition to the variables in the Data Appendix for Part II, for our group analyses, we used the follow combinations of education and test performance to measure overall human capital percentiles:

Group	Components
Human capital in top 20%	Graduate degree & Test in top 60% or missing Bachelor's degree & Test in top 40% Some college & Test in top 20%
Human capital in next 20%	Graduate degree & Test in bottom 40% Bachelor's degree & Test in bottom-middle 40% or missing Some college & Test in top 20% to 40% High school diploma & Test in top 40%
Human capital in middle 20%	Bachelor's degree & Test in bottom 20% Some college & Test in bottom-middle 40% or missing No high school diploma & Test in top 40%
Human capital in next 20%	Some college & Test in bottom 20% High school diploma & Test in bottom-middle 40% or missing
Human capital in bottom 20%	High-school diploma & Test in bottom 20% No high school diploma & Test in bottom-middle 60% or missing

First Amendment Rights for Anti-Religionists—Top 5 Model

34.6	8.8 White
11.8 Some college or more	8.6 Test in top 40%
11.0 No religion	−9.9 Age 65+

First Amendment Rights for Anti-Religionists—Full Model

45.5	−0.2 Population density in bottom 20%
6.6 Born outside the U.S. & Age 50+	−0.9 Born outside the U.S.
6.0 No religion	−3.9 Age 50+
6.0 Bachelor's degree or more & Age 50+	−4.0 No sex partners since age 18
5.8 Some college or more	−4.3 South region
5.7 Test in top 40%	−4.8 Church several times a year or more
5.6 Non-Catholic Christian & High school diploma or more	−5.0 Test in bottom 40%
4.7 White	−5.2 Non-Catholic Christian
3.6 5+ sex partners since age 18	−5.8 Non-Catholic Christian & Population density in bottom 20%
3.5 Bachelor's degree or more	−6.9 Age 65+
3.1 High school diploma or more	−8.1 Raised outside the U.S.

Table 5A.2. First Amendment Rights for Anti-Religionists—Groups

Group	Allow anti-religionist to speak	Allow anti-religionist book in library	Allow anti-religionist to teach
All	77%	74%	63%
Human capital in top 60%; No religious affiliation	93%	92%	88%
Human capital in top 40%; Some religious affiliation; White; Church less than about once a week	93%	92%	78%

(continues)

Table 5A.2. (*continued*)

Group	Allow anti-religionist to speak	Allow anti-religionist book in library	Allow anti-religionist to teach
Human capital in top 40%; Some religious affiliation; White; Church about once a week or more	89%	79%	71%
Human capital in bottom 40%; No religious affiliation	84%	78%	71%
Human capital in middle 20%; Some religious affiliation; White	80%	76%	64%
Human capital in top 60%; Some religious affiliation; Not White	74%	70%	57%
Human capital in bottom 20% to 40%; Some religious affiliation	69%	65%	50%
Human capital in bottom 20%; Some religious affiliation	51%	49%	39%

First Amendment Rights for Homosexuals—Top 5 Model

41.7		−7.3	Test in bottom 20%
8.5	High school diploma or more	−7.4	Age 65+
7.8	Some college or more	−13.6	Church more than once a week

First Amendment Rights for Homosexuals—Full Model

40.9		6.2	Catholic & Church about once a week or more
8.7	Non-Catholic Christian & African American	5.8	Some college or more & Age 65+
7.5	High school diploma or more		

5.4 Non-Catholic Christian & Test in Top 20%	−1.5 Catholic
4.4 White	−3.6 African American
4.2 Bachelor's degree or more	−3.9 South region
3.8 5+ sex partners since age 18	−5.0 Test in bottom 20%
3.7 Female	−5.2 Non-Catholic Christian
3.7 Test in top 40%	−6.4 Church more than once a week
3.5 Some college or more	−7.2 Church about once a week or more
−0.6 Test in top 20%	−9.1 Age 65+

Table 5A.3. First Amendment Rights for Homosexuals—Groups

Group	Allow homosexuals to speak	Allow homosexuals to teach	Allow homosexual books in library
All	85%	82%	77%
Human capital in top 40%; Church less than about once a week	97%	95%	92%
Human capital in top 40%; Church about once a week or more	90%	87%	82%
Human capital in lower-middle 40%; Church less than about once a week	87%	84%	81%
Human capital in lower-middle 40%; Church about once a week or more	75%	70%	64%
Human capital in bottom 20%; Church less than about once a week	73%	68%	63%
Human capital in bottom 20%; Church about once a week or more	55%	51%	42%

First Amendment Rights for Anti-American Muslims—Top 5 Model

41.4		10.8	Other religion
13.3	Test in top 40%	9.8	No religion
12.8	Bachelor's degree or more	−11.0	Raised outside the U.S.

First Amendment Rights for Anti-American Muslims—Full Model

47.1		−3.6	Female
11.2	Other Religion	−4.2	Church once a month or more
6.9	No religion		
6.8	Test in top 20%	−5.4	Population density in bottom 20%
6.6	Some college or more		
6.5	Test in top 40%	−6.8	Raised outside the U.S.
6.4	Bachelor's degree or more	−13.5	Raised outside the U.S. & Test in top 40%
4.7	Graduate degree		
−3.5	Test in bottom 20%	−18.9	Raised outside the U.S. & Graduate degree
−3.6	Test in bottom 40%		

Table 5A.4. First Amendment Rights for Anti-American Muslims—Groups

Group	Allow anti-American Muslim books in library	Allow anti-American Muslims to speak	Allow anti-American Muslims to teach
All	49%	42%	32%
Human capital in top 20%; Born and raised in the U.S.; No religious affiliation or religious affiliation is other than Christian or Jewish	88%	85%	69%
Human capital in top 20%; Born and raised in the U.S.; Christian or Jewish	77%	71%	55%
Human capital in top 20% to 40%; Born and raised in the U.S.; No religious affiliation or religious affiliation is other than Christian or Jewish	72%	64%	53%

Table 5A.4. (*continued*)

Group	Allow anti-American Muslim books in library	Allow anti-American Muslims to speak	Allow anti-American Muslims to teach
Human capital in top 20% to 40%; Born and raised in the U.S.; Christian or Jewish	56%	49%	35%
Human capital in bottom 60%; No religious affiliation or religious affiliation is other than Christian or Jewish	47%	42%	33%
Human capital in top 40%; Born or raised outside the U.S.	60%	36%	26%
Human capital in middle 20%; Christian or Jewish	41%	35%	23%
Human capital in bottom 40%; Christian or Jewish	28%	21%	16%

School Prayer—Top 5 Model

42.2		8.7	Bachelor's degree or more
15.0	Not Christian	6.5	Age 18–29
10.2	Test in top 20%	−7.6	Church more than once a week

School Prayer—Full Model

45.7		1.8	Church several times a year or more
12.2	Not Christian		
8.8	Test in top 20%	−2.4	Some college or more
6.9	High school diploma or more	−4.1	South region
		−5.0	Church more than once a week
6.4	Age 18–29	−6.4	High school diploma or more & Church several times a year or more
6.1	Some college or more & White		
5.3	Bachelor's degree or more	−6.4	White
4.5	Graduate degree	−7.8	African American

Table 5A.5. School Prayer—Groups

Group	Approve of ban
All	42%
Not Christian; Human capital in top 40%	83%
Not Christian; Human capital in bottom 60%	57%
Christian; Human capital in top 20%	56%
Christian; Human capital in upper-middle 40%; Not African American; Church less than about once a week	42%
Christian; Human capital in upper-middle 40%; Not African American; Church about once a week or more	30%
Christian; Human capital in bottom 40%; Not African American	27%
Christian; Human capital in bottom 80%; African American	18%

Homosexuality—Top 5 Model

50.8	−11.6 Non-Catholic Christian
17.0 Lesbian/gay/bisexual	−15.5 Church about once a week or more
10.3 Bachelor's degree or more	
8.5 High school diploma or more	

Homosexuality—Full Model

43.9	4.3 Test in top 40%
12.9 Lesbian/gay/bisexual	3.9 Graduate degree
7.7 Female	3.9 High school diploma or more
7.3 Age 18–29	
6.2 Bachelor's degree or more	1.3 Test in bottom 40%
6.2 White	−0.8 African American
6.1 5+ sex partners since age 18	−3.2 Church about every week or more
6.0 Some college or more	

−4.1 Has not been to a bar in the past year

−4.6 Church more than once a week

−5.1 South region

−5.2 Catholic

−5.3 Some college or more & African American

−5.6 5+ sex partners since age 18 & Age 18–29

−5.6 Church about once a week or more & Some college or more

−6.1 Bachelor's degree or more & Test in bottom 40%

−6.2 Non-Catholic Christian

−6.5 Church two or three times a month or more

−7.6 Non-Catholic Christian & White

Table 5A.6. Homosexuality—Groups

Group	Not wrong at all	Sometimes wrong	Almost always wrong	Always wrong
All	37%	7%	4%	**52%**
Not Christian or not heterosexual; Human capital in top 60%	**72%**	8%	3%	17%
Christian; Heterosexual; Church less than about once a week; Human capital in top 40%	**53%**	11%	4%	32%
Not Christian or not heterosexual; Human capital in bottom 40%	46%	**8%**	3%	43%
Catholic; Heterosexual; Church less than about once a week; Human capital in bottom 60%	37%	9%	**7%**	47%
Non-Catholic Christian; Heterosexual; Church less than about once a week; Human capital in bottom 60%	26%	6%	4%	**64%**
Catholic; Heterosexual; Church about once a week or more	24%	7%	5%	**64%**
Non-Catholic Christian; Heterosexual; Church about once a week or more	11%	4%	3%	**82%**

Same-Sex Marriage—Top 5 Model

55.4	−10.6 Non-Catholic Christian
21.3 Lesbian/gay/bisexual	−15.2 Church about once a week or more
9.4 Bachelor's degree or more	
8.7 Age 18–29	

Same-Sex Marriage—Full Model

45.2	−1.0 Population density in bottom 40%
14.2 Lesbian/gay/bisexual	−1.7 White
14.1 Lesbian/gay/bisexual & Church about once a week or more	−1.9 Population density in top 40%
9.3 Graduate degree	−2.1 Not Christian
9.0 Not Christian & White	−3.8 Raised outside the U.S.
6.6 High school diploma or more	−4.4 South region
5.1 Female & White	−5.6 Church two or three times a month or more
5.0 2+ sex partners since age 18	−7.0 Population density in bottom 40% & White
5.0 Bachelor's degree or more	−7.3 Non-Catholic Christian
5.0 Age 18–39	−7.8 Population density in top 40% & Graduate degree
4.7 Went to bars about once a month or more in the past year	−8.0 Church more than once a week
4.5 Female	−8.3 Church about once a week or more & High school diploma or more
3.8 Age 18–29	
0.5 Church about once a week or more	

Table 5A.7. Same-Sex Marriage—Groups

Group	Strongly agree	Agree	Neither	Disagree	Strongly disagree
All	18%	22%	**13%**	16%	31%
Not Christian or not heterosexual; Human capital in top 40%	44%	**28%**	10%	8%	10%
Christian; Heterosexual; Church less than about once a week; Human capital in top 40%; Female	26%	**29%**	15%	15%	15%
Not Christian or not heterosexual; Human capital in bottom 60%	23%	**29%**	15%	12%	21%
Catholic; Heterosexual; Church less than about once a week; Human capital in bottom 60%	18%	29%	**15%**	16%	22%
Christian; Heterosexual; Church less than about once a week; Human capital in top 40%; Male	16%	25%	**14%**	21%	24%
Non-Catholic Christian; Heterosexual; Church less than about once a week; Human capital in bottom 60%	11%	20%	15%	**17%**	37%
Catholic; Heterosexual; Church about once a week or more	8%	18%	19%	**20%**	35%
Non-Catholic Christian; Heterosexual; Church about once a week or more	5%	11%	8%	20%	**56%**

Immigration—Top 5 Model

49.2		8.8	Born outside the U.S.
11.7	Bachelor's degree or more	7.7	Parents born outside the U.S.
9.5	Latino American	−7.2	White

Immigration—Full Model

47.9

8.4 White & Bachelor's degree or more

8.3 Latino American

7.8 Born outside the U.S.

6.6 Parents born outside the U.S.

6.4 Raised outside the U.S.

5.9 Not Christian & Some college or more

5.7 Age 18–29

5.2 Age 65+ & Some college or more

4.9 No sex partners since age 18

4.9 Test in top 20%

3.9 Personal income in top 10%

3.7 Graduate degree

1.4 Test in top 40%

0.9 Not Christian

0.3 Some college or more

0.3 Bachelor's degree or more

−3.7 Age 65+

−8.5 Born outside the U.S. & Test in top 40%

−9.1 White

Table 5A.8. Immigration—Groups

Group	Increased a lot	Increased a little	Same as is	Reduced a little	Reduced a lot
All	4%	8%	36%	**25%**	27%
Born or raised outside the U.S.	11%	17%	**50%**	16%	6%
Born and raised in the U.S.; Human capital in top 20%; Not Christian or not heterosexual	5%	16%	**48%**	19%	12%
Born and raised in the U.S.; Human capital in top 20%; Christian; Heterosexual	1%	10%	**42%**	28%	19%
Born and raised in the U.S.; Human capital in bottom 80%; Not White	7%	10%	**38%**	22%	23%
Born and raised in the U.S.; Human capital in upper-middle 40%; White	1%	5%	32%	**31%**	31%
Born and raised in the U.S.; Human capital in bottom 40%; White	2%	4%	26%	**24%**	44%

Government Help for African Americans—Top 5 Model

54.9	7.6 Graduate degree
16.9 African American	5.5 Raised outside the U.S.
8.6 Lesbian/gay/bisexual	−10.6 White

Government Help for African Americans—Full Model

56.1	4.1 Bachelor's degree or more
12.7 African American	3.9 Population density in top 20%
9.1 Not Christian & High school diploma or more	3.8 Never married
8.6 African American & High school diploma or more	3.3 Graduate degree
6.3 Lesbian/gay/bisexual	−5.3 Not Christian
6.0 Not Christian & Graduate degree	−7.2 High school diploma or more
4.5 Raised outside the U.S.	−8.2 White
	−8.4 African American & Bachelor's degree or more

Table 5A.9. Government Help for African Americans—Groups

Group	Government help Blacks		Agree with both		No special treatment
All	8%	8%	32%	**20%**	32%
African American	30%	12%	**41%**	6%	11%
White; Born and raised in the U.S.; Not Christian or not heterosexual; Human capital in top 20%	9%	16%	**29%**	23%	23%
Latino/Asian/other American	13%	9%	**36%**	13%	29%
White; Born or raised outside the U.S.	7%	10%	**34%**	19%	30%

(continues)

Table 5A.9. (*continued*)

Group	Government help Blacks		Agree with both		No special treatment
White; Born and raised in the U.S.; Not Christian or not heterosexual; Human capital in bottom 80%	5%	8%	32%	**20%**	35%
White; Born and raised in the U.S.; Christian; Heterosexual; Human capital in top 20%	2%	8%	26%	**32%**	32%
White; Born and raised in the U.S.; Christian; Heterosexual; Human capital in bottom 80%	4%	5%	29%	**22%**	40%

Government Spending on African Americans—Top 5 Model

55.1	5.5 Lesbian/gay/bisexual
20.7 African American	−4.3 South region
6.2 Graduate degree	−9.3 White

Government Spending on African Americans—Full Model

48.7	−0.7 High school diploma or
22.9 African American	more
10.0 Latino American & High	−2.8 Latino American
school diploma or more	−3.5 South region
5.9 Graduate degree	−3.8 White
4.8 No children	−7.3 White & Non-Catholic
4.2 Lesbian/gay/bisexual	Christian
3.5 Female	−8.3 African American & No
3.1 Non-Catholic Christian	children

Table 5A.10. Government Spending on African Americans—Groups

Group	Too little	About right	Too much
All	31%	**49%**	20%
African American	**73%**	24%	3%
White; Not Christian or not heterosexual; Human capital in top 60%; Female	39%	**49%**	12%
Latino/Asian/other American	34%	**51%**	15%
White; Not Christian or not heterosexual; Human capital in top 60%; Male	30%	**49%**	21%
White; Not Christian or not heterosexual; Human capital in bottom 40%	25%	**48%**	27%
White; Christian; Heterosexual	20%	**55%**	25%

Race-Based Affirmative Action—Top 5 Model

57.5

7.7 Graduate degree

7.4 African American

6.8 Test in bottom 20%

6.3 Lesbian/gay/bisexual

−12.6 White

Race-Based Affirmative Action—Full Model

61.0

6.5 African American & High school diploma or more

5.9 Lesbian/gay/bisexual

5.8 Graduate degree

5.8 Not Christian & Test in top 20%

5.6 No sex partners since age 18

5.3 White & Test in bottom 20%

5.3 Test in bottom 20%

5.1 Not Christian & Some college or more

4.2 African American

3.4 Bachelor's degree or more

−0.2 Test in top 20%

−0.5 Not Christian

−2.6 Some college or more

−5.1 High school diploma or more

−8.7 Some college or more & Test in bottom 20%

−12.1 White

Table 5A.11. Race-Based Affirmative Action—Groups

Group	Strongly support	Support	Oppose	Strongly oppose
All	10%	7%	28%	55%
African American	33%	11%	26%	30%
Latino/Asian/other American; Human capital in bottom 20%	19%	10%	40%	31%
White; Human capital in top 20%; Not Christian or not heterosexual	9%	14%	33%	44%
Latino/Asian/other American; Human capital in top 80%	10%	9%	35%	46%
White; Human capital in bottom 20%	13%	9%	26%	52%
White; Human capital in middle 60%; Not Christian or not heterosexual	5%	5%	30%	60%
White; Human capital in top 80%; Christian; Heterosexual	3%	5%	25%	67%

Gender-Based Affirmative Action—Top 5 Model

70.2		−6.0	Some college or more
9.3	Test in bottom 20%	−7.2	High school diploma or more
7.3	Lesbian/gay/bisexual	−15.2	White

Gender-Based Affirmative Action—Full Model

62.5		4.2	Raised outside the U.S.
11.4	Some college or more & No religion	4.1	Test in bottom 40%
8.8	White & Test in the bottom 20%	0.1	Test in bottom 20%
7.1	Lesbian/gay/bisexual	−6.8	High school diploma or more
6.5	African American	−6.8	No religion
6.4	Family income in bottom 20%	−7.0	Some college
5.2	Female	−8.6	African American & Family income in bottom 20%
		−12.3	White

Table 5A.12. Gender-Based Affirmative Action—Groups

Group	Strongly for	For	Against	Strongly against
All	21%	11%	**27%**	41%
Not White; Female	42%	**14%**	24%	20%
Not White; Male	34%	15%	**24%**	27%
White; Human capital in bottom 40%; Female	26%	13%	**26%**	35%
White; Human capital in bottom 40%; Male	22%	11%	**30%**	37%
White; Human capital in top 60%; Female	11%	8%	**32%**	49%
White; Human capital in top 60%; Male	6%	8%	26%	**60%**

Death Penalty—Top 5 Model

46.1		8.2 Graduate degree
14.7 African American		8.2 Raised outside the U.S.
10.1 Latino American		5.4 Lesbian/gay/bisexual

Death Penalty—Full Model

49.7

15.8 African American

13.0 Latino American & Non-Catholic Christian

8.5 Latino American

7.9 Raised outside the U.S.

7.3 Lesbian/gay/bisexual & Some college or more

6.8 White & Bachelor's degree or more

6.3 No religion & Some college or more

5.3 Female

4.5 Graduate degree

0.1 Lesbian/gay/bisexual

−0.1 Some college or more

−1.3 Bachelor's degree or more

−1.6 White

−2.1 No religion

−4.2 High school diploma or more

−4.7 Non-Catholic Christian

−7.9 African American & Raised outside the U.S.

−8.5 Latino American & Female

Table 5A.13. Death Penalty—Groups

Group	Oppose
All	32%
African/Latino American	51%
White/Asian/other American; Born and raised in the U.S.; Human capital in top 20%; Catholic or not Christian or not heterosexual	45%
White/Asian/other American; Born or raised outside the U.S.	37%
White/Asian/other American; Born and raised in the U.S.; Human capital in top 20%; Non-Catholic Christian; Heterosexual	27%
White/Asian/other American; Born and raised in the U.S.; Human capital in bottom 80%; Female	27%
White/Asian/other American; Born and raised in the U.S.; Human capital in bottom 80%; Male	17%

Police Violence—Top 5 Model

69.5		−8.3	Asian American
12.4	Raised outside the U.S.	−10.6	High school diploma or more
−7.8	Personal income in top 10%	−14.4	White

Police Violence—Full Model

65.7		−3.3	Personal income in top 10%
11.0	Raised outside the U.S.	−3.5	Some college or more
6.1	High school diploma or more & Test in bottom 20%	−4.0	Test in top 40%
		−5.4	African American
5.8	Catholic	−5.6	Catholic & High school diploma or more
5.7	African American & Non-Catholic Christian		
		−6.4	High school diploma or more
4.9	Female	−7.6	Asian American
3.9	Ever widowed	−13.8	White
0.8	Test in bottom 20%	−14.1	African American & Personal income in top 10%
−2.0	Non-Catholic Christian		

Table 5A.14. Police Violence—Groups

Group	No
All	32%
Not White; Human capital in bottom 20%	74%
Not White; Human capital in top 80%; Born or raised outside the U.S.	60%
White; Human capital in bottom 20%	44%
Not White; Human capital in top 80%; Born and raised in the U.S.	42%
White; Human capital in top 80%; Born or raised outside the U.S.	33%
White; Human capital in bottom 20% to 40%; Born and raised in the U.S.	28%
White; Human capital in top 60%; Born and raised in the U.S.; Female	20%
White; Human capital in top 60%; Born and raised in the U.S.; Male	10%

B. World Values Survey

Tolerance toward the Nonreligious—Full Model

43.1

17.2 Western

16.8 Religiosity in bottom 20%

10.4 Religiosity in bottom 40%

−1.4 Education in bottom 40%

−2.4 Religiosity in top 20%

−3.9 United States & Religiosity in top 20%

−4.0 Education in bottom 20%

−4.2 United States

−4.5 Religiosity in top 40%

−5.9 United States & Education in bottom 40%

−7.2 Western & Religiosity in bottom 20%

Tolerance toward Immigrants—Full Model

48.7

10.7 Immigrant

8.8 Western & Education in top 40%

5.4 Western

4.3 Western & Immigrant

4.0 Education in top 20%

−1.2 Education in top 40%

−4.3 Education in bottom 40%

−7.1 United States

Table 5A.15. Summary of Regression Model for Tolerance toward the Nonreligious

	Education in top 60%	Education in bottom 20% to 40%	Education in bottom 20%
Religiosity in bottom 20%	United States: 76.0 West (not USA): 80.3 Other: 70.3	United States: 68.8 West (not USA): 78.9 Other: 68.9	United States: 64.8 West (not USA): 74.9 Other: 65.0
Religiosity in next 20%	United States: 66.5 West (not USA): 70.7 Other: 53.5	United States: 59.2 West (not USA): 69.3 Other: 52.1	United States: 55.3 West (not USA): 65.3 Other: 48.1
Religiosity in middle 20%	United States: 56.1 West (not USA): 60.3 Other: 43.1	United States: 48.8 West (not USA): 58.9 Other: 41.7	United States: 44.9 West (not USA): 55.0 Other: 37.8
Religiosity in next 20%	United States: 51.6 West (not USA): 55.8 Other: 38.6	United States: 44.3 West (not USA): 54.4 Other: 37.2	United States: 40.3 West (not USA): 50.4 Other: 33.2
Religiosity in top 20%	United States: 45.2 West (not USA): 53.4 Other: 36.2	United States: 38.0 West (not USA): 52.0 Other: 34.8	United States: 34.0 West (not USA): 48.0 Other: 30.8

Table 5A.16. Summary of Regression Model for Tolerance toward Immigrants

	Immigrant	Not Immigrant
Education in top 20%	United States: 73.6 West (not USA): 80.7 Other: 62.2	United States: 58.5 West (not USA): 65.6 Other: 51.5
Education it next 20%	United States: 69.6 West (not USA): 76.7 Other: 58.2	United States: 54.5 West (not USA): 61.7 Other: 47.5
Education in middle 20%	United States: 62.1 West (not USA): 69.2 Other: 59.5	United States: 47.0 West (not USA): 54.1 Other: 48.7
Education in bottom 40%	United States: 57.7 West (not USA): 64.9 Other: 55.2	United States: 42.7 West (not USA): 49.8 Other: 44.4

Data Appendix for Chapter 6

SEE THE DATA APPENDIX FOR PART II for general comments on variables and methods.

A. U.S. General Social Survey

The following groups are used in the GSS-based tables in this chapter 6 appendix:

Group	Description
1	White; Family income in bottom 40%; Heterosexual; Christian; Age 18–64; No children
2	White; Family income in bottom 40%; Heterosexual; Christian; Age 65+
3	White; Family income in bottom 40%; Heterosexual; Christian; Age 18–64; Has children
4	Latino/Asian/other American; Parent(s) born outside the U.S.; No high school diploma
5	African American
6	White; Income in bottom 90%; Not heterosexual and/or not Christian
7	Latino/Asian/other American; Parents born in the U.S.
8	Latino/Asian/other American; Parent(s) born outside the U.S.; High school diploma or more
9	White; Income in upper-middle 50%; Heterosexual; Christian; Age 65+
10	White; Income in upper-middle 50%; Heterosexual; Christian; Age 18–64; Not self-employed household
11	White; Income in upper-middle 50%; Heterosexual; Christian; Age 18–64; Self-employed household
12	White; Income in top 10%; Not heterosexual and/or not Christian
13	White; Income in top 10%; Heterosexual; Christian

Note: For these splits, "Income in the top 10%" includes those for whom either their personal income or their family income was in the top 10%. This group is in contrast with those for whom neither their personal income nor their family income was in the top 10%, a group that is further subdivided in most of these groups between those whose family income was in the bottom 40% or not. Thus, "Income in the upper-middle 50%" means (1) family income is below the top 10%, (2) personal income is below the top 10%, and (3) family income is above the bottom 40%.

The following table gives some basic information about these groups. The education information breaks out those without high school diplomas (No HS), those with high school diplomas but no college attendance (HS), those with some college or an associate's degree but no bachelor's degree (SC), those with bachelor's degrees but not graduate degrees (Bach), and those with graduate degrees (Grad).

Group	% of weighted sample	Family income (middle 50%)	Education	Female
1	4%	$12k to $35k	10% No HS; 31% HS; 38% SC; 18% Bach; 3% Grad	48%
2	4%	$15k to $35k	29% No HS; 45% HS; 16% SC; 7% Bach; 3% Grad	62%
3	8%	$17k to $37k	21% No HS; 42% HS; 29% SC; 6% Bach; 2% Grad	64%
4	4%	$15k to $42k	100% No HS	51%
5	13%	$19k to $73k	21% No HS; 29% HS; 35% SC; 10% Bach; 5% Grad	60%
6	14%	$25k to $82k	13% No HS; 28% HS; 31% SC; 19% Bach; 9% Grad	48%
7	3%	$25k to $90k	20% No HS; 28% HS; 36% SC; 13% Bach; 3% Grad	49%
8	7%	$35k to $106k	29% HS; 37% SC; 24% Bach; 10% Grad	52%
9	6%	$58k to $91k	15% No HS; 35% HS; 23% SC; 18% Bach; 9% Grad	58%
10	23%	$63k to $106k	6% No HS; 31% HS; 34% SC; 21% Bach; 8% Grad	57%
11	4%	$67k to $110k	6% No HS; 29% HS; 35% SC; 22% Bach; 8% Grad	59%
12	3%	$250k+	2% No HS; 9% HS; 21% SC; 37% Bach; 31% Grad	35%
13	7%	$250k+	2% No HS; 12% HS; 23% SC; 39% Bach; 24% Grad	41%

Government Equalize Incomes—Top 5 Model

56.1

6.1 Not Christian

5.7 Family income in bottom 40%

−5.5 Personal income in top 20%

−10.0 Family income in top 10%

−10.9 White

Government Equalize Incomes—Full Model

56.8

13.2 Age 65+ & Personal income in top 40%

7.3 Not Christian & Bachelor's degree or more

7.1 Graduate degree

6.4 Bachelor's degree or more & Test in top 20%

5.8 African American

5.0 White & Family income in bottom 40%

4.2 Union household

3.7 Family income in bottom 20%

3.4 Not Christian

2.2 Personal income in bottom 40%

−0.6 Family income in bottom 40%

−1.9 Personal income in top 40%

−4.9 Personal income in top 20%

−4.9 Self-employed household

−6.4 Bachelor's degree or more

−6.8 Age 65+

−7.4 Test in top 20%

−7.7 African American & Personal income in bottom 40%

−8.7 White

−9.4 Family income in top 10%

Table 6A.3. Government Equalize Incomes—Groups

Group	Gov. reduce diff.	3	4	5	No gov. action
All	30%	17%	**19%**	13%	21%
Latino/Asian/other American; Parent(s) born outside the U.S.; No high school diploma	47%	**15%**	20%	8%	10%
African American	44%	**15%**	22%	9%	10%
White; Family income in bottom 40%; Heterosexual; Christian; Age 18–64; Has children	37%	**18%**	19%	14%	12%

(*continues*)

Table 6A.3. (*continued*)

Group	Gov. reduce diff.	3	4	5	No gov. action
Latino/Asian/other American; Parent(s) born outside the U.S.; High school diploma or more	31%	**23%**	21%	12%	13%
White; Income in bottom 90%; Not heterosexual and/or not Christian	36%	**19%**	18%	12%	15%
White; Family income in bottom 40%; Heterosexual; Christian; Age 18–64; No children	26%	**25%**	18%	12%	19%
Latino/Asian/other American; Parents born in the U.S.	33%	17%	**22%**	12%	16%
White; Family income in bottom 40%; Heterosexual; Christian; Age 65+	28%	10%	**22%**	15%	25%
White; Income in upper-middle 50%; Heterosexual; Christian; Age 18–64; Not self-employed household	24%	18%	**18%**	16%	24%
White; Income in top 10%; Not heterosexual and/or not Christian	22%	18%	**14%**	10%	36%
White; Income in upper-middle 50%; Heterosexual; Christian; Age 65+	19%	13%	**21%**	15%	32%
White; Income in upper-middle 50%; Heterosexual; Christian; Age 18–64; Self-employed household	17%	12%	20%	**14%**	37%
White; Income in top 10%; Heterosexual; Christian	11%	14%	17%	**18%**	40%

Government Help for the Poor—Top 5 Model

57.6	−6.0	Age 65+
8.0 Lesbian/gay/bisexual	−6.2	Family income in top 10%
7.8 Family income in bottom 40%	−12.3	White

Government Help for the Poor—Full Model

54.4	3.3 Age 65+
9.0 Graduate degree & Age 65+	1.2 Family income in bottom 40%
8.4 Not Christian & Graduate degree	0.6 Graduate degree
	−0.4 High school diploma or more
7.5 African American	−1.2 Family income in bottom 20%
7.1 Family income in bottom 40% & White	−3.0 Non-Catholic Christian
	−3.1 White
6.9 Lesbian/gay/bisexual	−3.5 Family income in top 40%
6.3 Family income in bottom 20% & Non-Catholic Christian	−4.7 Family income in top 10%
	−7.3 White & High school diploma or more
5.8 Not Christian & White	
3.6 Raised outside the U.S.	−8.0 White & Age 65+
3.5 Female	−9.3 Age 65+ & Family income in bottom 40%
3.5 Northeast region	

Table 6A.4. Government Help for the Poor—Groups

Group	Gov. action	2	Agree with both	4	People help selves
All	17%	12%	**45%**	14%	12%
Latino/Asian/other American; Parent(s) born outside the U.S.; No high school diploma	45%	5%	**33%**	4%	13%
African American	33%	11%	**46%**	4%	6%
White; Family income in bottom 40%; Heterosexual; Christian; Age 18–64; Has children	28%	12%	**43%**	8%	9%
Latino/Asian/other American; Parent(s) born outside the U.S.; High school diploma or more	20%	13%	**47%**	13%	7%
White; Income in bottom 90%; Not heterosexual and/or not Christian	17%	15%	**47%**	13%	8%

(continues)

Table 6A.4. (*continued*)

Group	Gov. action	2	Agree with both	4	People help selves
Latino/Asian/other American; Parents born in the U.S.	19%	12%	**47%**	10%	12%
White; Family income in bottom 40%; Heterosexual; Christian; Age 18–64; No children	14%	16%	**44%**	18%	8%
White; Income in top 10%; Not heterosexual and/or not Christian	7%	21%	**46%**	16%	10%
White; Income in upper-middle 50%; Heterosexual; Christian; Age 18–64; Not self-employed household	8%	12%	**46%**	21%	13%
White; Family income in bottom 40%; Heterosexual; Christian; Age 65+	12%	5%	**50%**	11%	22%
White; Income in upper-middle 50%; Heterosexual; Christian; Age 65+	10%	6%	**45%**	17%	22%
White; Income in upper-middle 50%; Heterosexual; Christian; Age 18–64; Self-employed household	7%	10%	**42%**	23%	18%
White; Income in top 10%; Heterosexual; Christian	5%	4%	**42%**	29%	17%

Government Help for the Sick—Top 5 Model

45.9

13.5 African American

7.9 Born outside the U.S.

7.5 Lesbian/gay/bisexual

7.1 Not Christian

−8.3 Personal income in top 10%

Government Help for the Sick—Full Model

45.8	−0.6 Graduate degree
15.6 African American	−2.9 Bachelor's degree or more
7.9 Graduate degree & White	−3.1 Non-Catholic Christian
7.6 Not Christian & Bachelor's degree	−3.8 Test in top 20%
	−3.9 Self-employed household
7.5 White	−6.0 Personal income in top 10%
7.5 Non-Catholic Christian & Family income in bottom 20%	−6.4 Family income in bottom 20% & Personal income in bottom 40%
6.3 Born outside the U.S.	
6.1 Lesbian/gay/bisexual	−7.0 Age 65+ & Family income in bottom 40%
5.6 Family income in bottom 40%	
3.8 Age 65+	−7.9 White & High school diploma or more
3.2 Not Christian	
2.7 Personal income in bottom 40%	−8.2 African American & Family income in bottom 40%
1.6 High school diploma or more	
1.0 Family income in bottom 20%	−9.6 White & Age 65+

Table 6A.5. Government Help for the Sick—Groups

Group	Gov. action	2	Agree with both	4	People help selves
All	32%	**19%**	32%	9%	8%
African American	**51%**	15%	27%	3%	4%
Latino/Asian/other American; Parent(s) born outside the U.S.; No high school diploma	**50%**	**6%**	31%	4%	9%
White; Income in bottom 90%; Not heterosexual and/or not Christian	40%	**21%**	25%	8%	6%
White; Family income in bottom 40%; Heterosexual; Christian; Age 18–64; Has children	38%	**19%**	32%	5%	6%

(*continues*)

Table 6A.5. (*continued*)

Group	Gov. action	2	Agree with both	4	People help selves
Latino/Asian/other American; Parent(s) born outside the U.S.; High school diploma or more	36%	**19%**	34%	6%	5%
White; Family income in bottom 40%; Heterosexual; Christian; Age 18–64; No children	29%	**26%**	30%	9%	6%
White; Income in top 10%; Not heterosexual and/or not Christian	29%	**26%**	27%	10%	8%
Latino/Asian/other American; Parents born in the U.S.	26%	15%	**44%**	8%	7%
White; Income in upper-middle 50%; Heterosexual; Christian; Age 18–64; Not self-employed household	23%	23%	**32%**	14%	8%
White; Family income in bottom 40%; Heterosexual; Christian; Age 65+	26%	12%	**34%**	12%	16%
White; Income in upper-middle 50%; Heterosexual; Christian; Age 18–64; Self-employed household	18%	16%	**35%**	17%	14%
White; Income in top 10%; Heterosexual; Christian	14%	22%	**34%**	21%	9%
White; Income in upper-middle 50%; Heterosexual; Christian; Age 65+	19%	11%	**43%**	9%	18%

Government Spending on the Poor/Welfare—Top 5 Model

51.9

6.0 African American

5.7 Lesbian/gay/bisexual

4.7 Family income in bottom 40%

−3.2 Personal income in top 10%

−5.8 White

Government Spending on the Poor/Welfare—Full Model

57.4	3.7 Family income in bottom 40%
7.1 Born outside the U.S. & High school diploma or more	3.2 Graduate degree
	1.6 Not Christian
5.6 African American	0.4 Catholic
5.0 Age 65+ & Bachelor's degree or more	−3.3 Bachelor's degree or more
	−3.3 Personal income in top 10%
5.0 Born outside the U.S. & White	−4.0 Personal income in top 40%
4.9 Not Christian & Bachelor's degree or more	−4.3 High school diploma or more
	−4.5 Age 65+
4.9 Lesbian/gay/bisexual	−6.3 White
4.5 Age 65+ & Catholic	−9.1 Born outside the U.S.
4.2 Personal income in top 40% & Bachelor's degree or more	

Table 6A.6. Government Spending on the Poor/Welfare—Groups

Group	Too little	About right	Too much
All	**68%**	24%	8%
	23%	**36%**	41%
African American	**89%**	9%	2%
	38%	**34%**	28%
Latino/Asian/other American; Parents born in the U.S.	**78%**	20%	2%
	26%	**42%**	32%
White; Family income in bottom 40%; Heterosexual; Christian; Age 18–64; Has children	**78%**	18%	4%
	28%	**33%**	39%
Latino/Asian/other American; Parent(s) born outside the U.S.; High school diploma or more	**72%**	23%	5%
	25%	**41%**	34%
Latino/Asian/other American; Parent(s) born outside the U.S.; No high school diploma	**66%**	26%	8%
	27%	**42%**	31%
White; Income in bottom 90%; Not heterosexual and/or not Christian	**72%**	20%	8%
	25%	**35%**	40%
White; Family income in bottom 40%; Heterosexual; Christian; Age 18–64; No children	**68%**	25%	7%
	22%	**37%**	41%

(*continues*)

Table 6A.6. (*continued*)

Group	Too little	About right	Too much
White; Family income in bottom 40%; Heterosexual; Christian; Age 65+	**62%** 22%	28% **36%**	10% 42%
White; Income in top 10%; Not heterosexual and/or not Christian	**52%** 22%	36% **45%**	12% 34%
White; Income in upper-middle 50%; Heterosexual; Christian; Age 18–64; Not self-employed household	**63%** 16%	26% 33%	11% **51%**
White; Income in upper-middle 50%; Heterosexual; Christian; Age 65+	**56%** 17%	33% **39%**	11% 44%
White; Income in upper-middle 50%; Heterosexual; Christian; Age 18–64; Self-employed household	**54%** 13%	32% **38%**	14% 49%
White; Income in top 10%; Heterosexual; Christian	**53%** 12%	33% 36%	14% **52%**

Government Spending on Health Care—Top 5 Model

47.3
  6.1 African American
  5.0 Lesbian/gay/bisexual

  4.1 Female
−3.9 Family income in top 10%
−5.1 No sex partners since age 18

Government Spending on Health Care—Full Model

50.6
  5.3 African American
  5.2 Born outside the U.S. & Some college or more
  5.0 Family income in bottom 40% & White
  4.2 Female & White
  4.0 Lesbian/Gay/Bisexual
  3.0 Test in top 20%
  2.1 Non-Catholic Christian
  1.0 Female
−0.2 White

−0.3 Catholic
−0.8 Some college or more
−0.9 Family income in bottom 40%
−1.5 Family income in bottom 20%
−3.5 Family income in top 10%
−4.3 Age 65+
−4.5 Catholic & Family income in bottom 20%
−5.1 No sex partners since age 18
−6.1 White & Non-Catholic Christian
−6.4 Born outside the U.S.
−7.2 White & Test in top 20%

Table 6A.7. Government Spending on Health Care—Groups

Group	Too little	About right	Too much
All	71%	19%	10%
African American	83%	12%	5%
White; Family income in bottom 40%; Heterosexual; Christian; Age 18–64; Has children	79%	14%	7%
White; Income in bottom 90%; Not heterosexual and/or not Christian	76%	16%	8%
Latino/Asian/other American; Parents born in the U.S.	74%	17%	9%
White; Family income in bottom 40%; Heterosexual; Christian; Age 18–64; No children	72%	21%	7%
White; Income in upper-middle 50%; Heterosexual; Christian; Age 18–64; Not self-employed household	71%	19%	10%
White; Income in top 10%; Not heterosexual and/or not Christian	69%	18%	13%
White; Family income in bottom 40%; Heterosexual; Christian; Age 65+	66%	26%	8%
Latino/Asian/other American; Parent(s) born outside the U.S.; High school diploma or more	66%	24%	10%
White; Income in upper-middle 50%; Heterosexual; Christian; Age 18–64; Self-employed household	67%	18%	15%
White; Income in upper-middle 50%; Heterosexual; Christian; Age 65+	61%	26%	13%
White; Income in top 10%; Heterosexual; Christian	59%	28%	13%
Latino/Asian/other American; Parent(s) born outside the U.S.; No high school diploma	56%	31%	13%

Government Spending on Social Security—Top 6 Model

54.3

  7.6 African American

−5.3 Age 18–29

−5.9 Test in top 20%

−5.9 Family income in top 10%

−6.7 Bachelor's degree or more

−7.7 Age 65+

Government Spending on Social Security—Full Model

53.3

  9.1 African American

  8.8 Latino American & Some
      college or more

  5.9 Family income in bottom
      40% & White

  5.7 Age 18–29 & Bachelor's degree
      or more

  5.6 Born outside the U.S. &
      Bachelor's degree or more

  4.9 Age 18–39 & White

  4.7 Age 18–29 & Some college
      or more

  4.2 Female

  3.3 Nonmarital cohabitation

  1.8 Test in bottom 40%

−0.9 Test in top 20%

−1.0 Latino American

−1.2 Some college or more

−1.9 White

−2.6 Born outside the U.S.

−3.0 Family income in bottom 40%

−3.7 Age 18–39

−4.4 Age 65+

−4.6 Family income in top 10%

−4.7 Age 65+ & White

−5.2 Test in top 20% & Some college
      or more

−7.0 Bachelor's degree or more

−7.1 Born outside the U.S. & Test in
      bottom 40%

−9.4 Age 18–29

Table 6A.8. Government Spending on Social Security—Groups

Group	Too little	About right	Too much
All	**61%**	33%	6%
African American	**77%**	19%	4%
White; Family income in bottom 40%; Heterosexual; Christian; Age 18–64; Has children	**76%**	21%	3%
Latino/Asian/other American; Parents born in the U.S.	**64%**	32%	4%
White; Income in upper-middle 50%; Heterosexual; Christian; Age 18–64; Not self-employed household	**63%**	31%	6%
White; Income in bottom 90%; Not heterosexual and/or not Christian	**61%**	32%	6%
White; Family income in bottom 40%; Heterosexual; Christian; Age 18–64; No children	**60%**	33%	7%
White; Family income in bottom 40%; Heterosexual; Christian; Age 65+	**56%**	42%	2%
Latino/Asian/other American; Parent(s) born outside the U.S.; High school diploma or more	**58%**	34%	8%
White; Income in upper-middle 50%; Heterosexual; Christian; Age 18–64; Self-employed household	**56%**	36%	8%
White; Income in top 10%; Not heterosexual and/or not Christian	48%	**43%**	9%
Latino/Asian/other American; Parent(s) born outside the U.S.; No high school diploma	49%	**38%**	13%
White; Income in top 10%; Heterosexual; Christian	46%	**43%**	11%
White; Income in upper-middle 50%; Heterosexual; Christian; Age 65+	42%	**53%**	5%

Government Spending on Education—Top 5 Model

51.4	−4.9 White
4.7 High school diploma or more	−5.2 Raised outside the U.S.
−4.8 Latino American	−6.3 Age 65+

Government Spending on Education—Full Model

54.3	−0.2 Female
7.8 White & Raised outside the U.S.	−0.7 Age 18–39
6.6 Latino American & High school diploma or more	−5.0 Age 18–39 & Raised outside the U.S.
6.3 White & Age 18–39	−5.3 Age 65+
5.6 Age 18–29 & High school diploma or more	−6.6 Age 18–29
4.3 White & Female	−6.7 Raised outside the U.S.
2.7 High school diploma or more	−8.4 Latino American
	−10.2 White

Table 6A.9. Government Spending on Education—Groups

Group	Too little	About right	Too much
All	75%	20%	5%
African American	84%	14%	2%
Latino/Asian/other American; Parents born in the U.S.	83%	14%	3%
White; Income in top 10%; Not heterosexual and/or not Christian	80%	15%	5%
White; Income in bottom 90%; Not heterosexual and/or not Christian	79%	16%	5%
Latino/Asian/other American; Parent(s) born outside the U.S.; High school diploma or more	75%	21%	4%
White; Income in upper-middle 50%; Heterosexual; Christian; Age 18–64; Not self-employed household	76%	18%	6%

Table 6A.9. (*continued*)

Group	Too little	About right	Too much
White; Family income in bottom 40%; Heterosexual; Christian; Age 18–64; No children	**74%**	22%	4%
White; Family income in bottom 40%; Heterosexual; Christian; Age 18–64; Has children	**74%**	21%	5%
White; Income in upper-middle 50%; Heterosexual; Christian; Age 18–64; Self-employed household	**72%**	19%	9%
White; Income in top 10%; Heterosexual; Christian	**72%**	20%	8%
White; Income in upper-middle 50%; Heterosexual; Christian; Age 65+	**62%**	27%	11%
White; Family income in bottom 40%; Heterosexual; Christian; Age 65+	**60%**	31%	9%
Latino/Asian/other American; Parent(s) born outside the U.S.; No high school diploma	**51%**	44%	5%

Government Spending on Child Care—Top 5 Model

47.6		3.3	Female
8.8	African American	−6.2	Age 65+
4.4	Northeast region	−6.2	Personal income in top 10%

Government Spending on Child Care—Full Model

50.4		3.5	Female
9.7	Latino American & High school diploma or more	−1.3	Not Christian
		−1.6	Family income in bottom 40%
8.4	African American	−1.8	High school diploma or more
5.2	Not Christian & White	−3.7	White
5.2	Family income in bottom 40% & White	−4.2	Latino American
		−5.0	Personal income in top 10%
4.4	Northeast region	−6.2	Age 65+

Table 6A.10. Government Spending on Child Care—Groups

Group	Too little	About right	Too much
All	**55%**	37%	8%
African American	**71%**	26%	3%
White; Family income in bottom 40%; Heterosexual; Christian; Age 18–64; Has children	**60%**	33%	7%
Latino/Asian/other American; Parents born in the U.S.	**61%**	30%	9%
White; Income in bottom 90%; Not heterosexual and/or not Christian	**59%**	34%	7%
White; Family income in bottom 40%; Heterosexual; Christian; Age 18–64; No children	**57%**	37%	6%
Latino/Asian/other American; Parent(s) born outside the U.S.; High school diploma or more	**57%**	37%	6%
Latino/Asian/other American; Parent(s) born outside the U.S.; No high school diploma	**52%**	41%	7%
White; Income in upper-middle 50%; Heterosexual; Christian; Age 18–64; Not self-employed household	**52%**	40%	8%
White; Income in upper-middle 50%; Heterosexual; Christian; Age 18–64; Self-employed household	46%	**44%**	10%
White; Family income in bottom 40%; Heterosexual; Christian; Age 65+	46%	**43%**	11%
White; Income in top 10%; Not heterosexual and/or not Christian	45%	**44%**	11%
White; Income in top 10%; Heterosexual; Christian	43%	**46%**	11%
White; Income in upper-middle 50%; Heterosexual; Christian; Age 65+	40%	**48%**	12%

B. World Values Survey

Economic Views—Full Model

54.0
  4.2 Income in bottom 20%
  3.7 United States & Education in
       top 20%
  3.4 Western & Education in top
       40%

−1.9 Education in top 20%
−3.7 Education in top 40%
−3.7 Western
−3.7 Income in top 20%
−4.1 Income in top 40%
−7.5 United States

Table 6A.11. Summary of Regression Model

	Education in bottom 60%	**Education in top 20% to 40%**	**Education in top 20%**
Income in bottom 20%	United States: 47.1 West (not USA): 54.6 Other: 58.3	United States: 46.8 West (not USA): 54.3 Other: 54.7	United States: 48.7 West (not USA): 52.4 Other: 52.8
Income in next 40%	United States: 42.7 West (not USA): 50.3 Other: 54.0	United States: 42.5 West (not USA): 50.0 Other: 50.4	United States: 44.4 West (not USA): 48.2 Other: 48.5
Income in next 20%	United States: 38.7 West (not USA): 46.2 Other: 50.0	United States: 38.4 West (not USA): 45.9 Other: 46.3	United States: 40.3 West (not USA): 44.1 Other: 44.4
Income in top 20%	United States: 35.0 West (not USA): 42.5 Other: 46.2	United States: 34.7 West (not USA): 42.2 Other: 42.6	United States: 36.6 West (not USA): 40.4 Other: 40.7

Data Appendix for Chapter 8

The following tables present information about different mutually exclusive demographic groups from the U.S. General Social Survey, including years 2002 to 2012. All of these groups favor (to one degree or another) the Republican party over the Democratic party, as indicated by the GSS's primary party identification variable (including individuals who identify primarily as "independent" but think of themselves as closer to one party or the other as favoring that party). Together with the groups described in the Data Appendix for Chapter 9, these groups include all individuals in the sample. The initial series of tables includes some basic information about the groups; the later series of tables includes information on some of the policy items described earlier in the Data Appendix for Part II.

In the text of chapter 8: (1) When we refer to "Boehners," this includes a combination of groups R1 and R2 (R1 is the upper-middle-human-capital group; R2 is the high-human-capital group); (2) when we refer to "Johnsons," this is to group R5; (3) when we refer to "Church Ladies," this is to group R4; (4) when we refer to "Boehner Women," this includes a combination of groups R3 and R7 (R3 is the upper-middle-human-capital group; R7 is the high-human-capital group); (5) when we refer to "Downscale Kansans," this is to group R12.

Group	Description
R1	White, heterosexual, Christian, church about once a week or more, human capital in upper-middle 40%, family income in top 60%, male
R2	White, heterosexual, Christian, church about once a week or more, human capital in top 20%, male
R3	White, heterosexual, Christian, church about once a week or more, human capital in upper-middle 40%, family income in top 60%, female
R4	White, heterosexual, Christian, church about once a week or more, human capital in upper-middle 40%, family income in bottom 40%
R5	White, heterosexual, Christian, church less than about once a week, human capital in top 20%, male
R6	White, heterosexual, Christian, church less than about once a week, human capital in upper-middle 40%, age 18–64, family income in top 60%, male
R7	White, heterosexual, Christian, church about once a week or more, human capital in top 20%, female
R8	White, heterosexual, Christian, church about once a week or more, human capital in bottom 40%, family income in top 60%
R9	White, heterosexual, Christian, church less than about once a week, human capital in bottom 40%, age 18–64, family income in top 40%
R10	White, heterosexual, Christian, church less than about once a week, human capital in upper-middle 40%, age 65+
R11	White, heterosexual, Christian, church less than about once a week, human capital in upper-middle 40%, age 18–64, family income in top 60%, female
R12	White, heterosexual, Christian, church about once a week or more, human capital in bottom 40%, family income in bottom 40%
R13	White, heterosexual, Christian, church less than about once a week, human capital in bottom 40%, age 18–64, family income in middle 20%

Group	% Republican	% Democratic	% Conservative	% Liberal	% of adult population	% who vote	% of voting population
R1	69%	16%	67%	8%	2.6%	84%	3.5%
R2	71%	22%	65%	15%	2.1%	90%	3.0%
R3	65%	24%	55%	11%	4.0%	87%	5.6%
R4	60%	26%	58%	10%	1.9%	77%	2.3%
R5	60%	27%	51%	21%	2.9%	84%	3.9%
R6	55%	27%	43%	19%	4.9%	74%	5.8%
R7	58%	32%	55%	21%	2.5%	93%	3.7%
R8	55%	30%	55%	10%	4.4%	76%	5.3%
R9	46%	29%	35%	15%	2.8%	64%	2.9%
R10	50%	39%	43%	18%	1.7%	86%	2.3%
R11	46%	36%	37%	22%	5.3%	73%	6.2%
R12	45%	38%	42%	17%	2.9%	70%	3.2%
R13	36%	33%	28%	20%	3.7%	45%	2.7%

Group	Age (middle 50%)	Female	High school diploma	Bachelor's degree	Family income (middle 50%)	Married	South
R1	36 to 60	0%	100%	41%	$67k to $137k	79%	43%
R2	40 to 62	0%	100%	87%	$67k to $145k	83%	36%
R3	38 to 60	100%	99%	34%	$71k to $121k	81%	42%
R4	30 to 67	64%	99%	22%	$20k to $39k	52%	37%
R5	35 to 58	0%	100%	81%	$67k to $170k	71%	33%
R6	34 to 54	0%	99%	28%	$70k to $133k	65%	37%
R7	39 to 61	100%	100%	84%	$63k to $132k	75%	35%
R8	42 to 70	61%	79%	0%	$60k to $106k	79%	44%
R9	35 to 52	48%	88%	0%	$87k to $133k	75%	29%
R10	68 to 77	54%	96%	26%	$32k to $82k	64%	33%
R11	32 to 51	100%	99%	27%	$67k to $132k	72%	33%
R12	48 to 75	64%	70%	0%	$15k to $36k	55%	43%
R13	33 to 54	54%	78%	0%	$54k to $67k	63%	39%

R1: White; Heterosexual; Christian; Church about once a week or more; Human capital in upper-middle 40%; Family income in top 60%; Male

Lifestyle issues	Conservative
Is premarital sex not wrong at all?	25% yes
Should pornography be legal for adults?	49% yes
Should abortion be legal in cases motivated by being poor, being single, or not wanting more children?	22% yes
Should teens have access to birth control without parental consent?	29% yes
Should marijuana be legal?	25% yes

Issues relating to sexual orientation and religion	Conservative
Allow a gay man to teach at college?	81% yes
Allow someone against religion to teach at college?	65% yes
Allow an anti-American Muslim to teach at college?	27% yes
Allow same-sex marriage?	22% yes
Is homosexual sex not wrong at all?	13% yes
Approve of the ban on school prayer?	36% yes

Issues relating to gender, race, immigration, and criminal justice	Very Conservative
Support affirmative action for women?	10% yes
Support affirmative action for African Americans?	7% yes
Should the government help African Americans?	35% yes

Issues relating to gender, race, immigration, and criminal justice	Very Conservative
Spend more on African Americans?	13% yes
Should immigration levels be left as is or even increased?	47% yes
Oppose the death penalty?	20% yes
Oppose police striking citizens?	7% yes

Economic issues	Very Conservative
Should the government reduce income differences?	24% yes; 56% no
Should the government help the poor?	58% yes
Spend more on welfare?	13% yes
Spend more on the poor?	52% yes
Should the government help with health care?	69% yes
Spend more on health care?	57% yes
Spend more on Social Security?	43% yes
Spend more on education?	67% yes
Spend more on child care?	37% yes

R2: White; Heterosexual; Christian; Church about once a week or more; Human capital in top 20%; Male

Lifestyle issues	Conservative
Is premarital sex not wrong at all?	17% yes
Should pornography be legal for adults?	63% yes
Should abortion be legal in cases motivated by being poor, being single, or not wanting more children?	28% yes
Should teens have access to birth control without parental consent?	19% yes
Should marijuana be legal?	28% yes

Issues relating to sexual orientation and religion	Lean Liberal
Allow a gay man to teach at college?	86% yes
Allow someone against religion to teach at college?	74% yes
Allow an anti-American Muslim to teach at college?	63% yes
Allow same-sex marriage?	27% yes
Is homosexual sex not wrong at all?	15% yes
Approve of the ban on school prayer?	55% yes

Issues relating to gender, race, immigration, and criminal justice	Conservative
Support affirmative action for women?	5% yes
Support affirmative action for African Americans?	7% yes
Should the government help African Americans?	36% yes
Spend more on African Americans?	17% yes
Should immigration levels be left as is or even increased?	47% yes
Oppose the death penalty?	28% yes
Oppose police striking citizens?	8% yes

Economic issues	Very Conservative
Should the government reduce income differences?	31% yes; 63% no
Should the government help the poor?	55% yes
Spend more on welfare?	15% yes
Spend more on the poor?	43% yes
Should the government help with health care?	67% yes
Spend more on health care?	47% yes
Spend more on Social Security?	34% yes
Spend more on education?	59% yes
Spend more on child care?	34% yes

R3: White; Heterosexual; Christian; Church about once a week or more; Human capital in upper-middle 40%; Family income in top 60%; Female

Lifestyle issues	Very Conservative
Is premarital sex not wrong at all?	21% yes
Should pornography be legal for adults?	31% yes
Should abortion be legal in cases motivated by being poor, being single, or not wanting more children?	21% yes
Should teens have access to birth control without parental consent?	38% yes
Should marijuana be legal?	23% yes

Issues relating to sexual orientation and religion	Conservative
Allow a gay man to teach at college?	84% yes
Allow someone against religion to teach at college?	66% yes
Allow an anti-American Muslim to teach at college?	18% yes
Allow same-sex marriage?	35% yes
Is homosexual sex not wrong at all?	19% yes
Approve of the ban on school prayer?	30% yes

Issues relating to gender, race, immigration, and criminal justice	Very Conservative
Support affirmative action for women?	17% yes
Support affirmative action for African Americans?	2% yes
Should the government help African Americans?	32% yes
Spend more on African Americans?	17% yes
Should immigration levels be left as is or even increased?	34% yes
Oppose the death penalty?	28% yes
Oppose police striking citizens?	18% yes

Economic issues	Lean Conservative
Should the government reduce income differences?	30% yes; 46% no
Should the government help the poor?	61% yes
Spend more on welfare?	17% yes
Spend more on the poor?	61% yes
Should the government help with health care?	74% yes
Spend more on health care?	72% yes
Spend more on Social Security?	65% yes
Spend more on education?	76% yes
Spend more on child care?	50% yes

R4: White; Heterosexual; Christian; Church about once a week or more; Human capital in upper-middle 40%; Family income in bottom 40%

Lifestyle issues	Very Conservative
Is premarital sex not wrong at all?	15% yes
Should pornography be legal for adults?	34% yes
Should abortion be legal in cases motivated by being poor, being single, or not wanting more children?	10% yes
Should teens have access to birth control without parental consent?	32% yes
Should marijuana be legal?	25% yes

Issues relating to sexual orientation and religion	Conservative
Allow a gay man to teach at college?	76% yes
Allow someone against religion to teach at college?	60% yes
Allow an anti-American Muslim to teach at college?	27% yes
Allow same-sex marriage?	20% yes
Is homosexual sex not wrong at all?	15% yes
Approve of the ban on school prayer?	19% yes

Issues relating to gender, race, immigration, and criminal justice	Conservative
Support affirmative action for women?	34% yes
Support affirmative action for African Americans?	11% yes
Should the government help African Americans?	34% yes
Spend more on African Americans?	20% yes
Should immigration levels be left as is or even increased?	47% yes
Oppose the death penalty?	30% yes
Oppose police striking citizens?	14% yes

Economic issues	Moderate
Should the government reduce income differences?	44% yes; 37% no
Should the government help the poor?	70% yes
Spend more on welfare?	21% yes
Spend more on the poor?	66% yes
Should the government help with health care?	74% yes
Spend more on health care?	73% yes
Spend more on Social Security?	60% yes
Spend more on education?	68% yes
Spend more on child care?	46% yes

R5: White; Heterosexual; Christian; Church less than about once a week; Human capital in top 20%; Male

Lifestyle issues	Lean Liberal
Is premarital sex not wrong at all?	53% yes
Should pornography be legal for adults?	82% yes
Should abortion be legal in cases motivated by being poor, being single, or not wanting more children?	58% yes
Should teens have access to birth control without parental consent?	58% yes
Should marijuana be legal?	52% yes

Issues relating to sexual orientation and religion	Liberal
Allow a gay man to teach at college?	96% yes
Allow someone against religion to teach at college?	80% yes
Allow an anti-American Muslim to teach at college?	57% yes
Allow same-sex marriage?	57% yes
Is homosexual sex not wrong at all?	54% yes
Approve of the ban on school prayer?	58% yes

Issues relating to gender, race, immigration, and criminal justice	Conservative
Support affirmative action for women?	6% yes
Support affirmative action for African Americans?	10% yes
Should the government help African Americans?	34% yes
Spend more on African Americans?	18% yes
Should immigration levels be left as is or even increased?	51% yes
Oppose the death penalty?	24% yes
Oppose police striking citizens?	7% yes

Economic issues	Very Conservative
Should the government reduce income differences?	29% yes; 47% no
Should the government help the poor?	53% yes
Spend more on welfare?	11% yes
Spend more on the poor?	54% yes
Should the government help with health care?	67% yes
Spend more on health care?	57% yes
Spend more on Social Security?	39% yes
Spend more on education?	72% yes
Spend more on child care?	40% yes

R6: White; Heterosexual; Christian; Church less than about once a week; Human capital in upper-middle 40%; Age 18–64; Family income in top 60%; Male

Lifestyle issues	Moderate
Is premarital sex not wrong at all?	67% yes
Should pornography be legal for adults?	80% yes
Should abortion be legal in cases motivated by being poor, being single, or not wanting more children?	44% yes
Should teens have access to birth control without parental consent?	50% yes
Should marijuana be legal?	44% yes

Issues relating to sexual orientation and religion	Lean Liberal
Allow a gay man to teach at college?	82% yes
Allow someone against religion to teach at college?	69% yes
Allow an anti-American Muslim to teach at college?	35% yes
Allow same-sex marriage?	47% yes
Is homosexual sex not wrong at all?	55% yes
Approve of the ban on school prayer?	41% yes

Issues relating to gender, race, immigration, and criminal justice	Very Conservative
Support affirmative action for women?	12% yes
Support affirmative action for African Americans?	7% yes
Should the government help African Americans?	31% yes
Spend more on African Americans?	19% yes
Should immigration levels be left as is or even increased?	36% yes
Oppose the death penalty?	11% yes
Oppose police striking citizens?	12% yes

Economic issues	Conservative
Should the government reduce income differences?	32% yes; 51% no
Should the government help the poor?	59% yes
Spend more on welfare?	12% yes
Spend more on the poor?	54% yes
Should the government help with health care?	72% yes
Spend more on health care?	65% yes
Spend more on Social Security?	59% yes
Spend more on education?	73% yes
Spend more on child care?	46% yes

R7: White; Heterosexual; Christian; Church about once a week or more; Human capital in top 20%; Female

Lifestyle issues	Conservative
Is premarital sex not wrong at all?	29% yes
Should pornography be legal for adults?	38% yes
Should abortion be legal in cases motivated by being poor, being single, or not wanting more children?	24% yes
Should teens have access to birth control without parental consent?	45% yes
Should marijuana be legal?	25% yes

Issues relating to sexual orientation and religion	Lean Liberal
Allow a gay man to teach at college?	93% yes
Allow someone against religion to teach at college?	78% yes
Allow an anti-American Muslim to teach at college?	49% yes
Allow same-sex marriage?	42% yes
Is homosexual sex not wrong at all?	28% yes
Approve of the ban on school prayer?	51% yes

Issues relating to gender, race, immigration, and criminal justice	Lean Conservative
Support affirmative action for women?	13% yes
Support affirmative action for African Americans?	9% yes
Should the government help African Americans?	38% yes
Spend more on African Americans?	25% yes
Should immigration levels be left as is or even increased?	60% yes
Oppose the death penalty?	37% yes
Oppose police striking citizens?	16% yes

Economic issues	Conservative
Should the government reduce income differences?	38% yes; 47% no
Should the government help the poor?	63% yes
Spend more on welfare?	15% yes
Spend more on the poor?	59% yes
Should the government help with health care?	76% yes
Spend more on health care?	61% yes
Spend more on Social Security?	47% yes
Spend more on education?	75% yes
Spend more on child care?	43% yes

R8: White; Heterosexual; Christian; Church about once a week or more; Human capital in bottom 40%; Family income in top 60%

Lifestyle issues	Very Conservative
Is premarital sex not wrong at all?	16% yes
Should pornography be legal for adults?	31% yes
Should abortion be legal in cases motivated by being poor, being single, or not wanting more children?	16% yes
Should teens have access to birth control without parental consent?	25% yes
Should marijuana be legal?	17% yes

Issues relating to sexual orientation and religion	Very Conservative
Allow a gay man to teach at college?	59% yes
Allow someone against religion to teach at college?	43% yes
Allow an anti-American Muslim to teach at college?	22% yes
Allow same-sex marriage?	23% yes
Is homosexual sex not wrong at all?	12% yes
Approve of the ban on school prayer?	17% yes

Issues relating to gender, race, immigration, and criminal justice	Conservative
Support affirmative action for women?	29% yes
Support affirmative action for African Americans?	11% yes
Should the government help African Americans?	33% yes
Spend more on African Americans?	16% yes
Should immigration levels be left as is or even increased?	40% yes
Oppose the death penalty?	26% yes
Oppose police striking citizens?	31% yes

Economic issues	Conservative
Should the government reduce income differences?	32% yes; 44% no
Should the government help the poor?	63% yes
Spend more on welfare?	16% yes
Spend more on the poor?	60% yes
Should the government help with health care?	73% yes
Spend more on health care?	66% yes
Spend more on Social Security?	57% yes
Spend more on education?	68% yes
Spend more on child care?	44% yes

R9: White; Heterosexual; Christian; Church less than about once a week; Human capital in bottom 40%; Age 18–64; Family income in top 40%

Lifestyle issues	Lean Liberal
Is premarital sex not wrong at all?	67% yes
Should pornography be legal for adults?	74% yes
Should abortion be legal in cases motivated by being poor, being single, or not wanting more children?	46% yes
Should teens have access to birth control without parental consent?	61% yes
Should marijuana be legal?	48% yes

Issues relating to sexual orientation and religion	Moderate
Allow a gay man to teach at college?	80% yes
Allow someone against religion to teach at college?	52% yes
Allow an anti-American Muslim to teach at college?	20% yes
Allow same-sex marriage?	48% yes
Is homosexual sex not wrong at all?	30% yes
Approve of the ban on school prayer?	33% yes

Issues relating to gender, race, immigration, and criminal justice	Very Conservative
Support affirmative action for women?	28% yes
Support affirmative action for African Americans?	14% yes
Should the government help African Americans?	31% yes
Spend more on African Americans?	17% yes
Should immigration levels be left as is or even increased?	26% yes
Oppose the death penalty?	14% yes
Oppose police striking citizens?	29% yes

Economic issues	Moderate
Should the government reduce income differences?	42% yes; 37% no
Should the government help the poor?	70% yes
Spend more on welfare?	9% yes
Spend more on the poor?	62% yes
Should the government help with health care?	81% yes
Spend more on health care?	72% yes
Spend more on Social Security?	69% yes
Spend more on education?	72% yes
Spend more on child care?	51% yes

R10: White; Heterosexual; Christian; Church less than about once a week; Human capital in upper-middle 40%; Age 65+

Lifestyle issues	Moderate
Is premarital sex not wrong at all?	47% yes
Should pornography be legal for adults?	47% yes
Should abortion be legal in cases motivated by being poor, being single, or not wanting more children?	47% yes
Should teens have access to birth control without parental consent?	42% yes
Should marijuana be legal?	35% yes

Issues relating to sexual orientation and religion	Lean Conservative
Allow a gay man to teach at college?	73% yes
Allow someone against religion to teach at college?	45% yes
Allow an anti-American Muslim to teach at college?	25% yes
Allow same-sex marriage?	38% yes
Is homosexual sex not wrong at all?	24% yes
Approve of the ban on school prayer?	32% yes

Issues relating to gender, race, immigration, and criminal justice	Conservative
Support affirmative action for women?	26% yes
Support affirmative action for African Americans?	6% yes
Should the government help African Americans?	37% yes
Spend more on African Americans?	20% yes
Should immigration levels be left as is or even increased?	36% yes
Oppose the death penalty?	28% yes
Oppose police striking citizens?	23% yes

Economic issues	Conservative
Should the government reduce income differences?	35% yes; 46% no
Should the government help the poor?	60% yes
Spend more on welfare?	20% yes
Spend more on the poor?	54% yes
Should the government help with health care?	72% yes
Spend more on health care?	65% yes
Spend more on Social Security?	44% yes
Spend more on education?	62% yes
Spend more on child care?	37% yes

R11: White; Heterosexual; Christian; Church less than about once a week; Human capital in upper-middle 40%; Age 18–64; Family income in top 60%; Female

Lifestyle issues	Lean Liberal
Is premarital sex not wrong at all?	60% yes
Should pornography be legal for adults?	66% yes
Should abortion be legal in cases motivated by being poor, being single, or not wanting more children?	53% yes
Should teens have access to birth control without parental consent?	66% yes
Should marijuana be legal?	45% yes

Issues relating to sexual orientation and religion	Liberal
Allow a gay man to teach at college?	93% yes
Allow someone against religion to teach at college?	75% yes
Allow an anti-American Muslim to teach at college?	33% yes
Allow same-sex marriage?	66% yes
Is homosexual sex not wrong at all?	52% yes
Approve of the ban on school prayer?	45% yes

Issues relating to gender, race, immigration, and criminal justice	Conservative
Support affirmative action for women?	16% yes
Support affirmative action for African Americans?	7% yes
Should the government help African Americans?	36% yes
Spend more on African Americans?	21% yes
Should immigration levels be left as is or even increased?	31% yes
Oppose the death penalty?	20% yes
Oppose police striking citizens?	23% yes

Economic issues	Lean Liberal
Should the government reduce income differences?	41% yes; 38% no
Should the government help the poor?	68% yes
Spend more on welfare?	18% yes
Spend more on the poor?	61% yes
Should the government help with health care?	83% yes
Spend more on health care?	75% yes
Spend more on Social Security?	68% yes
Spend more on education?	82% yes
Spend more on child care?	59% yes

R12: White; Heterosexual; Christian; Church about once a week or more; Human capital in bottom 40%; Family income in bottom 40%

Lifestyle issues	Very Conservative
Is premarital sex not wrong at all?	20% yes
Should pornography be legal for adults?	30% yes
Should abortion be legal in cases motivated by being poor, being single, or not wanting more children?	19% yes
Should teens have access to birth control without parental consent?	40% yes
Should marijuana be legal?	21% yes

Issues relating to sexual orientation and religion	Very Conservative
Allow a gay man to teach at college?	54% yes
Allow someone against religion to teach at college?	32% yes
Allow an anti-American Muslim to teach at college?	11% yes
Allow same-sex marriage?	24% yes
Is homosexual sex not wrong at all?	9% yes
Approve of the ban on school prayer?	16% yes

Issues relating to gender, race, immigration, and criminal justice	Lean Conservative
Support affirmative action for women?	36% yes
Support affirmative action for African Americans?	13% yes
Should the government help African Americans?	46% yes
Spend more on African Americans?	21% yes
Should immigration levels be left as is or even increased?	29% yes
Oppose the death penalty?	30% yes
Oppose police striking citizens?	35% yes

Economic issues	Lean Liberal
Should the government reduce income differences?	48% yes; 27% no
Should the government help the poor?	78% yes
Spend more on welfare?	25% yes
Spend more on the poor?	70% yes
Should the government help with health care?	83% yes
Spend more on health care?	72% yes
Spend more on Social Security?	69% yes
Spend more on education?	67% yes
Spend more on child care?	53% yes

R13: White; Heterosexual; Christian; Church less than about once a week; Human capital in bottom 40%; Age 18–64; Family income in middle 20%

Lifestyle issues	Moderate
Is premarital sex not wrong at all?	58% yes
Should pornography be legal for adults?	67% yes
Should abortion be legal in cases motivated by being poor, being single, or not wanting more children?	38% yes
Should teens have access to birth control without parental consent?	56% yes
Should marijuana be legal?	43% yes

Issues relating to sexual orientation and religion	Moderate
Allow a gay man to teach at college?	82% yes
Allow someone against religion to teach at college?	55% yes
Allow an anti-American Muslim to teach at college?	18% yes
Allow same-sex marriage?	55% yes
Is homosexual sex not wrong at all?	35% yes
Approve of the ban on school prayer?	30% yes

Issues relating to gender, race, immigration, and criminal justice	Conservative
Support affirmative action for women?	40% yes
Support affirmative action for African Americans?	13% yes
Should the government help African Americans?	48% yes
Spend more on African Americans?	26% yes
Should immigration levels be left as is or even increased?	36% yes
Oppose the death penalty?	15% yes
Oppose police striking citizens?	28% yes

Economic issues	Liberal
Should the government reduce income differences?	57% yes; 28% no
Should the government help the poor?	78% yes
Spend more on welfare?	20% yes
Spend more on the poor?	79% yes
Should the government help with health care?	83% yes
Spend more on health care?	79% yes
Spend more on Social Security?	70% yes
Spend more on education?	75% yes
Spend more on child care?	64% yes

Data Appendix for Chapter 9

THE FOLLOWING TABLES PRESENT INFORMATION about different mutually exclusive demographic groups from the U.S. General Social Survey, including years 2002 to 2012. All of these groups favor (to one degree or another) the Democratic party over the Republican party, as indicated by the GSS's primary party identification variable (including individuals who identify primarily as "independent" but think of themselves as closer to one party or the other as favoring that party). Together with the groups described in the Data Appendix for Chapter 8, these groups include all individuals in the sample. The initial series of tables includes some basic information about the groups; the later series of tables includes information on some of the policy items described earlier in the Data Appendix for Part II.

Group	Description
D1	African American, church about once a week or more, human capital in top 60%
D2	African American, church less than about once a week, human capital in top 60%
D3	African American, church about once a week or more, human capital in bottom 40%
D4	African American, church less than about once a week, human capital in bottom 40%
D5	White, not Christian and/or not heterosexual, human capital in top 20%, female
D6	White, not Christian and/or not heterosexual, human capital in top 20%, male
D7	Latino/Asian/other American, church less than about once a week, human capital in top 60%
D8	White, not Christian and/or not heterosexual, human capital in upper-middle 40%, female

(continued)

Group	Description
D9	Latino/Asian/other American, church less than about once a week, human capital in bottom 40%
D10	Latino/Asian/other American, church about once a week or more, human capital in bottom 40%
D11	White, not Christian and/or not heterosexual, human capital in bottom 40%, family income in bottom 40%
D12	Latino/Asian/other American, church about once a week or more, human capital in top 60%
D13	White, heterosexual, Christian, church less than about once a week, human capital in top 20%, female
D14	White, heterosexual, Christian, church less than about once a week, human capital in bottom 40%, age 65+
D15	White, heterosexual, Christian, church less than about once a week, human capital in bottom 40%, age 18–64, family income in bottom 40%
D16	White, not Christian and/or not heterosexual, human capital in upper-middle 40%, male
D17	White, heterosexual, Christian, church less than about once a week, human capital in upper-middle 40%, age 18–64, family income in bottom 40%
D18	White, not Christian and/or not heterosexual, human capital in bottom 40%, family income in top 60%

In the text of chapter 9: (1) African Americans appear in groups D1, D2, D3, and D4, with D1 and D3 constituting the groups we include among "churchgoing African Americans"; (2) when we refer to "Steinems," this is to group D5, when we refer to "Barneys," this is to group D6, and "Barney Steinems" refers to these groups combined; (3) Latino/Asian/other Americans appear in groups D7, D9, D10, and D12; (4) when we refer to "Hillarys," this is to group D13; (5) when we refer to "Springers," this is to group D15.

Group	% Democratic	% Republican	% Liberal	% Conservative	% of adult population	% who vote	% of voting population
D1	82%	6%	25%	26%	2.7%	80%	3.5%
D2	81%	5%	35%	19%	3.5%	69%	3.9%
D3	75%	8%	35%	31%	2.8%	64%	2.9%
D4	71%	9%	30%	24%	4.2%	45%	3.0%
D5	73%	13%	72%	13%	2.1%	84%	2.8%
D6	61%	19%	55%	21%	2.5%	80%	3.2%
D7	59%	19%	37%	20%	4.6%	48%	3.5%
D8	54%	18%	53%	13%	3.3%	60%	3.2%
D9	43%	14%	35%	26%	5.3%	18%	1.5%
D10	44%	21%	22%	43%	2.2%	29%	1.0%
D11	40%	20%	33%	18%	2.5%	34%	1.4%
D12	49%	30%	22%	39%	1.9%	54%	1.6%
D13	52%	36%	41%	31%	3.2%	82%	4.2%
D14	50%	36%	15%	39%	2.8%	75%	3.4%
D15	41%	29%	21%	32%	4.3%	37%	2.5%
D16	42%	31%	39%	25%	3.8%	62%	3.8%
D17	43%	38%	21%	33%	3.1%	48%	2.4%
D18	33%	31%	19%	30%	2.7%	44%	1.9%

Group	Age (middle 50%)	Female	High school diploma	Bachelor's degree	Family income (middle 50%)	Married	South
D1	33 to 53	69%	99%	35%	$33k to $94k	52%	60%
D2	29 to 49	58%	98%	29%	$27k to $86k	32%	49%
D3	34 to 62	68%	62%	0%	$17k to $54k	42%	68%
D4	27 to 53	50%	61%	0%	$12k to $47k	25%	61%
D5	34 to 59	100%	100%	85%	$50k to $154k	52%	23%
D6	34 to 60	0%	100%	82%	$58k to $170k	54%	24%
D7	27 to 45	45%	98%	43%	$37k to $121k	47%	24%
D8	27 to 50	100%	97%	27%	$31k to $110k	45%	22%
D9	26 to 44	48%	43%	0%	$17k to $54k	49%	35%
D10	30 to 54	65%	46%	0%	$18k to $57k	61%	40%
D11	25 to 50	47%	62%	0%	$12k to $32k	31%	25%
D12	32 to 51	57%	97%	47%	$39k to $114k	68%	29%
D13	35 to 56	100%	100%	80%	$57k to $145k	65%	33%
D14	68 to 79	60%	62%	0%	$17k to $50k	51%	37%
D15	30 to 53	55%	64%	0%	$14k to $35k	36%	42%
D16	28 to 52	0%	97%	28%	$34k to $110k	44%	27%
D17	25 to 50	58%	97%	11%	$15k to $37k	23%	35%
D18	26 to 51	44%	74%	0%	$60k to $110k	51%	29%

**D1: African American; Church about once a week or more;
Human capital in top 60%**

Lifestyle issues	Lean Conservative
Is premarital sex not wrong at all?	26% yes
Should pornography be legal for adults?	59% yes
Should abortion be legal in cases motivated by being poor, being single, or not wanting more children?	35% yes
Should teens have access to birth control without parental consent?	52% yes
Should marijuana be legal?	24% yes

Issues relating to sexual orientation and religion	Conservative
Allow a gay man to teach at college?	81% yes
Allow someone against religion to teach at college?	61% yes
Allow an anti-American Muslim to teach at college?	31% yes
Allow same-sex marriage?	35% yes
Is homosexual sex not wrong at all?	12% yes
Approve of the ban on school prayer?	16% yes

Issues relating to gender, race, immigration, and criminal justice	Very Liberal
Support affirmative action for women?	53% yes
Support affirmative action for African Americans?	37% yes
Should the government help African Americans?	81% yes
Spend more on African Americans?	78% yes
Should immigration levels be left as is or even increased?	55% yes
Oppose the death penalty?	52% yes
Oppose police striking citizens?	46% yes

Economic issues	Very Liberal
Should the government reduce income differences?	56% yes; 24% no
Should the government help the poor?	92% yes
Spend more on welfare?	29% yes
Spend more on the poor?	89% yes
Should the government help with health care?	93% yes
Spend more on health care?	87% yes
Spend more on Social Security?	79% yes
Spend more on education?	87% yes
Spend more on child care?	75% yes

D2: African American; Church less than about once a week; Human capital in top 60%

Lifestyle issues	Liberal
Is premarital sex not wrong at all?	60% yes
Should pornography be legal for adults?	83% yes
Should abortion be legal in cases motivated by being poor, being single, or not wanting more children?	57% yes
Should teens have access to birth control without parental consent?	61% yes
Should marijuana be legal?	54% yes

Issues relating to sexual orientation and religion	Lean Liberal
Allow a gay man to teach at college?	90% yes
Allow someone against religion to teach at college?	68% yes
Allow an anti-American Muslim to teach at college?	32% yes
Allow same-sex marriage?	57% yes
Is homosexual sex not wrong at all?	36% yes
Approve of the ban on school prayer?	40% yes

Issues relating to gender, race, immigration, and criminal justice	Very Liberal
Support affirmative action for women?	49% yes
Support affirmative action for African Americans?	45% yes
Should the government help African Americans?	84% yes
Spend more on African Americans?	71% yes
Should immigration levels be left as is or even increased?	54% yes
Oppose the death penalty?	50% yes
Oppose police striking citizens?	38% yes

Economic issues	Very Liberal
Should the government reduce income differences?	64% yes; 17% no
Should the government help the poor?	88% yes
Spend more on welfare?	32% yes
Spend more on the poor?	88% yes
Should the government help with health care?	96% yes
Spend more on health care?	86% yes
Spend more on Social Security?	79% yes
Spend more on education?	90% yes
Spend more on child care?	74% yes

D3: African American; Church about once a week or more; Human capital in bottom 40%

Lifestyle issues	Lean Conservative
Is premarital sex not wrong at all?	29% yes
Should pornography be legal for adults?	49% yes
Should abortion be legal in cases motivated by being poor, being single, or not wanting more children?	25% yes
Should teens have access to birth control without parental consent?	49% yes
Should marijuana be legal?	20% yes

Issues relating to sexual orientation and religion	Very Conservative
Allow a gay man to teach at college?	57% yes
Allow someone against religion to teach at college?	39% yes
Allow an anti-American Muslim to teach at college?	20% yes
Allow same-sex marriage?	24% yes
Is homosexual sex not wrong at all?	9% yes
Approve of the ban on school prayer?	17% yes

Issues relating to gender, race, immigration, and criminal justice	Very Liberal
Support affirmative action for women?	62% yes
Support affirmative action for African Americans?	46% yes
Should the government help African Americans?	81% yes
Spend more on African Americans?	71% yes
Should immigration levels be left as is or even increased?	54% yes
Oppose the death penalty?	57% yes
Oppose police striking citizens?	66% yes

Economic issues	Very Liberal
Should the government reduce income differences?	55% yes; 22% no
Should the government help the poor?	90% yes
Spend more on welfare?	41% yes
Spend more on the poor?	86% yes
Should the government help with health care?	90% yes
Spend more on health care?	78% yes
Spend more on Social Security?	76% yes
Spend more on education?	76% yes
Spend more on child care?	65% yes

D4: African American; Church less than about once a week; Human capital in bottom 40%

Lifestyle issues	Moderate
Is premarital sex not wrong at all?	56% yes
Should pornography be legal for adults?	80% yes
Should abortion be legal in cases motivated by being poor, being single, or not wanting more children?	43% yes
Should teens have access to birth control without parental consent?	67% yes
Should marijuana be legal?	41% yes

Issues relating to sexual orientation and religion	Conservative
Allow a gay man to teach at college?	79% yes
Allow someone against religion to teach at college?	50% yes
Allow an anti-American Muslim to teach at college?	18% yes
Allow same-sex marriage?	49% yes
Is homosexual sex not wrong at all?	23% yes
Approve of the ban on school prayer?	26% yes

Issues relating to gender, race, immigration, and criminal justice	Very Liberal
Support affirmative action for women?	66% yes
Support affirmative action for African Americans?	47% yes
Should the government help African Americans?	84% yes
Spend more on African Americans?	72% yes
Should immigration levels be left as is or even increased?	49% yes
Oppose the death penalty?	57% yes
Oppose police striking citizens?	62% yes

Economic issues	Very Liberal
Should the government reduce income differences?	58% yes; 17% no
Should the government help the poor?	89% yes
Spend more on welfare?	48% yes
Spend more on the poor?	91% yes
Should the government help with health care?	94% yes
Spend more on health care?	81% yes
Spend more on Social Security?	76% yes
Spend more on education?	82% yes
Spend more on child care?	70% yes

D5: White; Not Christian and/or not heterosexual; Human capital in top 20%; Female

Lifestyle issues	Very Liberal
Is premarital sex not wrong at all?	78% yes
Should pornography be legal for adults?	83% yes
Should abortion be legal in cases motivated by being poor, being single, or not wanting more children?	83% yes
Should teens have access to birth control without parental consent?	85% yes
Should marijuana be legal?	76% yes

Issues relating to sexual orientation and religion	Very Liberal
Allow a gay man to teach at college?	98% yes
Allow someone against religion to teach at college?	88% yes
Allow an anti-American Muslim to teach at college?	57% yes
Allow same-sex marriage?	87% yes
Is homosexual sex not wrong at all?	87% yes
Approve of the ban on school prayer?	85% yes

Issues relating to gender, race, immigration, and criminal justice	Lean Liberal
Support affirmative action for women?	17% yes
Support affirmative action for African Americans?	27% yes
Should the government help African Americans?	64% yes
Spend more on African Americans?	39% yes
Should immigration levels be left as is or even increased?	69% yes
Oppose the death penalty?	55% yes
Oppose police striking citizens?	18% yes

Economic issues	Liberal
Should the government reduce income differences?	62% yes; 26% no
Should the government help the poor?	82% yes
Spend more on welfare?	26% yes
Spend more on the poor?	72% yes
Should the government help with health care?	89% yes
Spend more on health care?	79% yes
Spend more on Social Security?	53% yes
Spend more on education?	86% yes
Spend more on child care?	61% yes

D6: White; Not Christian and/or not heterosexual; Human capital in top 20%; Male

Lifestyle issues	Very Liberal
Is premarital sex not wrong at all?	83% yes
Should pornography be legal for adults?	91% yes
Should abortion be legal in cases motivated by being poor, being single, or not wanting more children?	86% yes
Should teens have access to birth control without parental consent?	73% yes
Should marijuana be legal?	76% yes

Issues relating to sexual orientation and religion	Very Liberal
Allow a gay man to teach at college?	99% yes
Allow someone against religion to teach at college?	88% yes
Allow an anti-American Muslim to teach at college?	67% yes
Allow same-sex marriage?	84% yes
Is homosexual sex not wrong at all?	78% yes
Approve of the ban on school prayer?	88% yes

Issues relating to gender, race, immigration, and criminal justice	Moderate
Support affirmative action for women?	21% yes
Support affirmative action for African Americans?	21% yes
Should the government help African Americans?	49% yes
Spend more on African Americans?	33% yes
Should immigration levels be left as is or even increased?	69% yes
Oppose the death penalty?	45% yes
Oppose police striking citizens?	10% yes

Economic issues	Moderate
Should the government reduce income differences?	51% yes; 34% no
Should the government help the poor?	73% yes
Spend more on welfare?	24% yes
Spend more on the poor?	58% yes
Should the government help with health care?	84% yes
Spend more on health care?	68% yes
Spend more on Social Security?	42% yes
Spend more on education?	79% yes
Spend more on child care?	46% yes

D7: Latino/Asian/other American; Church less than about once a week; Human capital in top 60%

Lifestyle issues	Lean Liberal
Is premarital sex not wrong at all?	64% yes
Should pornography be legal for adults?	74% yes
Should abortion be legal in cases motivated by being poor, being single, or not wanting more children?	58% yes
Should teens have access to birth control without parental consent?	59% yes
Should marijuana be legal?	42% yes

Issues relating to sexual orientation and religion	Liberal
Allow a gay man to teach at college?	90% yes
Allow someone against religion to teach at college?	72% yes
Allow an anti-American Muslim to teach at college?	31% yes
Allow same-sex marriage?	76% yes
Is homosexual sex not wrong at all?	55% yes
Approve of the ban on school prayer?	64% yes

Issues relating to gender, race, immigration, and criminal justice	Lean Liberal
Support affirmative action for women?	36% yes
Support affirmative action for African Americans?	21% yes
Should the government help African Americans?	58% yes
Spend more on African Americans?	36% yes
Should immigration levels be left as is or even increased?	77% yes
Oppose the death penalty?	37% yes
Oppose police striking citizens?	38% yes

Economic issues	Lean Liberal
Should the government reduce income differences?	55% yes; 27% no
Should the government help the poor?	80% yes
Spend more on welfare?	22% yes
Spend more on the poor?	71% yes
Should the government help with health care?	88% yes
Spend more on health care?	69% yes
Spend more on Social Security?	59% yes
Spend more on education?	81% yes
Spend more on child care?	59% yes

D8: White; Not Christian and/or not heterosexual; Human capital in upper-middle 40%; Female

Lifestyle issues	Very Liberal
Is premarital sex not wrong at all?	75% yes
Should pornography be legal for adults?	82% yes
Should abortion be legal in cases motivated by being poor, being single, or not wanting more children?	68% yes
Should teens have access to birth control without parental consent?	79% yes
Should marijuana be legal?	62% yes

Issues relating to sexual orientation and religion	Very Liberal
Allow a gay man to teach at college?	95% yes
Allow someone against religion to teach at college?	82% yes
Allow an anti-American Muslim to teach at college?	49% yes
Allow same-sex marriage?	93% yes
Is homosexual sex not wrong at all?	81% yes
Approve of the ban on school prayer?	70% yes

Issues relating to gender, race, immigration, and criminal justice	Moderate
Support affirmative action for women?	26% yes
Support affirmative action for African Americans?	11% yes
Should the government help African Americans?	49% yes
Spend more on African Americans?	38% yes
Should immigration levels be left as is or even increased?	52% yes
Oppose the death penalty?	39% yes
Oppose police striking citizens?	29% yes

Economic issues	Liberal
Should the government reduce income differences?	50% yes; 22% no
Should the government help the poor?	78% yes
Spend more on welfare?	28% yes
Spend more on the poor?	75% yes
Should the government help with health care?	90% yes
Spend more on health care?	85% yes
Spend more on Social Security?	68% yes
Spend more on education?	87% yes
Spend more on child care?	68% yes

D9: Latino/Asian/other American; Church less than about once a week; Human capital in bottom 40%

Lifestyle issues	Moderate
Is premarital sex not wrong at all?	52% yes
Should pornography be legal for adults?	68% yes
Should abortion be legal in cases motivated by being poor, being single, or not wanting more children?	32% yes
Should teens have access to birth control without parental consent?	61% yes
Should marijuana be legal?	22% yes

Issues relating to sexual orientation and religion	Lean Conservative
Allow a gay man to teach at college?	72% yes
Allow someone against religion to teach at college?	49% yes
Allow an anti-American Muslim to teach at college?	15% yes
Allow same-sex marriage?	60% yes
Is homosexual sex not wrong at all?	28% yes
Approve of the ban on school prayer?	39% yes

Issues relating to gender, race, immigration, and criminal justice	Liberal
Support affirmative action for women?	60% yes
Support affirmative action for African Americans?	25% yes
Should the government help African Americans?	62% yes
Spend more on African Americans?	32% yes
Should immigration levels be left as is or even increased?	73% yes
Oppose the death penalty?	44% yes
Oppose police striking citizens?	71% yes

Economic issues	Lean Liberal
Should the government reduce income differences?	57% yes; 19% no
Should the government help the poor?	82% yes
Spend more on welfare?	29% yes
Spend more on the poor?	73% yes
Should the government help with health care?	87% yes
Spend more on health care?	62% yes
Spend more on Social Security?	55% yes
Spend more on education?	64% yes
Spend more on child care?	54% yes

D10: Latino/Asian/other American; Church about once a week or more; Human capital in bottom 40%

Lifestyle issues	Conservative
Is premarital sex not wrong at all?	26% yes
Should pornography be legal for adults?	50% yes
Should abortion be legal in cases motivated by being poor, being single, or not wanting more children?	21% yes
Should teens have access to birth control without parental consent?	54% yes
Should marijuana be legal?	16% yes

Issues relating to sexual orientation and religion	Very Conservative
Allow a gay man to teach at college?	68% yes
Allow someone against religion to teach at college?	43% yes
Allow an anti-American Muslim to teach at college?	19% yes
Allow same-sex marriage?	34% yes
Is homosexual sex not wrong at all?	10% yes
Approve of the ban on school prayer?	36% yes

Issues relating to gender, race, immigration, and criminal justice	Liberal
Support affirmative action for women?	62% yes
Support affirmative action for African Americans?	23% yes
Should the government help African Americans?	54% yes
Spend more on African Americans?	31% yes
Should immigration levels be left as is or even increased?	75% yes
Oppose the death penalty?	53% yes
Oppose police striking citizens?	71% yes

Economic issues	Lean Liberal
Should the government reduce income differences?	56% yes; 26% no
Should the government help the poor?	81% yes
Spend more on welfare?	24% yes
Spend more on the poor?	67% yes
Should the government help with health care?	86% yes
Spend more on health care?	62% yes
Spend more on Social Security?	56% yes
Spend more on education?	62% yes
Spend more on child care?	57% yes

D11: White; Not Christian and/or not heterosexual; Human capital in bottom 40%; Family income in bottom 40%

Lifestyle issues	Liberal
Is premarital sex not wrong at all?	68% yes
Should pornography be legal for adults?	76% yes
Should abortion be legal in cases motivated by being poor, being single, or not wanting more children?	41% yes
Should teens have access to birth control without parental consent?	74% yes
Should marijuana be legal?	56% yes

Issues relating to sexual orientation and religion	Liberal
Allow a gay man to teach at college?	81% yes
Allow someone against religion to teach at college?	73% yes
Allow an anti-American Muslim to teach at college?	30% yes
Allow same-sex marriage?	65% yes
Is homosexual sex not wrong at all?	49% yes
Approve of the ban on school prayer?	47% yes

Issues relating to gender, race, immigration, and criminal justice	Moderate
Support affirmative action for women?	41% yes
Support affirmative action for African Americans?	21% yes
Should the government help African Americans?	51% yes
Spend more on African Americans?	32% yes
Should immigration levels be left as is or even increased?	37% yes
Oppose the death penalty?	27% yes
Oppose police striking citizens?	45% yes

Economic issues	Very Liberal
Should the government reduce income differences?	66% yes; 19% no
Should the government help the poor?	90% yes
Spend more on welfare?	35% yes
Spend more on the poor?	83% yes
Should the government help with health care?	91% yes
Spend more on health care?	78% yes
Spend more on Social Security?	68% yes
Spend more on education?	73% yes
Spend more on child care?	67% yes

D12: Latino/Asian/other American; Church about once a week or more; Human capital in top 60%

Lifestyle issues	Lean Conservative
Is premarital sex not wrong at all?	29% yes
Should pornography be legal for adults?	50% yes
Should abortion be legal in cases motivated by being poor, being single, or not wanting more children?	24% yes
Should teens have access to birth control without parental consent?	51% yes
Should marijuana be legal?	20% yes

Issues relating to sexual orientation and religion	Lean Conservative
Allow a gay man to teach at college?	78% yes
Allow someone against religion to teach at college?	56% yes
Allow an anti-American Muslim to teach at college?	22% yes
Allow same-sex marriage?	39% yes
Is homosexual sex not wrong at all?	25% yes
Approve of the ban on school prayer?	38% yes

Issues relating to gender, race, immigration, and criminal justice	Lean Liberal
Support affirmative action for women?	37% yes
Support affirmative action for African Americans?	17% yes
Should the government help African Americans?	54% yes
Spend more on African Americans?	34% yes
Should immigration levels be left as is or even increased?	77% yes
Oppose the death penalty?	44% yes
Oppose police striking citizens?	56% yes

Economic issues	Lean Liberal
Should the government reduce income differences?	47% yes; 29% no
Should the government help the poor?	79% yes
Spend more on welfare?	27% yes
Spend more on the poor?	72% yes
Should the government help with health care?	91% yes
Spend more on health care?	68% yes
Spend more on Social Security?	59% yes
Spend more on education?	72% yes
Spend more on child care?	55% yes

D13: White; Heterosexual; Christian; Church less than about once a week; Human capital in top 20%; Female

Lifestyle issues	Liberal
Is premarital sex not wrong at all?	62% yes
Should pornography be legal for adults?	74% yes
Should abortion be legal in cases motivated by being poor, being single, or not wanting more children?	63% yes
Should teens have access to birth control without parental consent?	73% yes
Should marijuana be legal?	45% yes

Issues relating to sexual orientation and religion	Very Liberal
Allow a gay man to teach at college?	99% yes
Allow someone against religion to teach at college?	83% yes
Allow an anti-American Muslim to teach at college?	53% yes
Allow same-sex marriage?	75% yes
Is homosexual sex not wrong at all?	70% yes
Approve of the ban on school prayer?	61% yes

Issues relating to gender, race, immigration, and criminal justice	Lean Conservative
Support affirmative action for women?	16% yes
Support affirmative action for African Americans?	13% yes
Should the government help African Americans?	41% yes
Spend more on African Americans?	30% yes
Should immigration levels be left as is or even increased?	51% yes
Oppose the death penalty?	38% yes
Oppose police striking citizens?	18% yes

Economic issues	Moderate
Should the government reduce income differences?	42% yes; 45% no
Should the government help the poor?	67% yes
Spend more on welfare?	20% yes
Spend more on the poor?	59% yes
Should the government help with health care?	79% yes
Spend more on health care?	74% yes
Spend more on Social Security?	51% yes
Spend more on education?	83% yes
Spend more on child care?	52% yes

D14: White; Heterosexual; Christian; Church less than about once a week; Human capital in bottom 40%; Age 65+

Lifestyle issues	Lean Conservative
Is premarital sex not wrong at all?	33% yes
Should pornography be legal for adults?	36% yes
Should abortion be legal in cases motivated by being poor, being single, or not wanting more children?	36% yes
Should teens have access to birth control without parental consent?	42% yes
Should marijuana be legal?	25% yes

Issues relating to sexual orientation and religion	Very Conservative
Allow a gay man to teach at college?	62% yes
Allow someone against religion to teach at college?	34% yes
Allow an anti-American Muslim to teach at college?	12% yes
Allow same-sex marriage?	42% yes
Is homosexual sex not wrong at all?	19% yes
Approve of the ban on school prayer?	18% yes

Issues relating to gender, race, immigration, and criminal justice	Conservative
Support affirmative action for women?	41% yes
Support affirmative action for African Americans?	16% yes
Should the government help African Americans?	41% yes
Spend more on African Americans?	21% yes
Should immigration levels be left as is or even increased?	25% yes
Oppose the death penalty?	19% yes
Oppose police striking citizens?	43% yes

Economic issues	Lean Conservative
Should the government reduce income differences?	40% yes; 39% no
Should the government help the poor?	68% yes
Spend more on welfare?	18% yes
Spend more on the poor?	65% yes
Should the government help with health care?	73% yes
Spend more on health care?	66% yes
Spend more on Social Security?	58% yes
Spend more on education?	61% yes
Spend more on child care?	44% yes

D15: White; Heterosexual; Christian; Church less than about once a week; Human capital in bottom 40%; Age 18–64; Family income in bottom 40%

Lifestyle issues	Moderate
Is premarital sex not wrong at all?	56% yes
Should pornography be legal for adults?	65% yes
Should abortion be legal in cases motivated by being poor, being single, or not wanting more children?	33% yes
Should teens have access to birth control without parental consent?	62% yes
Should marijuana be legal?	48% yes

Issues relating to sexual orientation and religion	Conservative
Allow a gay man to teach at college?	73% yes
Allow someone against religion to teach at college?	51% yes
Allow an anti-American Muslim to teach at college?	10% yes
Allow same-sex marriage?	49% yes
Is homosexual sex not wrong at all?	27% yes
Approve of the ban on school prayer?	31% yes

Issues relating to gender, race, immigration, and vcriminal justice	Lean Conservative
Support affirmative action for women?	43% yes
Support affirmative action for African Americans?	15% yes
Should the government help African Americans?	47% yes
Spend more on African Americans?	19% yes
Should immigration levels be left as is or even increased?	35% yes
Oppose the death penalty?	19% yes
Oppose police striking citizens?	38% yes

Economic issues	Liberal
Should the government reduce income differences?	54% yes; 26% no
Should the government help the poor?	83% yes
Spend more on welfare?	30% yes
Spend more on the poor?	81% yes
Should the government help with health care?	90% yes
Spend more on health care?	78% yes
Spend more on Social Security?	74% yes
Spend more on education?	74% yes
Spend more on child care?	63% yes

D16: White; Not Christian and/or not heterosexual; Human capital in upper-middle 40%; Male

Lifestyle issues	Very Liberal
Is premarital sex not wrong at all?	76% yes
Should pornography be legal for adults?	92% yes
Should abortion be legal in cases motivated by being poor, being single, or not wanting more children?	64% yes
Should teens have access to birth control without parental consent?	72% yes
Should marijuana be legal?	69% yes

Issues relating to sexual orientation and religion	Very Liberal
Allow a gay man to teach at college?	91% yes
Allow someone against religion to teach at college?	83% yes
Allow an anti-American Muslim to teach at college?	51% yes
Allow same-sex marriage?	66% yes
Is homosexual sex not wrong at all?	61% yes
Approve of the ban on school prayer?	69% yes

Issues relating to gender, race, immigration, and criminal justice	Conservative
Support affirmative action for women?	21% yes
Support affirmative action for African Americans?	8% yes
Should the government help African Americans?	38% yes
Spend more on African Americans?	27% yes
Should immigration levels be left as is or even increased?	44% yes
Oppose the death penalty?	28% yes
Oppose police striking citizens?	18% yes

Economic issues	Moderate
Should the government reduce income differences?	46% yes; 36% no
Should the government help the poor?	76% yes
Spend more on welfare?	22% yes
Spend more on the poor?	59% yes
Should the government help with health care?	82% yes
Spend more on health care?	70% yes
Spend more on Social Security?	57% yes
Spend more on education?	77% yes
Spend more on child care?	51% yes

D17: White; Heterosexual; Christian; Church less than about once a week; Human capital in upper-middle 40%; Age 18–64; Family income in bottom 40%

Lifestyle issues	Lean Liberal
Is premarital sex not wrong at all?	57% yes
Should pornography be legal for adults?	73% yes
Should abortion be legal in cases motivated by being poor, being single, or not wanting more children?	45% yes
Should teens have access to birth control without parental consent?	67% yes
Should marijuana be legal?	51% yes

Issues relating to sexual orientation and religion	Lean Liberal
Allow a gay man to teach at college?	90% yes
Allow someone against religion to teach at college?	71% yes
Allow an anti-American Muslim to teach at college?	28% yes
Allow same-sex marriage?	64% yes
Is homosexual sex not wrong at all?	44% yes
Approve of the ban on school prayer?	42% yes

Issues relating to gender, race, immigration, and criminal justice	Conservative
Support affirmative action for women?	26% yes
Support affirmative action for African Americans?	7% yes
Should the government help African Americans?	43% yes
Spend more on African Americans?	24% yes
Should immigration levels be left as is or even increased?	35% yes
Oppose the death penalty?	23% yes
Oppose police striking citizens?	20% yes

Economic issues	Liberal
Should the government reduce income differences?	56% yes; 27% no
Should the government help the poor?	80% yes
Spend more on welfare?	23% yes
Spend more on the poor?	72% yes
Should the government help with health care?	87% yes
Spend more on health care?	77% yes
Spend more on Social Security?	72% yes
Spend more on education?	77% yes
Spend more on child care?	60% yes

D18: White; Not Christian and/or not heterosexual; Human capital in bottom 40%; Family income in top 60%

Lifestyle issues	Liberal
Is premarital sex not wrong at all?	73% yes
Should pornography be legal for adults?	80% yes
Should abortion be legal in cases motivated by being poor, being single, or not wanting more children?	53% yes
Should teens have access to birth control without parental consent?	71% yes
Should marijuana be legal?	51% yes

Issues relating to sexual orientation and religion	Liberal
Allow a gay man to teach at college?	83% yes
Allow someone against religion to teach at college?	68% yes
Allow an anti-American Muslim to teach at college?	29% yes
Allow same-sex marriage?	65% yes
Is homosexual sex not wrong at all?	52% yes
Approve of the ban on school prayer?	45% yes

Issues relating to gender, race, immigration, and criminal justice	Conservative
Support affirmative action for women?	33% yes
Support affirmative action for African Americans?	14% yes
Should the government help African Americans?	44% yes
Spend more on African Americans?	20% yes
Should immigration levels be left as is or even increased?	37% yes
Oppose the death penalty?	18% yes
Oppose police striking citizens?	31% yes

Economic issues	Lean Liberal
Should the government reduce income differences?	49% yes; 32% no
Should the government help the poor?	77% yes
Spend more on welfare?	13% yes
Spend more on the poor?	68% yes
Should the government help with health care?	82% yes
Spend more on health care?	72% yes
Spend more on Social Security?	66% yes
Spend more on education?	73% yes
Spend more on child care?	50% yes

Notes

Chapter 1: Agendas in Action

1. Clarence Page (Nov. 18, 2012), Romney's "gifts" gaffe, *Chicago Tribune*.
2. Ira Stoll (Nov. 19, 2012), Defending Romney's "gift" remarks, reason.com.
3. Michael Kinsley (Apr. 23, 1988), Commentary: The gaffer speaks, *The Times*.
4. Chuck Todd (Nov. 7, 2012), live appearance on MSNBC.
5. Abramowitz 2013.
6. Abramowitz (2013) makes the point that the marriage gap and the gender gap flow in part from the fact that single people and younger people are more liberal on religious/lifestyle issues. We would add as well that single people and younger people also tend to have lower incomes and less economic stability.
7. Judis and Teixeira 2002.
8. Our data here come from the U.S. General Social Survey for 2002 to 2012.
9. Stewart et al. 2004, 108.
10. Caplan 2007, 153.
11. Steven Pinker (Oct. 24, 2012), Why are states so red and blue? nytimes.com.
12. E.g., Bardes & Oldendick 2003; Feldman 2003; Jessee 2012; Zaller 1992.
13. As an empirical matter—i.e., looking at how issue opinions correlate with calling one's views "liberal" versus "conservative" in representative samples—Americans these days use the terms such that, for the main items we explore in this book: (1) views opposing legal limits on or the moral condemnation of premarital sex, pornography, birth control, abortion, and recreational drugs are generally "liberal" and views that do want to limit or moralize these areas are generally "conservative"; (2) views that support traditionally subordinate groups (e.g., non-Christians, homosexuals, immigrants, racial minorities, and women), whether that support comes through measures to equalize group treatment or engage in affirmative efforts to advance such groups, are generally "liberal" and views that oppose such support are generally "conservative"; and (3) views that call for relatively higher levels of income redistribution and spending on safety-net and entitlement programs are generally "liberal" and views that oppose such higher levels are generally "conservative." We understand that internationally, historically, and in some corners of the academy these terms often appear with very different meanings.
14. Political scientists talk about this kind of split in various ways, pointing out, for example, that ideological coherence is higher among people with greater political knowledge (Jessee 2012) or among whites (Bowler & Segura 2012) or among political elites (Ellis & Stimson 2012).
15. Henry & Sears 2002.
16. E.g., Altemeyer 2003.
17. E.g., Flanigan & Zingale 2002; Jacoby 2010; Jessee 2012; Lewis-Beck et al. 2008.
18. E.g., Cottam et al. 2004; Ellis & Stimson 2012; Feldman 2003; Hibbing et al. 2013; Lewis-Beck et al. 2008; Zaller 1992.

19. Conover & Feldman 1981.
20. Achen 2002. We are broadly in agreement with political scientists who see party affiliations as in part causes and in part effects of issue opinions (e.g., Carsey & Layman 2006; Sniderman & Stiglitz 2012).
21. Huang & Liu 2005; Schmitt et al. 2003.
22. Bartels 2002.
23. Bullock 2011.
24. Part of our concern here involves somewhat technical matters we allude to in chapter 2 and discuss in part B of the Data Appendix for Chapter 2. In short, we think researchers in political science often don't worry as much as they should about the impact of including noncausal correlates (like, we would argue, DERP variables and, in many circumstances [especially when it comes to predicting well-known and widely contested policy opinions], party identifications and ideological labels) as predictors in their models.

Chapter 2: Investigating Interests

1. Sears & Funk 1990, 170.
2. Taber 2003, 448.
3. Lewis-Beck et al. 2008, 197.
4. Bryan Caplan (Sept. 18, 2012), Will false beliefs in the SIVH destroy Romney's candidacy? econlog.econlib.org. See also Caplan 2007.
5. Haidt 2012.
6. Ross Douthat (Jul. 1, 2013), The media, immigration and G.O.P. donorism, douthat.blogs.nytimes.com.
7. Will Wilkinson (Jun. 25, 2013), Market forces and appeals to fairness, economist.com.
8. Jonathan Chait (Aug. 23, 2013), Can't get enough of the libertarian populism debate? nymag.com.
9. Ezra Klein (Jun. 19, 2012), The individual mandate: What happened? washingtonpost.com.
10. Kinder 1998, 801–802 (citations omitted).
11. Haidt 2012, ch. 4.
12. Owens & Pedulla 2013; see also Bowler & Segura 2012.
13. Ellis & Stimson 2012.
14. E.g., Becker 1996.
15. Kenrick & Griskevicius 2013.
16. Ibid.
17. Lau & Redlawsk 2006, 6. Lane (2003) provides a look at how self-interest has typically been restricted to material interests, relating primarily to money and other property. Kinder's (1998, p. 801) self-interest definition includes "wealth and power"—something that expands beyond the strictly tangible—but is limited to "the immediate future" and "the short-run."
18. Dawkins 1989.

19. Richerson & Boyd 1998.
20. Tajfel et al. 1971.
21. Page, Putterman, and Unel (2005) use this example.
22. Charness & Yang 2010.
23. Some political scientists have made related calls for expanding the notion of self-interest, including Lane (2003), who argued against limiting self-interest to material matters, and Ellis and Stimson (2012), who view self-interest as encompassing self, children, grandchildren, and communities.
24. Kinder 1998, 808.
25. Haidt 2012.
26. Cf. Abramson et al. 2010; Alvarez & Brehm 2002.

Chapter 3: Machiavellian Minds

1. Mercier & Sperber 2011.
2. Some of the material in this chapter echoes topics presented in Kurzban's *Why Everyone (Else) Is a Hypocrite*. Readers of that book will certainly have a head start in understanding this chapter, but will find new ways to connect ideas about divided minds to modern political debates.
3. Seeing is one of those things that can seem easy, because people do it so effortlessly, but it is in fact incredibly complex. Chapter 4 of Steven Pinker's *How the Mind Works* provides a great overview.
4. Some of the most fascinating work in modern psychology, including the growing field of cognitive neuroscience, involves sorting through the complex ways the brain divides its work (Gazzaniga, Ivry, & Mangun 2013).
5. Nisbett & Wilson 1977.
6. See Kurzban (2010) footnotes 28 and 29, p. 107, for concern about the breadth of this effect.
7. Riess et al. 1981.
8. Libet et al. 1983.
9. Gazzaniga 1998; Gazzaniga, Ivry, & Magnum 2013.
10. This is, roughly, our rephrasing of a leading definition from Keltner and Shiota (2003), discussed at length in Shiota and Kalat (2012): "An emotion is a universal, functional reaction to an external stimulus event, temporally integrating physiological, cognitive, phenomenological, and behavioral channels to facilitate a fitness-enhancing, environment-shaping response to the current situation."
11. MacKuen et al. 2007; Neuman et al. 2007; Spezio & Adolphs 2007.
12. Schreiber 2007.
13. Cohen 2003.
14. Ibid., 811. For a similar effect among Danes, see Slothuus and de Vreese (2010). They conclude: "We found that citizens tend to respond more favorably to an issue frame if sponsored by a party they vote for than if the frame was promoted by another party" (p. 642). See also Petersen et al. 2010.

15. For similar findings, see Pronin et al. (2007).
16. Haidt 2012.
17. Epley & Dunning 2000, Study 4.
18. Ibid., 867, statistical tests omitted.
19. Ibid., 867–68.
20. Heath 1999.
21. Miller & Ratner 1998, 54.
22. Taber & Lodge 2006, 764.
23. Kahan et al. 2013.
24. Weeden 2003.
25. For example, the *New York Times* obituary of Jerry Falwell said: "But, at his core, he remained through his career what he was at the beginning: a preacher and moralist, a believer in the Bible's literal truth, with convictions about religious and social issues rooted in his reading of Scripture." Peter Applebome (May 15, 2007), Jerry Falwell, Moral Majority founder, dies at 73, nytimes.com. Research has also used biblical literalism as an assumed causal predictor of abortion attitudes (e.g., Gay & Lynxwiler 1999).
26. E.g., Brewer & Stonecash 2007.

Chapter 4: Fighting over Sex

1. Unless otherwise indicated, the data for numerical claims in this chapter come from the U.S. General Social Survey.
2. E.g., Kate Taylor (Jul. 12, 2013), Sex on campus: She can play that game, too, nytimes.com.
3. These figures come from recent U.S. Census data.
4. Weeden et al. 2006.
5. Divorce rates discussed in this paragraph and the next come from our analyses of the U.S. National Survey of Family Growth.
6. Both Edsall (2006) and Douthat and Salam (2008) make the point that the working class is particularly vulnerable to the effects of family instability on financial stability, and indicate that this has contributed to a rejection of liberal social views among many working-class people. We'll see later that this isn't really so clear. Of the five lifestyle issues we cover in this chapter (premarital sex, pornography, abortion, teen birth control, and marijuana), the only major effects that exist as a function of socioeconomic differences are with regard to abortion.
7. Casper & Bianchi 2002.
8. Again, here, the divorce statistics come from our analyses of data from the U.S. National Survey of Family Growth.
9. Kurzban et al. 2010; Quintelier et al. 2013.
10. Weeden 2003.

11. Dawkins 2006; Dennett 2006.
12. Haidt 2012; Norenzayan 2013; Wilson 2002.
13. Atran 2002; Boyer 2001.
14. Sniderman & Stiglitz 2012.
15. The data on patterns of church attendance among the current generation of young adults come from the National Longitudinal Surveys of Youth 1997. Otherwise, our data on church attendance come from the GSS.
16. Weeden 2014; Weeden et al. 2008; Weeden & Kurzban 2013.
17. Our analyses of the NLSY data come from Weeden (2014), where more detail can be found.
18. Kenrick 2011.
19. Dennett 2006, 279–80.
20. Our data on these points come from the GSS, years 2002 to 2012.
21. Weeden & Kurzban 2013.

Chapter 5: Rules of the Game

1. E.g., Douthat & Salam 2008; Hayes 2012.
2. E.g., Cottam et al. 2004; Ellis & Stimson 2012; Feldman 2003; Lewis-Beck et al. 2008; Zaller 1992.
3. Pratto et al. 2006.
4. Huang & Liu 2005.
5. Dupper 2013.
6. Bowler & Segura 2012.
7. E.g., Converse 1964; Ellis & Stimson 2012; Jessee 2012.

Chapter 6: Money Matters

1. Ross Douthat (Sept. 18, 2012), Our revolting elites, nytimes.com.
2. Abramson et al. 2010; Sabato 2013.
3. Data on income in this paragraph come from 2012 U.S. Census estimates.
4. Casper & Bianchi 2002.
5. Social Security Administration (Jan. 2013), Monthly Statistical Snapshot, December 2012.
6. Office of Family Assistance, U.S. Department of Health and Human Services (Aug. 2012), Characteristics and Financial Circumstances of TANF Recipients, Fiscal Year 2010.
7. C. Eugene Steuerle & Caleb Quakenbush (Nov. 2013), Social Security and Medicare Taxes and Benefits over a Lifetime, Urban Institute.

8. Philip Rucker (Jul. 28, 2009), Sen. DeMint of S.C. is voice of opposition to health-care reform, washingtonpost.com.
9. Office of Family Assistance, U.S. Department of Health and Human Services (Aug. 2012), Characteristics and Financial Circumstances of TANF Recipients, Fiscal Year 2010.
10. Alesina & Glaeser 2004.
11. Political researchers sometimes comment on the fact that it is rational for minorities to support redistributive programs, though researchers are less likely to highlight the other side of that coin (e.g., Alvarez & Brehm 2002; Bowler & Segura 2012).
12. Douthat 2012; Edsall 2006.
13. Alesina & Glaeser 2004.

Chapter 7: The Many Shades of Red and Blue

1. Solnick & Hemenway 1998.
2. For example, among class members who have household incomes of $250,000 or less, 90% favor raising income tax rates on those making more than $250,000; only 63% agree among those with household incomes of $500,000 or more.
3. Converse 1964. Even those whose arguments rely on a single left-right dimension nonetheless generally acknowledge that ideological coherence is stronger among some groups than others (e.g., Jessee 2012).

Chapter 8: The Republican Coalition

1. Campbell et al. 1960.
2. Noel 2013.
3. Lewis-Beck et al. 2008.
4. Brewer & Stonecash 2007.
5. Douthat & Salam 2008.
6. Brewer & Stonecash 2007; Gelman et al. 2010; Greenberg 2004; Sabato 2013.
7. Brewer & Stonecash 2007; Ellis & Stimson 2012.
8. Douthat 2012.
9. Cohn 2013; Judis & Teixeira 2002.
10. Abramson et al. 2010.
11. Cohn 2013; Douthat & Salam 2008.
12. Martinez 2010.
13. Noel 2013.
14. Miller & Schofield 2003.
15. We don't mean to imply any judgment in using the term "downscale"—we just mean it as a simple description of those with less education and lower incomes.

Chapter 9: The Democratic Coalition

1. Abramson et al. 2010; Edsall 2006.
2. Gloria Steinem (interviewed by Susan Dominus) (1998), Gloria Steinem: First feminist, nymag.com.
3. Brewer & Stonecash 2007.
4. Cf. Douthat & Salam 2008.
5. Gilens 2012; Hacker & Pierson 2010.
6. Althaus 2003.

Chapter 10: An Uncomfortable Take on Political Positions

1. Haidt 2012.
2. Caplan 2007.
3. Our discussions of the demographic correlates of views on environmental spending (in this paragraph) and military spending (in the next paragraph) are based on our analyses of GSS data.
4. Weeden at al. 2008.
5. Erikson et al. 2002; Stimson 1991.
6. Petersen at al. 2013.
7. E.g., Cottam et al. 2004; Ellis & Stimson 2012; Feldman 2003; Lewis-Beck et al. 2008; Zaller 1992.
8. Bartels 2010.
9. E.g., Sniderman & Stiglitz 2012.
10. E.g., Jacoby 2010. Jessee (2012) makes a similar argument about liberal/conservative ideology, i.e., that its stability over time is indicative of its causal priority.
11. E.g., Abramson et al. 2010; Green et al. 2002; Lewis-Beck et al. 2008.
12. Consider this admission from Feldman (2003), a leading proponent of the view that values are important causes of political opinions: "Most work on values begins with the assumption that values influence attitudes but not the reverse. At this point, there is little hard evidence to support this assumption."
13. Pinker 2002.
14. Smith et al. 2012, 18. Several studies reach similar conclusions, including recent ones using extended family design that better enables researchers to investigate potential heightened environmental similarity between identical twins compared with fraternal twins (Hatemi et al. 2010; Kandler, Bleidorn, & Riemann 2012).
15. Smith et al. 2012, 17.
16. Hibbing et al. 2013; Smith at al. 2012.
17. Haworth et al. 2010.
18. McGue & Lykken 1992.

19. Bailey et al. 2000.
20. Erick Erickson (Jun. 26, 2013), Call them back, @GovernorPerry, redstate.com.
21. Gail Collins (Jun. 28, 2013), Expect the unexpected, nytimes.com.
22. Erick Erickson (Oct. 2, 2013), This is about shutting down Obamacare, redstate
    .com.
23. Gail Collins (Sept. 25, 2013), Meet dilly and dither, nytimes.com.
24. Smith & Park 2013.

References

Abramowitz, A. (2013). Voting in a time of polarization: Why Obama won and what it means. In L. J. Sabato (ed.), *Barack Obama and the new America: The 2012 election and the changing face of politics*. Lanham, MD: Rowman & Littlefield Publishers.

Abramson, P. R., Aldrich, J. H., & Rohde, D. W (2010). *Change and continuity in the 2008 elections*. Washington, DC: CQ Press.

Achen, C. C. (2002). Parental socialization and rational party identification. *Political Behavior*, 24, 151–70.

Alesina, A., & Glaeser, E. L. (2004). *Fighting poverty in the US and Europe: A world of difference*. Oxford: Oxford University Press.

Altemeyer, B. (2004). The other "authoritarian personality." In J. T. Jost & J. Sidanius (eds.), *Political psychology: Key readings*. New York: Psychology Press.

Althaus, S. L. (2003). *Collective preferences in democratic politics: Opinion surveys and the will of the people*. Cambridge: Cambridge University Press.

Alvarez, R. M., & Brehm, J. (2002). *Hard choices, easy answers: Values, information, and American public opinion*. Princeton: Princeton University Press.

Atran, S. (2002). *In gods we trust: The evolutionary landscape of religion*. Oxford: Oxford University Press.

Bailey, J. M., Kirk, K. M., Zhu, G., Dunne, M. P., & Martin, N.G. (2000). Do individual differences in sociosexuality represent genetic or environmentally contingent strategies? Evidence from the Australian Twin Registry. *Journal of Personality and Social Psychology*, 78, 537–45.

Bardes, B. A., & Oldendick, R. W. (2003). *Public opinion: Measuring the American mind* (2nd ed.). Belmont, CA: Wadsworth.

Bartels, L. M. (2002). Beyond the running tally: Partisan bias in political perceptions. *Political Behavior*, 24, 117–50.

———. (2010). The study of electoral behavior. In J. E. Leighley (ed.), *The Oxford handbook of American elections and political behavior*. Oxford: Oxford University Press.

Becker, G. S. (1996). *Accounting for tastes*. Cambridge: Harvard University Press.

Bowler, S., & Segura, G. M. (2012). *The future is ours: Minority politics, political behavior, and the multiracial era of American politics*. Los Angeles: CQ Press.

Boyer, P. (2001). *Religion explained: The evolutionary origins of religious thought*. New York: Basic Books.

Brewer, M. D., & Stonecash, J. M. (2007). *Split: Class and cultural divides in American politics*. Washington, DC: CQ Press.

Bullock, J. G. (2011). Elite influence on public opinion in an informed electorate. *American Political Science Review*, 105, 496–515.

Campbell, A., Converse, P. E., Miller, W. E., & Stokes, D. E. (1960). *The American voter*. Chicago: University of Chicago Press.

Caplan, B. (2007). *The myth of the rational voter: Why democracies choose bad policies*. Princeton: Princeton University Press.

Carsey, T. M., & Layman, G. C. (2006). Changing sides or changing minds? Party identification and policy preferences in the American electorate. *American Journal of Political Science*, 50, 464–77.

Casper, L. M., & Bianchi, S. M. (2002). *Continuity and change in the American family.* Thousand Oaks, CA: Sage Publications.

Charness, G., & Yang, C. L. (2010). Endogenous group formation and efficiency: An experimental study. In *Proceedings of the Behavioral and Quantitative Game Theory: Conference on Future Directions.*

Cohen, G. L. (2003). Party over policy: The dominating impact of group influence on political beliefs. *Journal of Personality and Social Psychology,* 85, 808–22.

Cohn, N. (2013). America's evolving electorate. In L. J. Sabato (ed.), *Barack Obama and the new America: The 2012 election and the changing face of politics.* Lanham, MD: Rowman & Littlefield Publishers.

Conover, P. J., & Feldman, S. (1981). The origins and meaning of liberal-conservative self-identification. *American Journal of Political Science,* 25, 617–45.

Converse, P. E. (1964). The nature of belief systems in mass publics. In D. E. Apter (ed.), *Ideology and discontent.* New York: Free Press

Cottam, M., Dietz-Uhler, B., Mastors, E., & Preston, T. (2004). *Introduction to political psychology.* Mahwah, NJ: Lawrence Erlbaum Associates.

Dawkins, R. (1989). *The selfish gene* (new ed.). Oxford: Oxford University Press.

———. (2006). *The God delusion.* Boston: Houghton Mifflin.

Dennett, D. (2006). *Breaking the spell: Religion as a natural phenomenon.* London: Viking.

Douthat, R. (2012). *Bad religion: How we became a nation of heretics.* New York: Free Press.

Douthat, R., & Salam, R. (2008). *Grand new party: How Republicans can win the working class and save the American dream.* New York: Doubleday.

Dupper, D. R. (2013). *School bullying: New perspectives on a growing problem.* Oxford: Oxford University Press.

Edsall, T. B. (2006). *Building red America: The new conservative coalition and the drive for permanent power.* New York: Basic Books.

Ellis, C., & Stimson, J. A. (2012). *Ideology in America.* Cambridge: Cambridge University Press.

Epley, N., & Dunning, D. (2000). Feeling "holier than thou": Are self-serving assessments produced by errors in self- or social prediction? *Journal of Personality and Social Psychology,* 79, 861–75.

Erikson, R. S., MacKuen, M. B., & Stimson, J. A. (2002). *The macro polity.* New York: Cambridge University Press.

Feldman, S. (2003). Values, ideology, and the structure of political attitudes. In D. O. Sears, L. Huddy, & R. Jervis (eds.), *Oxford handbook of political psychology.* Oxford: Oxford University Press.

Flanigan, W. H., & Zingale, N. H. (2002). *Political behavior of the American electorate* (10th ed.). Washington, DC: CQ Press.

Frank, R. (1988). *Passions within reason: The strategic role of the emotions.* New York: W. W. Norton.

Frank, T. (2004). *What's the matter with Kansas? How conservatives won the heart of America.* New York: Owl Books.

Gay, D., & Lynxwiler, J. (1999). The impact of religiosity on race variations in abortion attitudes. *Sociological Spectrum,* 19, 359–77.

Gazzaniga, M. S. (1998). *The mind's past.* Berkeley: University of California Press.

Gazzaniga, M. S., Ivry, R. B., & Mangun, G. R. (2013). *Cognitive neuroscience: The biology of the mind* (4th ed.). New York: W. W. Norton & Company.

Gelman, A., Park, D., Shor, B., & Cortina, J. (2010). *Red state, blue state, rich state, poor state: Why Americans vote the way they do* (expanded ed.). Princeton: Princeton University Press.

Gilens, M. (2012). *Affluence and influence: Economic inequality and political power in America.* Princeton: Princeton University Press.

Gladwell, M. (2005). *Blink: The power of thinking without thinking.* New York: Little, Brown and Company.

Green, D., Palmquist, B., & Schickler, E. (2002). *Partisan hearts and minds: Political parties and the social identities of voters.* New Haven: Yale University Press.

Greenberg, S. B. (2004). *The two Americas: Our current political deadlock and how to break it.* New York: Thomas Dunne Books.

Hacker, J. S., & Pierson, P. (2010). *Winner-take-all politics: How Washington made the rich richer and turned its back on the middle class.* New York: Simon & Schuster.

Haidt, J. (2012). *The righteous mind: Why good people are divided by politics and religion.* New York: Pantheon Books.

Hatemi, P. K., Hibbing, J. R., Medland, S. E., Keller, M. C., Alford, J. R., Smith, K. B., Martin, N. G., & Eaves, L. J. (2010). Not by twins alone: Using the extended family design to investigate genetic influence on political beliefs. *American Journal of Political Science, 54,* 798–814.

Haworth, C. M. A., Wright, M. J., Luciano, M., Martin, N. G., de Geus, E. J. C., van Beijsterveldt, C. E. M., Bartels, M., Posthuma, D., Boomsma, D. I., Davis, O. S. P., Kovas, Y., Corley, R. P., DeFries, J. C., Hewitt, J. K., Olson, R. K., Rhea, S. A., Wadsworth, S. J., Iacono, W. G., McGue, M., Thompson, L. A., Hart, S. A., Petrill, S. A., Lubinski, D., & Plomin, R. (2010). The heritability of general cognitive ability increases linearly from childhood to young adulthood. *Molecular Psychiatry, 15,* 1112–20.

Hayes, C. L. (2012). *Twilight of the elites: America after meritocracy.* New York: Crown Publishers.

Heath, C. (1999). On the social psychology of agency relationships: Lay theories of motivation overemphasize extrinsic incentives. *Organizational Behavior and Human Decision Processes, 78,* 25–62.

Henry, P. J., & Sears, D. O. (2002). The symbolic racism 2000 scale. *Political Psychology, 23,* 253–83.

Hibbing, J. R., Smith. K. B., & Alford, J. R. (2013). *Predisposed: Liberals, conservatives, and the biology of political differences.* New York: Routledge.

Huang, L., & Liu, J. H. (2005). Personality and social structure implications of the situational priming of social dominance orientation. *Personality and Individual Differences, 38,* 267–76.

Issenberg, S. (2012). *The victory lab: The secret science of winning campaigns.* New York: Crown Publishing Group.

Jacoby, W. G. (2010). The American voter. In J. E. Leighley (ed.), *The Oxford handbook of American elections and political behavior.* Oxford: Oxford University Press.

Jessee, S. A. (2012). *Ideology and spatial voting in American elections.* Cambridge University Press.

Judis, J. B., & Teixeira, R. (2002). *The emerging Democratic majority*. New York: Scribner.

Kahan, D. M., Peters, E., Dawson, E. C., & Slovic, P. (2013). Motivated numeracy and enlightened self-government. Working paper.

Kandler, D., Bleidorn, W., & Riemann, R. (2012). Left or right? Sources of political orientation: The roles of genetic factors, cultural transmission, assortative mating, and personality. *Journal of Personality and Social Psychology*, 102, 633–45.

Keltner, D., & Shiota, M. N. (2003). New displays and new emotions: A commentary on Rozin and Cohen (2003). *Emotion*, 3, 86–91.

Kenrick, D. T. (2011). *Sex, murder, and the meaning of life: A psychologist investigates how evolution, cognition, and complexity are revolutionizing our view of human nature*. New York: Basic Books.

Kenrick, D. T., & Griskevicius, V. (2013). *The rational animal: How evolution made us smarter than we think*. New York: Basic Books.

Kinder, D. R. (1998). Opinion and action in the realm of politics. In D. T. Gilbert, S. T. Fiske, & G. Lindzey (eds.), *The handbook of social psychology* (4th ed.). Boston: McGraw-Hill.

Kurzban, R. (2010). *Why everyone (else) is a hypocrite: Evolution and the modular mind*. Princeton: Princeton University Press.

Kurzban, R., Dukes, A., & Weeden, J. (2010). Sex, drugs and moral goals: Reproductive strategies and views about recreational drugs. *Proceedings of the Royal Society B: Biological Sciences*, 277, 3501–08.

Lane, R. E. (2003). Rescuing political science from itself. In D. O. Sears, L. Huddy, & R. Jervis (eds.), *Oxford handbook of political psychology*. Oxford: Oxford University Press.

Lau, R. R., & Redlawsk, D. P. (2006). *How voters decide: Information processing during election campaigns*. Cambridge: Cambridge University Press.

Lewis-Beck, M. S., Jacoby, W. G., Norpoth, H., & Weisberg, H. F. (2008). *The American voter revisited*. Ann Arbor: University of Michigan Press.

Libet, B., Gleason, C. A., Wright, E. W., & Pearl, D. K. (1983). Time of conscious intention to act in relation to onset of cerebral activity (readiness-potential): The unconscious initiation of a freely voluntary act. *Brain*, 106, 623–42.

Luker, K. (1984). *Abortion and the politics of motherhood*. Berkeley: University of California Press.

MacKuen, M., Marcus, G. E., Neuman, W. R., & Keele, L. (2007). The third way: The theory of affective intelligence and American democracy. In W. R. Neuman, G. E. Marcus, A. N. Crigler, & M. MacKuen (eds.), *The affect effect: Dynamics of emotion in political thinking and behavior*. Chicago: University of Chicago Press.

Martinez, M. D. (2010). Why is American turnout so low, and why should we care? In J. E. Leighley (ed.), *The Oxford handbook of American elections and political behavior*. Oxford: Oxford University Press.

McGue, M., & Lykken, D. T. (1992). Genetic influence on risk of divorce. *Psychological Science*, 3, 368–73.

Mercier, H., & Sperber, D. (2011). Why do humans reason? Arguments for an argumentative theory. *Behavioral and Brain Sciences*, 34, 57–111.

Miller, D. T., & Ratner, R. K. (1998). The disparity between the actual and assumed power of self-interest. *Journal of Personality and Social Psychology*, 74, 53–62.

Miller, G., & Schofield, N. (2003). Activists and partisan realignment in the United States. *American Political Science Review*, 97, 245–60.

Neuman, W. R., Marcus, G. E., Crigler, A. N., & MacKuen, M. (2007). Theorizing affect's effects. In W. R. Neuman, G. E. Marcus, A. N. Crigler, & M. MacKuen (eds.), *The affect effect: Dynamics of emotion in political thinking and behavior*. Chicago: University of Chicago Press.

Nisbett, R., & Wilson, T. (1977). Telling more than we can know: Verbal reports on mental processes. *Psychological Review*, 84, 231–59.

Noel, H. (2013). *Political ideologies and political parties in America*. Cambridge University Press.

Norenzayan, A. (2013). *Big gods: How religion transformed cooperation and conflict*. Princeton: Princeton University Press.

Owens, L. A., & Pedulla, D. S. (2014). Material welfare and changing political preferences: The case of support for redistributive social policies. *Social Forces*, 92, 1087–13.

Page, T., Putterman, L., & Unel, B. (2005). Voluntary association in public goods experiments: Reciprocity, mimicry, and efficiency. *Economic Journal*, 115, 1032–53.

Petersen, M. B., Aaroe, L., Jensen, N. H., & Curry, O. (2014). Social welfare and the psychology of food sharing: Short-term hunger increases support for social welfare. *Political Psychology*, doi: 10.1111/pops.12062.

Petersen, M. B., Slothuus, R., & Togeby, L. (2010). Political parties and value consistency in public opinion formation. *Public Opinion Quarterly*, 74, 530–50.

Pinker, S. (1997). *How the mind works*. New York: W. W. Norton & Company.

———. (2002). *The blank slate: The modern denial of human nature*. New York: Viking Penguin.

Pratto, F., Sidanius, J., & Levin, S. (2006). Social dominance theory and the dynamics of intergroup relations: Taking stock and looking forward. *European Review of Social Psychology*, 17, 271–320.

Pronin, E., Berger, J. A., & Molouki, S. (2007). Alone in a crowd of sheep: Asymmetric perceptions of conformity and their roots in an introspection illusion. *Journal of Personality and Social Psychology*, 92, 585–95.

Quintelier, K. J., Ishii, K., Weeden, J., Kurzban, R., & Braeckman, J. (2013). Individual differences in reproductive strategy are related to views about recreational drug use in Belgium, the Netherlands, and Japan. *Human Nature*, 24, 196–217.

Richerson, P. J., & Boyd, R. (1998). The evolution of human ultra-sociality. In I. Eibl-Eibisfeldt and F. Salter (eds.), *Ideology, warfare, and indoctrinability*. Berghan Books.

Riess, M., Rosenfeld, P., Melburg, V., & Tedeschi, J. T. (1981). Self-serving attributions: Biased private perceptions and distorted public perceptions. *Journal of Personality and Social Psychology*, 41, 224–31.

Sabato, L. J. (2013). The Obama encore that broke some rules. In L. J. Sabato (ed.), *Barack Obama and the new America: The 2012 election and the changing face of politics*. Lanham, MD: Rowman & Littlefield Publishers.

Schmitt, M. T., Branscombe, N. R., & Kappen, D. M. (2003). Attitudes toward group-based inequality: Social dominance or social identity? *British Journal of Social Psychology*, 42, 161–86.

Schreiber, D. (2007). Political cognition as social cognition: Are we all political sophisticates? In W. R. Neuman, G. E. Marcus, A. N. Crigler, & M. MacKuen (eds.), *The affect effect: Dynamics of emotion in political thinking and behavior.* Chicago: University of Chicago Press.

Sears, D. O., & Funk, C. L. (1990). Self-interest in Americans' political opinions. In J. L. Mansbridge (ed.), *Beyond self-interest.* Chicago: University of Chicago Press.

Shiota, M. N., & Kalat, J. W. (2012). *Emotion* (2nd ed.). Belmont, CA: Wadsworth, Cengage Learning.

Slothuus, R., & de Vreese, C. H. (2010). Political parties, motivated reasoning, and issue framing effects. *The Journal of Politics, 72,* 630–45.

Smith, K., Alford, J. R., Hatemi, P. K., Eaves, L. J., Funk, C., & Hibbing, J. R. (2012). Biology, ideology, and epistemology: How do we know political attitudes are inherited and why should we care? *American Journal of Political Science, 56,* 17–33.

Smith, S. S., & Park, H. M. (2013). Americans' attitudes about the senate filibuster. *American Politics Research, 41,* 735–60.

Sniderman, P. M., & Stiglitz, E. H. (2012). *The reputational premium: A theory of party identification and policy reasoning.* Princeton: Princeton University Press.

Solnick, S. J., & Hemenway, D. (1998). Is more always better? A survey on positional concerns. *Journal of Economic Behavior & Organization, 37,* 373–83.

Spezio, M. L., & Adolphs, R. (2007). Emotion processing and political judgment: Toward integrating political psychology and decision neuroscience. In W. R. Neuman, G. E. Marcus, A. N. Crigler, & M. MacKuen (eds.), *The affect effect: Dynamics of emotion in political thinking and behavior.* Chicago: University of Chicago Press.

Stewart, J., Karlin, B., & Javerbaum, D. (2004). *America (the book): A citizen's guide to democracy inaction.* New York: Warner Books.

Stimson, J. A. (1991). *Public opinion in America: Moods, cycles, and swings.* Boulder, CO: Westview Press.

Taber, C. S. (2003). Information processing and public opinion. In D. O. Sears, L. Huddy, & R. Jervis (eds.), *Oxford handbook of political psychology.* Oxford: Oxford University Press.

Taber, C., & Lodge, M. (2006). Motivated skepticism in the evaluation of political beliefs. *American Journal of Political Science, 50,* 755–69.

Tajfel, H., Billig, M. G., Bundy, R. P., & Falment, C. (1971). Social categorization and intergroup behaviour. *European Journal of Social Psychology, 1,* 149–78.

Weeden, J. (2003). *Genetic interests, life histories, and attitudes towards abortion* (Ph.D. diss.). University of Pennsylvania.

———. (2014). Losing my religion: A life-history analysis of the decline in religious attendance from childhood to adulthood. In J. Slone & J. Van Slyke (eds.), *The attraction of religion: Evolutionary theories of religion.* New York: Bloomsbury Academic.

Weeden, J., Abrams, M., Green, M. C., & Sabini, J. (2006). Do high-status people really have fewer children? Education, income, and fertility in the contemporary U.S. *Human Nature, 17,* 377–92.

Weeden, J., Cohen, A. B., & Kenrick, D. T. (2008). Religious attendance as reproductive support. *Evolution and Human Behavior, 29,* 327–34.

Weeden, J., & Kurzban, R. (2013). What predicts religiosity? A multinational analysis of reproductive and cooperative morals. *Evolution and Human Behavior, 34,* 440–45.

Wilson, D. S. (2002). *Darwin's cathedral: Evolution, religion and the nature of society.* Chicago: University of Chicago Press.

Wilson, T. D. (2002). *Strangers to ourselves: Discovering the adaptive unconscious.* Cambridge, MA: Belknap Press of Harvard University Press.

Zaller, J. R. (1992). *The nature and origins of mass opinion.* Cambridge: Cambridge University Press.

Index